Frank Weitenkampf, Albert Bleunard

Babylon electrified

The history of an expedition undertaken to restore ancient Babylon

Frank Weitenkampf, Albert Bleunard

Babylon electrified

The history of an expedition undertaken to restore ancient Babylon

ISBN/EAN: 9783744722964

Printed in Europe, USA, Canada, Australia, Japan

Cover: Foto ©ninafisch / pixelio.de

More available books at **www.hansebooks.com**

Babylon Electrified

THE HISTORY OF AN EXPEDITION UNDERTAKEN TO RESTORE ANCIENT
BABYLON BY THE POWER OF ELECTRICITY AND HOW IT RESULTED

BY

A. BLEUNARD

DOCTOR OF SCIENCES

TRANSLATED FROM THE FRENCH BY FRANK LINSTOW WHITE

ILLUSTRATED BY MONTADER

PHILADELPHIA
GEBBIE & CO., Publishers
1889

CONTENTS.

FIRST PART.

MESOPOTAMIA.

			PAGE
CHAPTER	I.	CAPTAIN LAYCOCK'S PROJECT	1
"	II.	A DREAM	9
"	III.	A CALCULATION WITH A NEGATIVE RESULT	14
"	IV.	A GREAT DISCOVERY	22
"	V.	AT SEA	30
"	VI.	ON THE BANKS OF THE ORONTES	39
"	VII.	FATMA	57
"	VIII.	THE EUPHRATES	68
"	IX.	BABYLON	76
"	X.	THE DISCOVERY OF GRIMMITSCHOFFER	85
"	XI.	FROM BAGDAD TO MOSUL	94
"	XII.	THE GROTTO OF BAVIAN	109
"	XIII.	THE HYDRAULIC WORKS	120
"	XIV.	ACROSS THE HIGH MOUNTAINS	130
"	XV.	A SAD EVENT	143
"	XVI.	THE VALLEY OF THE DYALAH	154

SECOND PART.

THE ELECTRIC WORKS.

CHAPTER	I.	LIBERTY	161
"	II.	THE KASR AND BABEL	169
"	III.	THE SAM	182

CONTENTS.

			PAGE
Chapter IV.	From Babylon to the Persian Gulf	.	. 191
" V.	The Electric Lighthouse	. . .	. 206
" VI.	The Lighting of Liberty	. . .	. 217
" VII.	The Great Works	. . .	. 226
" VIII.	Tillage and Cooking by Electricity		. 235
" IX.	The End of an Archæologist	. .	. 242
" X.	A Revolt	. . . . .	. 249
" XI.	The Thermo-Solar Pile	. .	. 254
" XII.	The Calm before the Storm	. .	. 262
" XIII.	New Causes for Anxiety	. .	. 270
" XIV.	Jack Adams	. . . .	. 276
" XV.	Destruction of the Hydraulic Works	.	. 281
" XVI.	The Revenge	. . . .	. 285
" XVII.	Ruin and Desolation	. .	. 295
" XVIII.	A Year After	. . .	. 301

LIST OF ILLUSTRATIONS.

	PAGE
Discussing the captain's project	1
Captain Laycock	2
The geologist	4
His lordship	6
Tail-piece	8
A vision	9
Tail-piece—In the desert	13
In Badger's study	14
"Jack Adams was alone in the library of his lordship"	18
Tail-piece—An important calculation	21
"Babylon will be reconstructed"	22
The French electrician	25
The reporter	25
Engineer Blacton	26
Tail-piece—The Davy and the Faraday	29
"At sea"	30
"A magnificent bolis"	36
Tail-piece—"She could not tear herself away from her contemplation"	38
On the banks of the Orontes	39
The caravan	43
A rough road	47
Marrah	51
"The sheikh came to meet them"	53
"*My lady* Mohammed"	54
Tail-piece—A dowar	56
Aleppo	57
A ruined city	59
"Fatma . . . had fallen at the foot of the tomb"	61
"The chief of the band"	63
A caravan	66
Tail-piece	67
The kalak	68
The ruined bridge of Deir	72
Tail-piece—A Mesopotamian turtle	75
Hillah	76
"Badger . . . was looking anxiously in the direction of the city"	78
Flatnose at work	80
Tail-piece—*Chef* Green	84
"The discovery of Grimmitschoffer"	85
A native husbandman	88
Tail-piece—Mr. Grimmitschoffer	93
An eastern court-yard	94
"It seemed to him that the young girl's eyes were wet"	95
The Bagdad of the *Arabian Nights*	98
The Bagdad of reality	100
"From Tekrit to Mosul"	105
Tail-piece	108
The grotto of Bavian	109
Nebbi-Yunus	111
"Grimmitschoffer was beside himself with joy"	113
A subterranean cascade	118
Tail-piece—The governess	119
Among the mountains	120
A picturesque road	125
Wild flowers	128
At Rowandiz	129
"They entered a deep hollow"	136
Flatnose's fall	141
Tail-piece	142
Kurds	143

	PAGE		PAGE
"Flatnose . . . had been killed instantly"	146	On the road to Babylon	224
		The future canals	226
"Don't move, please"	152	"He drew the name of Nedjef"	228
Tail-piece—A factor in civilization	153	Digging canals	232
The Lesser Zab	154	A native laborer	233
"Grimmitschoffer . . . discovered a colossal head of stone"	159	An electric kitchen	235
		The editor's table	239
Tail piece—The camp	160	Tail-piece—An electric roast	241
Liberty	161	The mad archæologist	242
"You treat me like the little princesses in the fairy tales"	166	Grimmitschoffer's discovery	246
		Tail-piece—Cail & Co.'s make	248
Tail-piece — "Protection against sunstroke"	168	A strike	249
		Tail-piece—The refractory Moslem	253
On the Kasr	169	The riot	254
Monsieur Cornillé	174	A malignant native	256
"An improvised lunch"	177	Tail-piece—The moving power	261
Tail-piece—The Mouchot apparatus	181	The calm before the storm	262
The hunt	182	The congregation of the faithful	267
"The horses were tied to some palms"	184	Tail-piece—The two friends	269
"They advanced only with extreme difficulty"	186	On the road to Bagdad	270
		"Death to the Christians"	274
"Cabuzac . . . came back, pushing a hamper before him"	188	Tail-piece—The electric road	275
		Jack Adams and Fatma	276
An unfortunate savant	189	Tail-piece—Fatma	280
Tail-piece—Game	190	"Destruction of the hydraulic works"	281
To the Persian Gulf	191		
Chaldeans	196	The work of destruction	283
At Waraba and Bubian	200	The revenge	285
A rare native	204	On a war footing	287
The electric lighthouse	206	"This is my will"	290
Miss Nelly	210	Tail-piece	294
The silent bearer of dispatches	213	The explosion	295
Tail-piece—The electric lamp	216	A miraculous escape	299
The lighting of Liberty	217	Tail-piece—The Kasr in flames	300
Grimm at work	220	A year after	301
"They showed themselves unveiled"	221	Tail-piece—An opponent to progress	304

FIRST PART.

MESOPOTAMIA.

CHAPTER I.

CAPTAIN LAYCOCK'S PROJECT.

A LARGE gathering was assembled that evening at the London house of Sir James Badger, baronet. The principal members of Parliament, of the bar, of the financial world, were there. The arts, literature, and the sciences had also furnished their most illustrious representatives.

Lord Badger was a man of about fifty years of age, robust and tall. He had been early bereft of a wife whom he had loved tenderly; but there was left to him a young daughter, between twenty and twenty-two years of age, Miss Nelly, on whom all his strength of affection was concentrated. One of the richest proprietors in England—his fortune was estimated at over twenty millions of pounds, sterling—Lord Badger took pleasure in promoting daring enterprises, if they seemed to him in the least to have a useful aim. Proud of the adventurous spirit of his countrymen, he could be extremely liberal with his money when some distant voyage or important discovery was in question.

"Gladstone," an influential member of Parliament was saying at this moment, "Gladstone makes too many concessions with regard to Egypt. We must remain the masters of that country, if we do not wish to be driven from the Indies by the Russians."

"The English," replied a little old man with a clean-shaven face, "are most assuredly making all efforts to guard the roads which lead to the Indies. Cyprus belongs to us, and we have the protectorate of Asia Minor. As to Egypt, it is to be hoped that we shall soon emerge victorious from the present difficulties. England, when her interests are at stake, never flinches."

Applause greeted these patriotic words, which gained in importance from the fact that they were uttered by one who was a public favorite and who held a high position in the Ministry.

The conversation then took another turn. The latest novel, the exhibition of paintings, the play in vogue at the moment, became the subjects of discussion.

"Gentlemen," suddenly said a person who had not taken part in the conversation before, "permit me to recur for an instant to the Egyptian question."

The speaker was a tall man, with a red and sun-burnt face, and flowing whiskers. His energetic physiognomy proclaimed him to be a man accustomed to brave danger. It was Captain Laycock, of the Royal Navy, who had made the tour of the world five times, and had been in many a scrimmage.

"England," he continued, "seeks to get possession of the two routes which lead to the Indies. The first and most important at the present time is Egypt: it may be said to belong to us. As to the second, that begins opposite to Cyprus, passes round Arabia, and ends at the Persian Gulf. This route, in the near future, may become the rival of the first. I ask you, gentlemen, if it is not time for England to begin to think of preparing the roads of the future by improving a route which will be among the most effective for the exchange of our products. Some persons have already thought of constructing a railway to connect the Mediterranean with the Indies. Several plans have already been proposed, but all met with grave obstacles."

"Did you not make one of an expedition to Asia Minor and Mesopotamia?" interrupted Badger, addressing the captain.

"Yes, my lord."

"Will you, then, please to give us some information about this curious country, so that our ideas on the subject may be more clearly defined?"

"With pleasure," said the captain. "We see that Mesopotamia, from the earliest times, was the rival of Egypt, to which country, moreover, its physical form gives it more than one point of resemblance. By turns these two favored countries disputed the monopoly of the exchange between Europe and Asia. History tells us that under the reign of Nebuchadnezzar Babylon became the great mart of the world. Teredon, on the Persian Gulf, and Tyre, on the Mediterranean, were the two extreme points at which the thoroughfare between Asia and Europe began and ended."

At this point the captain was interrupted by Miss Nelly, who invited Lord Badger's guests to draw nearer to the tea-table which two servants had just brought in. Nothing could be more charming than the modest grace with which this young girl, a perfect type of English beauty, did the honors of her father's *salon*. While rising and coming forward in answer to her call, the men continued their conversation.

"Permit me to call your attention to the fact, my dear captain," a celebrated geologist interposed at this point, "that the superiority of the road from Teredon to Tyre is due to the natural configuration of that part of Asia. Mesopotamia is a vast plain which abuts at the northwest on the Mediterranean. It is true that a mountain chain skirts the borders of that sea. But, opposite to the island of Cyprus, this chain diminishes in height to admit of easy communication between the valley of the Euphrates and that of the Orontes. Thus you see that the route of Nebuchadnezzar was wholly laid out by nature."

"Your remark proves but one thing, my dear Mr. Monaghan," resumed the captain, "and that is that Mesopotamia is inevitably destined to regain one day the station from which it has fallen. Commercial routes cannot depart from natural lines. The course of history proves the truth of what I have just asserted. At the time of the conquest of Mesopotamia by the Persians the new occupants, it is true, obstructed the river Euphrates for purposes of defence; but as soon as Alexander had driven out the Persians he made haste to re-establish the commercial routes. He caused an immense basin to be dug at Babylon, and that city became an important port, where thousands of ships unloaded their merchandise. Several centuries afterward the Arabs drove out the Greeks; nevertheless, the prosperity of Babylon continued during the early years of the Mussulman occupation, and it remained for the Turkish conquest to reduce this country to the miserable state in which we see it to-day.

Thus, gentlemen, you see that Babylonia for many centuries remained the principal route of commerce between Asia and Europe. It is true that this splendor has wholly disappeared in our day: where once there stood numerous rich and populous cities nothing is now to be seen but heaps of rubbish scattered about in the sands of the desert. But that which has been may be again. Why could not our daring countryman, Lord Badger, who is stopped by no obstacles, why could he not undertake the resurrection of this vast country?"

Captain Laycock's proposition was certainly calculated to please the adventurous spirit of his lordship; yet Badger was not the man to become enthusiastic and to take up the matter in this way without considering all the difficulties of the undertaking. He desired, therefore, to have an exact account of the state of the country in question.

"Captain," he replied immediately to him who had called upon him to take the initiative in the matter, "can you tell me why Mesopotamia has become a desert after so long a period of prosperity? You understand the importance of my question. It is to be feared, in fact, that the causes of its decadence are irremediable. It seems strange to me that a country inhabited during a long succession of centuries should by degrees have become a sterile desert. If the decadence of the country is due to the faults of the inhabitants or to the migrations of civilization, it is possible to revive its ancient prosperity. But if nature has become modified, if the rivers are less full, if the sources have dried up, if the sands of Arabia have invaded the rich cultivated lands of bygone times, I think these regions must be left in their condition, for it is not within the power of man to restore the former order of nature."

"My lord," replied the captain, "this is what I noted during my voyage in Mesopotamia. To-day, as formerly, the soil is remarkably fertile wherever there is water. I believe, therefore, that it is simply necessary to repair the canals in order to cover Mesopotamia with a vegetation as luxurious as it was in antiquity and to enable the country to maintain millions of inhabitants."

Monaghan then began to speak:

"I cannot," said he, "allow what Captain Laycock has said to pass by without submitting a few observations which may, perhaps, be of a nature to modify his opinion. In travelling through Asia Minor and along the coast of Palestine it soon becomes evident that changes have taken place in the nature of the climate since past ages. There where, as history tells us, rich cultivated lands formerly gave support to numerous populations the dismal desert now extends far and wide. It is the lack of water that causes this sterility. There is less rainfall in our day, and the old river-beds are either altogether dried up or contain but an insignificant stream of water. Hills which were formerly cultivated from base to summit are to-day scorched by the rays of an implacable sun."

"And is the cause of this scarcity of water known?" asked some one.

"Yes," replied Monaghan. "It is due to the disappearance of the ancient forests, and, what is much more important, to the change in the direction of the atmospheric currents, which no longer bring the vapors with which they become charged in passing over the seas."

During the whole of this conversation between Captain Laycock and the geologist Monaghan, James Badger had remained silent; one would have said that he was balancing in his mind the hope which the first had given him and the discouraging reasons which the other seemed to suggest to him.

"Captain," he said, suddenly, addressing honest Laycock, "I think that your proposition deserves to be studied very attentively, and, whatever objections it may call forth, I thank you for having communicated it and for having thought of me as the one to put it into execution. And now, gentlemen, I invite you to take a cup of tea."

The conversation once more became general, and covered the most varying subjects.

But Lord Badger and Captain Laycock remained silent, each absorbed in his thoughts. Lord Badger reflected on the project of the captain; the more he thought of it the more the execution of this project pleased him by its grandeur and by the advantages which his country would derive from it. Laycock, on the other hand, could not call the assertions of the geologist, Monaghan, into question. The climate of this western portion of Asia had evidently undergone great changes. In order to revive civilization in the midst of these deserts, it would be necessary to restore artificially what nature had herself destroyed, by making use of the power given to man by modern science, and supplying the deficiency in the rainfall by raising the waters of the Tigris and the Euphrates, so as to spread the fertilizing liquid throughout the country by means of more numerous canals.

While the conversation around him became more animated, Captain Laycock was lost more and more in contemplation of this work of the future. He saw Mesopotamia becoming, in a short time, the public granary of all Europe. Besides grain, a large number of other useful plants might be cultivated. The North would furnish the finest fruit-trees: the cherry, apple, pear, plum, orange, lemon, pomegranate—all natives of Asia Minor and of Mesopotamia. Lower down, other plants, still more useful, would be added—the sugar-cane and the cotton plant, both sources of industries of the greatest importance. Finally, in Lower Mesopotamia, around Babylon itself, forests of date-palms could be cultivated.

The Holy Scriptures located the terrestrial Paradise in Mesopotamia, and not without reason. Where could a land be found better adapted to the welfare of man? Here, the sky is of a splendor unknown in the misty countries of Europe; the soil, as fertile as that of Egypt, lends itself to the cultivation of the most varying products. Why delay longer a pacific conquest which would furnish an outlet for the crowded populations of the old continent?

Unfortunately, to dig canals, to raise the waters, to construct and work manufactories, would require an enormous force, and Mesopotamia itself offered no resources. Deprived of forests and of coal-mines, it lacked fuel, the first requisite of all operations.

Thus Captain Laycock was obliged to admit that, notwithstanding the fascinating grandeur of the work, its execution was well-nigh impossible. Lord Badger, who, by a natural coincidence, had himself arrived at a similar conclusion, approached the sailor and said abruptly:

"Captain Laycock, I shall undertake the execution of your project if you find coal in Mesopotamia."

"Alas, my lord," exclaimed the captain, who was not surprised by Badger's words, so exactly did they correspond with his own thoughts, "that is impossible."

"Then," replied Badger, "your project is likewise impossible of realization?"

"Pardon me," said one of those present, who had been listening attentively to the words exchanged between the captain and Badger; "you lack coal, but you have electricity."

He who spoke was a tall young man, with a black beard, sharp eyes, and a physiognomy that was southern rather than Anglo-Saxon in character.

It was an engineer; one Jack Adams.

"Explain yourself, Mr. Adams," said his lordship, who did not fully understand the significance of the engineer's remark.

"That is quite simple, my lord," replied the latter. "Although coal is wanting, natural forces abound in the very heart of Mesopotamia. Now, at this day, science is sufficiently advanced to enable you to transform all the natural forces into electricity, and this again into new forces which will replace advantageously the coal which you lack."

At this point Jack Adams was suddenly interrupted by the voice of a stout person, who called to his lordship:

"We are waiting only for you to complete a party at whist. Come, now, make haste; you can talk of serious things to-morrow."

"That is true," said Badger, addressing the captain and Jack Adams; "this evening I must devote myself to my guests. But call on me to-morrow morning, if you please, Mr. Adams. We can then talk of the means of reconstructing ancient Babylon."

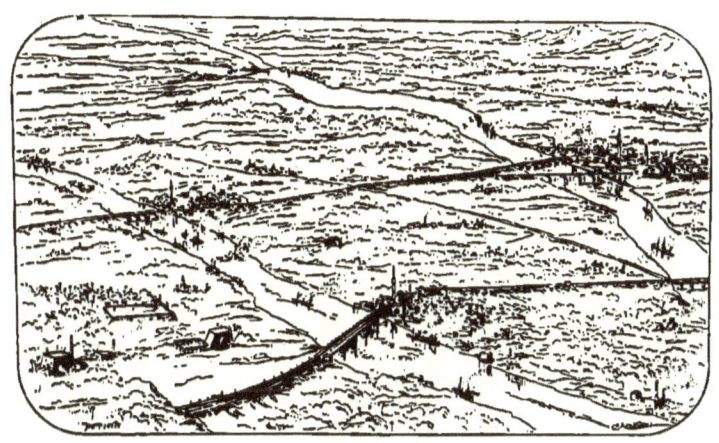

CHAPTER II.

A DREAM.

JACK ADAMS' words had produced a deep impression on Lord Badger. But little versed in matters of electricity, that science which, though so modern, had already been so fruitful in results, he could have but an imperfect idea of the consequences of that which the engineer had revealed to him. Yet it was enough to enable him to perceive the possibility of bringing the project of Captain Laycock to a successful issue.

When the last of his guests had taken leave, and he had embraced his dear Nelly more tenderly than usual, his lordship went down into his garden. He felt the need of being alone and breathing more freely. The over-heated air in the rooms seemed to obscure the ideas that thronged his brain.

As he walked slowly down the paths, he thought of the numerous incidents of the evening. The captain's proposition, the objections made by Monaghan, had left him wavering between hope and fear, when the magic word *electricity*, uttered by Jack Adams, had restored his confidence by offering new vistas to his mind. It appeared to him then that the resurrection of Mesopotamia, the restoration of Babylon to its original power and splendor, were matters possible of realization, and he saw in himself the one marked out for that work.

While he was abandoning himself to these thoughts, which the profound silence that reigned about him seemed to favor, the coolness of the night and the perfume-laden air of the garden restored order and calm to his ideas, which had just been in such a state of ebullition.

Badger retired to rest with his heart full of faith in the future. Nevertheless, the night had only momentarily quieted him; he was hardly in bed before this feverishness seized upon him.

He fancied himself transported suddenly into this Mesopotamia which he wished to restore. He was not on the ground; he hovered in the air at a height of several thousand yards. The atmosphere was of an admirable purity; in spite of the distance, he could clearly distinguish the smallest details.

An immense desert lay stretched below him. The sands undulated like the waves of a raging sea. Some islets of verdure stood out, at long intervals, from the grayish ground of the soil; and these islets were inhabited by families of nomadic shepherds, who were pasturing their flocks. He saw some of these shepherds travelling through the desert, mounted on camels, and going from one oasis to another.

Raising his eyes, he perceived nothing in the distance, at first, but a confused mass of mountain-chains. The day was beginning to break. The mountain-tops, which obstructed the horizon towards the east, was tinged with the colors of the rainbow. The desert appeared to continue with the same uniformity to the very base of this long chain.

He then perceived that a light breath of air was carrying him gradually towards the East. The mountains became more and more visible, their outlines more clearly defined.

The desert was transformed as he advanced. Immense plains of lemon-trees now succeeded the uncultivated sands. The tufts of trees became more and more rare. Two broad rivers, silvery white, wound along parallel to the mountain-chain. Following their course towards the south, he saw them lose themselves in the sea which sparkled on the far horizon.

It suddenly appeared to him that he was not alone in the air. A whirr of wings struck his ears. He turned around and saw nothing but the boundless desert through which he had passed. Nevertheless there soon arose a voice, which said to him:

"Fear nothing, mortal; I am the genius of the place which thou beholdest. It is I who have brought thee hither. Thou dost not see me, for the spirits do not take upon them a material form; thou canst only hear me. The sun is rising in the midst of the brilliant dawn;

thou wilt distinguish the smallest details. The desert over which thou wert hovering before is Arabia. The two rivers are the Tigris and the Euphrates; the mountains which border the horizon separate Persia from Mesopotamia. Thou wilt now easily understand why this country has so long been a centre of civilization. Mesopotamia is narrowly confined between the desert of Arabia and the mountain-chains. Thanks to the two rivers which irrigate it, it is like a second Egypt, a belt of land of an incomparable fertility in the midst of barren sands. The populations of Arabia, of the high plateaus of Asia Minor, of Persia, have always sought to descend towards these fertile plains. If I add further that the Tigris and the Euphrates place the Mediterranean in almost direct communication with the Indian Ocean, thou hast the secret of the prosperity of ancient Mesopotamia.

"The cities," continued the spirit, after a moment of silence, "have here attained an incomparable splendor. The names of Babylon and Nineveh have come down through the centuries, giving to men the idea of strange and marvellous cities. Yet thou wilt seek in vain for the ruins of these ancient capitals. Their palaces are reduced to dust. Look at these small hillocks scattered throughout the plain: those are the last remains of the cities of Mesopotamia.

"The spectacle before thine eyes is a sad one. Nowhere has man so turned up the soil and transformed nature; but nowhere else, on the other hand, has nature with such rapidity regained possession of her empire and destroyed the works of man. The bricks of which the houses were constructed have been reduced to dust by the action of the elements. As to the canals dug so laboriously to distribute water everywhere and fertilize the soil, they have been filled up by the sands of the desert carried in by the winds.

"So long as the populations of Mesopotamia were active and industrious man overcame the barrenness of the soil; this country was flourishing and prosperous. But since a weakened people has governed the land the ancient splendor has disappeared to give place to ruin and desolation.

"The time is close at hand, O mortal! Civilization will recover the dominion lost for so many years. Look: thou shalt be permitted to behold the wonders of the future."

The spirit ceased to speak and the most profound silence continued to reign for a brief time. Suddenly a fearful noise was heard in the sky, like a terrific peal of thunder. The air became suddenly dark. Light vapors arose slowly from the earth and rolled like the waves of the sea.

But all at once a new phenomenon was produced. The vapors oscillate and break up in all directions, and the wind carries them off beyond the mountains. The sun is radiant in the sky; its rays flood a magic spectacle.

All of Mesopotamia is transformed.

The Tigris and the Euphrates now flow in the midst of an ocean of verdure; Mesopotamia resembles a forest of palm-trees. Sumptuous cities rise on all sides, with magnificent palaces towering towards the sky. Numerous canals wind about among the trees; innumerable ships sail in all directions. Everywhere the mixed crowd is active and busy.

Babylon is reconstructed. It has again become an immense port, where all the ships of the world come to load and unload their wares. The Euphrates and the Tigris, connected by a thousand canals, bear fleets towards the two seas. The Mediterranean communicates with the rivers which have become the principal artery of the world.

The voice of the genius was heard again:

"See, O mortal, what the efforts of man can accomplish. He has known how to employ the forces of nature, and prosperity has promptly taken the place of desolation. I shall reveal to thee the secret of the power of this people. Science has made them free. They live conformably to the laws of reason. Impregnated with all noble ideas, they have become the most civilized people on earth. They have known how to avail themselves of the greatest force of the universe—electricity. This has increased the forces of man a hundredfold. This small corner of Asia shows thee what later on the surface of the globe will become."

"I must go nearer," exclaimed Badger, "and see this marvellous spectacle closer at hand. From the height at which I hover the details are effaced, and I can but see the general effect."

"Impossible," replied the spirit; "I cannot let thee view the future closer by. It is thus that the genius of man divines future ages without being conscious of the details."

"I shall then approach in spite of you!" cried Badger, suddenly seized with an insane desire to know all. "I need but let myself fall to the ground!"

"Be it so," said the spirit, "it shall be done according to thy wish."

Badger now felt himself falling gradually. The descent began slowly, but he soon saw, to his dismay, that it accelerated rapidly.

What a surprise! The nearer he approached to the earth the more the panorama which he had admired a moment before dimmed and vanished. What a deception! The cities crumbled and sank, the forests disappeared and gave place to the sands of the desert. The canals dried up and became filled with earth.

The rapidity of his fall still increased. Space whirled round madly; a sharp, whistling noise filled his ears. His head swam round. He touched the ground at last with a frightful crash!

Lord Badger awoke with a start. He had sprung with one bound to the middle of his chamber.

Somewhat stunned, his first care was to make sure that he was not hurt. The sun's bright rays penetrated into the apartment. His lordship then remembered the appointment which he had made with Jack Adams, and went at once to his dressing-room, so that he might be ready to receive the engineer. While dressing Badger recalled to mind the various events of the dream which had troubled him during the night, and he seemed to discover a prophetic meaning in it. "No matter," he said at length, as if replying to his own thoughts, "even though my part should be but the daily struggle with nature and with men, without ever being permitted to judge my work in its entirety; even though I should have to leave the enjoyment and success to those who will come after me—I shall try."

CHAPTER III.

A CALCULATION WITH A NEGATIVE RESULT.

WE are now in the spacious library, which serves also as study.

Lord Badger, as we have already perceived, was not only a man of great and strong imagination; he was also practical to a high degree. A combination less rare than is generally supposed, and which alone produces truly superior men. As soon as he had conceived some grand project, and had thoroughly considered it, he felt the need of causing it to pass from pure theory into the domain of fact, subjecting it to the test of practice.

He had the good sense to understand that, as the education he had received, though, it is true, very complete, was general in character, he was not qualified to judge for himself to what extent his projects were capable of realization, no more than he would have been able to carry them out alone, when once the possibility of realizing them had been recognized. He therefore took care to surround himself with specialists, and he was almost always fortunate in his choice of men. This he had proven once again by applying to the electrician, Jack Adams, who had allowed him to perceive the possibility of realizing his project.

Jack Adams had already attained celebrity by several brilliant inventions. Still young, hardly thirty-five years of age, he possessed the ardent confidence which sustains courage and enables one to perform wonders. He believed in the future of his favorite science, in the good which electricity would bestow some day on civilization. Bound by no ties, he would devote himself body and soul to a great enterprise such as the one which now occupied Badger's thoughts.

It will thus be understood with what impatience the latter, now seated in his study, awaited the engineer. Badger's dream was very vague; it floated among clouds of purple, sparkling in the golden light of the sun; but its indistinct forms were fleeting and seemed to vanish whenever he attempted to determine them.

Was it not to be feared that a thorough discussion would set all these fine illusions at naught? Would his conference with the engineer give substance to the spirit, or was it going to destroy his chimera by proving to him that it was not capable of realization? Was the science of electricity sufficiently advanced to authorize an experiment on so grand a scale?

Fortunately, Jack Adams was himself a visionary—science claims such as well as faith. This dream of his lordship, he had often had it, but without ever having fixed his thoughts upon it; for he saw no possibility of a realization. He lacked money. A communion of ideas between these two men was thus inevitable; Badger and Jack Adams had the same aspiration. The first brought to the second the wherewithal to realize their common ideal.

At the time appointed for the interview the door-bell rang, and, almost immediately after, Jack Adams was ushered into the presence of his lordship. The latter stepped forward eagerly to meet him, and they had hardly shaken hands when the thought uppermost in his mind found expression in the question:

"Well! night brings counsel, it is said; do you still believe this morning, as you affirmed you did last night, that the science of electricity is sufficiently advanced to enable us to reconquer the deserts of Mesopotamia for civilization? Can man manage this fluid with sufficient facility to enable us to direct towards Babylon the natural forces of its surroundings?"

"I believe in the success of the enterprise," replied Jack Adams. "The natural forces which we can find with certainty in the vicinity of Mesopotamia are: the rays of the sun, the streams and rivers, the winds, the waves of the sea and its tides. Perhaps we shall have the good fortune to discover coal and petroleum. If these are found in large quantities, our work will be simplified. But we must not count too much on these auxiliaries, so rare in that part of Asia. Besides, the other forces will be amply sufficient. By means of Mouchot's solar apparatus we will produce the steam necessary for setting the electric machines in motion. Turbines will serve to obtain the power of the torrents and rivers; windmills will utilize the force of the winds. As to the waves and tides of the ocean, we can transform them into a utilizable motion by very ingenious operations."

"I perceive very well," resumed his lordship, " on what you depend for obtaining the necessary quantity of electricity. But, supposing that you obtained it in sufficient quantity, could you make suitable use of it?"

"Undoubtedly," replied the engineer. "The cables, tracing their passage in the air, in the sands, in the depths of the seas, will bring the fluid for us into immense reservoirs where it will accumulate. Then, renewing our store of electricity proportionally to our needs, we shall make it work according to our wishes. With it, we shall move about with rapidity among the new cities and the plains of Mesopotamia; with it, we shall illuminate our dwellings with a brilliancy comparable to that of the sun. It shall draw our plows and turn up the furrows, from which abundant harvests will spring. Thanks to electricity, we shall become modern demi-gods. Then, we shall indeed have carried off the lightning from heaven, to make it descend to the earth. We shall have transformed into an arm of civilization that which was formerly only a terrible agent of death!"

"See how you excite yourself," said his lordship, smiling. "Calm yourself, for I still fear that the reality may not be equal to the dream. Are you absolutely certain that Mesopotamia will offer the resources of which you have just spoken to me?"

"Yes," replied the engineer. "Have you a map of the country?"

"An excellent one," said Badger. "Let us go up to my study; we shall find maps and books there which will give us accurate information."

Lord James Badger was a scholar. His library contained everything remarkable that had appeared in several centuries. Geography, especially, occupied several shelves.

A gigantic atlas was spread out on the table. Jack Adams opened it at the map of the world.

"My lord," said the engineer, "on this map of the world you see a great white belt, parallel to the equator. It represents the space occupied by the tropical deserts. This belt commences in North Africa, on the shores of the Atlantic Ocean, and it extends across the whole width of the continent. It is the desert of Sahara, the dryness and aridity of which are hardly disturbed by a few oases covered with verdure and by the lovely valley of the Nile. It then traverses the Red Sea, and loses itself in Asia, passing through Arabia, Persia, Bokhara and Mongolia."

"What is the cause of these vast deserts?" asked his lordship.

"These tropical deserts," replied Adams, "are the regions of the earth in which the azure skies are rarely darkened by clouds. They lie between two parallel rings, beyond which rain-storms are frequent; but here it hardly ever rains."

"Why have you drawn my attention especially to this belt of barren territory?"

"Because," replied the engineer, immediately, "it is only here that the force of the solar rays can be utilized. Here nature, more than anywhere else, is active, replete with power and force. The deserts of Sahara, of Arabia, and of Persia, thanks to the power of electricity, thanks to the transformation of heat into this tractable agent, will be sooner or later converted into great manufactories. The fiery rays of the sun, which to-day scorch everything, will be converted into electricity. Populous and rich cities will arise in all directions. Water will circulate in abundance and give fertility to the soil. Monstrous cables will traverse these ancient deserts like endless aqueducts. They will sink into the sea and land on the coasts of old Europe, now become the ruler of the whole world. From these cables smaller cables will spread out in all directions, like the branches of an immense tree, leading to the cities, the villages, to every inhabited spot. And thus heat, light and motive power, used in any part of Europe, shall have had their source in the desert of Sahara, in the heart of Africa! But what conflicts will convulse the earth before such results are attained! The axis of civilization cannot be displaced thus without difficulty. The conflict has already begun; it will only be emphasized in course of time. The nations of the north have a vague intuition of the part which they are called upon to play in the land of the sun. England guards India, and extends her conquests to all parts of the earth. France has taken possession of Tunis, reaches out to Senegal, and establishes herself in Madagascar and Indo-China. All the nations feel that the time is near, and turn their eyes towards the Equator. They

divine that the future lies there. The ancient cradles of humanity will become centres of civilization. The nations of the north, at present doomed to unfruitful restlessness, will gain renewed vigor by this contact, and the standard of progress will rise gloriously over the regenerated world!"

Jack Adams was really glorious in his enthusiasm. He had become quite transfigured. As he stood before the map he seemed to rule the world, to command the elements. His gaze, lost in the infinite, saw the sublime spectacles conjured up by his words.

James Badger looked at him with admiration. His dream was more grandly developed than before; science completed admirably that which had been inspired by his imagination.

The engineer was the first to break the silence:

"Let us return to that which interests us, my lord," said he. "You see that Mesopotamia lies in the zone of the deserts of the old continent. The sun, therefore, will not fail us. The Persian Gulf, with its tides and waves, is at our doors. That sea, however, cannot be of much use to us; its tides are not very perceptible nor its waves very nigh. As to the winds, they are very regular in these regions. From May to September we shall have the southern monsoon; during the other half of the year the northern winds will not cease to blow. Rivers and streams abound in Mesopotamia. Besides the Tigris and the Euphrates, which flow through its whole length, a large number of streams run down the mountains. On the north there is the Batman-Soo, whose waters are as torrent-like as those of the Tigris at its rise. The Arzen-Soo, the Boutan-Soo, the Bitlis, the Greater Zab, the Lesser Zab and the Diyalah are important tributaries of the Tigris. The Mourad, the Kara-Soo and the Tokma-Soo are tributaries of the Euphrates. We shall not want for waterfalls, for there are numerous cascades in the mountains. The Euphrates itself forms several important cataracts. Here you see the forty passes where more than three hundred rapids succeed each other within a distance of about one hundred miles."

"I see with pleasure," said Lord Badger, "that Mesopotamia is situated favorably for our projects. It seems that nature has accumulated here the most appropriate means for our assistance. Please set to work as promptly as possible, sir engineer. Make your calculations; don't let us begin anything carelessly. I wish to rebuild Babylon; I wish to raise this city from the dust and restore Mesopotamia to its ancient splendor. You have caused me to perceive the possibility of this resurrection by means of electricity. It remains for you to calculate our chances of success. The day is still little advanced. It has not struck twelve yet. Please to come down with me to the dining-room where a frugal repast awaits us. You can devote the evening to your calculations. Let us never wait until the morrow before coming to a resolution—great works are quickly decided upon. Human thought loses its vigor in waiting."

Jack Adams was alone in the library of his lordship. Heaps of paper, covered with figures and algebraical calculations, were spread out before him. Long equations, bristling with x's and y's, all a cabalistic language, curled around the end of his pen. He seemed like a magician evoking the spirits of earth and heaven.

And was he not in truth a magician, this man bent over his work? Oh, surprising power of mind! he was fathoming nature, that eternal enigma.

A modern Titan, he combined and amalgamated the power of the mysterious element in his mathematical formulas. Under his skilful hands heat and light, movement and chemical force, were transformed at will into that unseizable fluid, electricity. Guided by the formulas of the illustrious physicists of our century—Ampère, Faraday, Laplace, Joule, Ohm, Coulomb—he manipulated at pleasure the various manifestations of force.

Worn out with fatigue, covered with perspiration, he still strung out figures on figures. Not a moment of rest had he yet granted himself to quiet his overstrained nerves.

At six o'clock his lordship entered his study. Adams, lost to sight and sound, was not aware of his presence. Lord Badger did not dare to interrupt him; he comprehended that the moment was decisive.

A long quarter of an hour passed in complete silence. Night had gradually set in. Only a faint light now filtered through the mist that had risen from the Thames. At last the engineer stirred. He perceived his lordship, who was anxiously regarding him.

"My lord," exclaimed he, rising and stepping hastily toward him, "my lord, I have but one more equation to resolve. It embodies all my investigations and will decide the fate of our work."

"Very well; go on," said Badger. "I await with impatience the results of your last calculations."

It was now completely dark. His lordship rang the bell. A servant brought in a lighted lamp.

Ten minutes passed, a century for Badger. He seemed to hear the beatings of his heart, grown more rapid under the influence of his emotion.

Finally, pale, with dimmed eyes, Jack Adams said in a low voice:

"My lord, your project must be abandoned, at least for the present. Science is as yet unable to furnish us with the means of realizing our dream. Our apparatus are too imperfect to provide us with the amount of caloric which we should need. I had hoped too soon; but the reality shows the impossibility of realizing our hopes at present."

CHAPTER IV.

A GREAT DISCOVERY.

Two weeks have passed since the occurrence of the events which we have just related. Time has somewhat quieted the agitation of Lord Badger, struck so cruelly by the negative result to which the calculations of Jack Adams had led. The disillusionment was hard for a daring man, accustomed to overcome all obstacles. Badger had tried hard to fight against it at first and had gone over the calculations with Adams in due form. But he was compelled finally to submit to the evidence.

His lordship had seen Captain Laycock again and had made known to him the vicissitudes through which his project had successively passed. The idea of making use of electricity had appeared very original to Laycock, and he deeply regretted the impossibility that had been encountered. He said to Badger that there was still room for hope and that, perhaps, a better means for accomplishing the work would be found.

Let us now transfer ourselves to Lord Badger's dwelling: we find him sitting in an arm-chair, absently reading the *Times*. Not that the paper is lacking in interest: no, but his lordship's thoughts are elsewhere. Always under the influence of a fixed idea, he reads whole sentences and pages without attempting to understand the sense. Badger's body is in London; his mind is in Asia.

But see how his eye suddenly brightens. He rises precipitately. He approaches the window in order to read more clearly a paragraph which has just met his eyes.

This paragraph contained but these few lines:

"It is announced that a French electrician has discovered a new *thermo-electric* pile of great power. The invention is still a secret. It seems that by means of this pile it is possible to transform sixty hundredths of the heat of the solar rays into electricity."

His lordship's agitation will be understood. If the discovery was true, it would modify the situation entirely: his project might at last be realized. Jack Adams must be informed at once, and his opinion obtained.

He hastily wrote a line asking the engineer to come to him, rang for a servant and told him to take the letter to its address.

The servant was about to go, when his lordship was informed that Jack Adams wished to see him. The engineer entered hurriedly, and hastened towards Badger.

"Victory!" cried he. "Babylon will be reconstructed."

His lordship and the engineer shook hands effusively. They were transported with joy.

"So you have heard of the new discovery?" said his lordship.

"I have just received a letter about it from Paris," replied Adams. "My correspondent was himself present at the experiments of the inventor, a Mr. Cornillé. He gives me details from which I may determine with certainty the possibility of undertaking your project with success."

"God be praised!" said his lordship. "And now, please to explain to me exactly how this new discovery will enable us to realize our plans. I had just foreseen this result when reading the paragraph in the *Times;* and that is the reason I was about to send for you, when you came yourself."

His lordship and the engineer both sat down.

"Nothing can be easier, my lord," said the engineer. "I had supposed, in my calculations, that the rays of the sun would serve to heat the water in a boiler, according to the ingenious system of Mr. Mouchot. But it appeared that, by this process, I could but transform six or seven hundredths of the solar heat into electricity. This quantity was much too small."

"I understand the rest now," interrupted Badger. "Cornillé's discovery permits the conversion of sixty hundredths of solar heat into electricity. We are now in possession of a sufficient quantity of electricity."

"Exactly," replied the engineer. "I have, besides, made new calculations. They show that we can go ahead."

Jack Adams opened his note-book and took from it a leaf covered with calculations. He explained fully to his lordship the changes which he had found it necessary to make in his operations, and how he had arrived at the final result.

"I read in the *Times*," said Badger, "that the engineer had kept the secret of his discovery."

"That is true," replied Jack Adams, "but I do not think that that will prove an obstacle to you. It will be easy for you to buy the inventor's secret. Besides, when Cornillé knows the motive from which you act, it is certain that he will not hesitate to join forces with you. The French, my lord, are as adventurous in spirit as the English; and when some noble action is on foot the two nations can stretch out a friendly hand to each other."

"Well, at all events," said Badger, "I shall write immediately to Cornillé, make my propositions to him, and ask him to come here. He will reply without delay; we shall soon know where we stand in the matter."

Ten days after the sending of Sir James Badger's letter, Cornillé arrived in London. He was a tall man, with sharp and intelligent eyes, black hair, and a dark complexion. He was two or three years younger than Jack Adams.

Cornillé had accepted his lordship's propositions with enthusiasm. He loved the Orient by instinct, and would be delighted to go there to test his discovery.

As to selling this discovery to Badger, he would not hear of such a thing. His ambition lay higher; he would be contented at present with glory if his lordship's projects succeeded. Prosperity would come naturally afterwards.

On such a basis, the mutual understanding between Badger and Cornillé could not fail to be quickly established. As the co-operation of the other associates was already assured, it remained but to proceed to work. Accordingly, hardly two days after the young French engineer's arrival in London, we find him with his lordship, in the study, where are also our two old acquaintances, Captain Laycock and the geologist Monaghan, to whom have been added two new persons, who are likewise to take part in the expedition. The first, Flatnose, is a famous reporter on one of the largest papers in London. Stout and fat, his bulky body supported by two short legs, his face beaming perpetually with a broad smile, twinkling eyes, and swinging in his walk from one leg to the other, and, besides all this, no mean gourmand, our journalist has a vague and distant resemblance to Shakespeare's Falstaff. Let us hasten to add that this resemblance ceases at these physical peculiarities. Cheerful, jovial, a good companion, Flatnose is, besides, a brave and loyal soul, whom no one would think of making game of, and who is always ready to place his pen at the service of a good action. When you see him for the first time, you ask yourself how this fat person finds it possible to move about. Always red in the face, always mopping his brow with a handkerchief with large checks, he yet practices conscientiously his profession as a reporter, and returns each evening to the office with a note-book crammed with

various facts and anecdotes. The second is a Mr. Blacton, an eminent engineer, at the head of one of the most important manufactories in London. He is a man of about forty, grown old prematurely by incessant work. From bending over his desk during all of the day and part of the night, his back has become slightly rounded; an excellent man, well informed, who has travelled far and observed much, serious and yet interesting in his conversation.

Before a table in the centre of the room, on which are placed a  pamphlet formed of several large-sized sheets of paper with broad margins, joined together, and covered with close and legible writing, and a pen and ink-stand, stands Sir James Badger; his habitually serious face is yet more grave than usual.

The others, ranged around him in a semicircle, are motionless, as serious as his lordship. We feel that the moment is solemn for all. The gravity of the party has even extended to Flatnose.

Badger took the pamphlet from the table.

"Gentlemen," he began, in a slow voice, "we all know beforehand the object of this meeting; we all pursue the same end: the resurrection of Babylon and of Mesopotamia. We swear to remain faithful to our work, faithful unto death."

"We swear it," repeated those who surrounded him.

"The agent by means of which we hope to attain this end is electricity. We swear to keep the secret of our associate and friend,

Charles Cornillé, until the completion of our experiments. These once ended, each of us becomes free again."

"We swear it!"

"Each one of us, furthermore, binds himself to execute faithfully and zealously the part of the programme which is assigned to him in the general work!"

"We pledge ourselves!"

"I shall now read to you for the last time our act of association, after which it will but remain for each of us to affix his signature to this document."

Badger slowly read the terms of the pamphlet, stopping after each paragraph, in order to give time for any observations that might be made. He met only with signs of assent. When he had finished reading, he replaced the pamphlet on the table, and, dipping the pen into the ink, he was the first to sign, in his beautiful writing, firm and clear. The others followed his example, and came forward to sign in their turn.

"And now, gentlemen," said his lordship, when all was finished, "you know what each man's *rôle* is. Let us hasten, and let each one perform his task. Everything must be ready in six months."

After these words, it but remained for them to take leave of his lordship.

What resolutions had been taken? What had been the *rôle* assigned to each of our characters? Why was it desired to keep the secret of Cornillé's discovery?

So many questions, to which we shall reply successively.

We have seen that an association had been formed for the execution of the projects suggested by Captain Laycock. Jack Adams was intrusted with the general superintendence of the work. Cornillé, whose discovery had made the execution of the project possible, had for his special duty the perfecting of his thermo-solar pile and the construction of a gigantic one.

As for Badger, he reserved for himself the supreme management of the work. It was he, moreover, who devoted a large part of his fortune to the enterprise and who took charge of the diplomatic proceedings.

It had been decided that the first years should be devoted to trials which were indispensable to avoid meeting with certain failure. It was necessary to test on a large scale Cornillé's pile, which as yet was but an attempt. The basis of the association might be broadened and an appeal made to public subscription when preliminary trials had demonstrated the possibility of accomplishing the intended transformations.

The reason will now be understood which led his lordship to exact secrecy in regard to Cornillé's discovery. It was not an object in speculation, since he proposed to make it public as soon as his experiments in Mesopotamia were ended. But, if the secret of Cornillé's pile had been made known immediately, a swarm of inventors would have seized upon a prize so easy to work out. New improvements would have been announced every day with much display, and would have thrown disturbance into the work undertaken at Babylon. Now, to bring this work to a safe end, it was necessary to preserve all calmness and serenity of mind.

Cornillé was to set to work immediately to seek for the final improvements of his marvellous discovery. Lord Badger placed all the necessary credit at his disposal. The experiments were to take place in a part of his lordship's garden, transformed into works. They were thus certain to be secure from inquisitive persons and from spies who would seek to detect the secret.

Jack Adams was also to be in no want of work during six these months. He would have to procure or cause to be constructed the apparatus which were to be set up in Mesopotamia: turbines, dynamo-electric machines, condensators, cables, windmills, etc. It was necessary to think of everything, even to the smallest detail, for down there would be found neither works to make up the wanting material, nor a tradesman to furnish a screw or a bolt that had been forgotten. What a number of materials to be collected in this short space of time!

Jack Adams was furthermore charged with engaging the hands necessary for setting up the apparatus and working them afterward. What skill it would be necessary to display! Workmen and superiors would have to show untiring zeal and courage to contend with a people who detest science.

Badger's duty was relatively simpler. It was necessary to obtain the Sultan's authority to found a city and a colony on the banks of the Euphrates, on the site formerly occupied by Babylon. In order to hasten the conclusion of the treaty, Badger took the resolution of going to Constantinople himself; he thus placed himself directly in communication with the influential people of whom he would stand in need.

As to Captain Laycock, the first promoter of the project, he was appointed to manage the ships intended for the transport of the travelers and the material. Two large steamships were to reach the Indian Ocean by the Suez Canal, and unload their cases in the port of Bassorah, on the Shat-el-Arab.

A third small steamer, with light draught, was to take Sir James Badger and his companions to the coasts of Syria. From there, it would in its turn reach the port of Bassorah and serve for transporting the machines on the shallow waters of the Tigris and the Euphrates.

The place of the geologist, Monaghan, was necessary among the members of the expedition. His profound knowledge of the country which was to be traveled over and inhabited, would often be of great use.

Blacton was to be intrusted with the general management of the electric motors. Having for some years made a specialty of this kind of motors, he had been introduced to Badger as an indispensable auxiliary.

Flatnose's duties were fully indicated: he was to send to his paper, following the occurrence, notes, information, narratives, which would result in preventing public attention from being diverted from an enterprise the preparations for which would without doubt excite curiosity to a high degree, but which would not fail to be soon forgotten if the interest excited by its beginnings were not kept alive constantly. What enterprise to-day can hope to succeed without the co-operation of the press? Besides, Flatnose formed a gay note in this grave and learned society, a ray of fine and joyous humor.

Such were the personages and the *rôles* assigned to each, at the moment when Badger caused the document to be signed which seemed like a preface to the resurrection of Babylon.

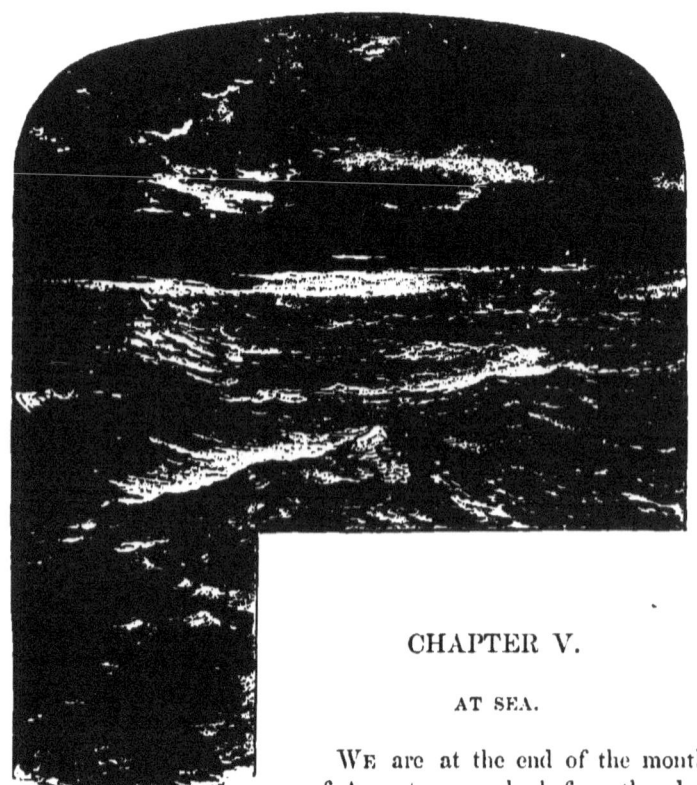

CHAPTER V.

AT SEA.

WE are at the end of the month of August, a week before the day of departure, set on the third of September. The preparations are completed.

Lord Badger has returned from Constantinople, having obtained all he desired. His task had been easy. The Turkish government, in want of money, had seen in his lordship's project a means of enriching itself.

Lord Badger had placed himself in communication with several important personages, who had given him letters of recommendation to the chiefs of the countries where he would set up his apparatus. He was the holder of a firman which granted him the proprietorship of the site of ancient Babylon, and of the portions of territory where he would see fit to establish his works. Besides, the firman ordered the governors of the provinces to aid, by all possible means, in supplying the needs and establishing the security of the enterprise directed by his lordship. The order was explicit, and no one would dare to evade it.

Cornillé's researches had been perfectly successful. Important improvements had been made in the thermo-electric pile. It had been possible to raise its original yield of sixty hundredths to seventy-five. The construction of a gigantic pile of fifty thousand elements had been completed. Jack Adams, on his part, had purchased or caused to be constructed all the necessary apparatus.

Miss Nelly was to accompany her father. She wished to follow him in this daring expedition, to share fatigue and danger with him. She kept her governess with her, the spare and tall Miss Jenny Ross, who could not have separated herself from her young mistress.

Captain Laycock had easily obtained leave of absence for three years.

A very useful member had furthermore been added to the expedition: it is the cook, Green. His modest office was neither the least important nor the easiest; but, having already traveled much, Green knew the culinary secrets of all parts of the earth. They might, therefore, trust to him to keep them from dying of hunger.

During this last week it was intended to put the apparatus on board of the two large transports, the *Davy* and the *Faraday*. The small steamer, the *Electricity*, was specially destined to carry the leaders of the expedition, with their luggage.

The three ships were to sail at the same time. The *Davy* and the *Faraday* were to carry, besides the plant, the numerous hands engaged by Jack Adams. Sixty men, workmen and foremen, had been divided between the two ships. Their destination, as we have already said, was Bassorah, at the lower end of the Persian Gulf.

As to the *Electricity*, it was to land Badger and his daughter, with Miss Ross, as well as Cornillé, Monaghan, Blacton, Flatnose and Green at Iskanderoon, on the coast of Syria. Laycock and Jack Adams would rejoin the *Davy* and the *Faraday* at Suez, to go with these two ships to Bassorah.

The third of September arrived at last. On that day the sun rose radiant, as if to salute the departing voyagers with his rays. Was he not king of the feast, this star which was to give a portion of his heat to resuscitate the empire of Semiramis? His presence was thus a happy omen, and he seemed to say to all: "You can count on me."

The *Electricity* rocked softly under a light wind. Already under steam, a light cloud of smoke issued from its wide smoke-stack. Near by, two other ships, of much greater tonnage, were completing their preparations for departure. They were the *Davy* and the *Faraday*, which were to follow the *Electricity* at an interval of a few hours.

A little before six Captain Laycock appeared on St. Katharine's Docks, walking with a resolute step and whistling a martial air. His hands in the two pockets of his jacket, his cap perched jauntily on his head, his whiskers flying in the wind, he replied with a friendly good morning to the salute of the sailors. The brave seaman, who was wearied by the turbulent life of the cities, was happy to return again to the sea, which he had not seen for several months.

He went on board of the ship, and inspected it minutely to its smallest details, wishing to assure himself with his own eyes that nothing was wanting and everything was in order. He finally took possession of his cabin, and awaited the arrival of the other travellers.

The time of departure was fixed at eleven o'clock precisely, the time of high-tide. The docks of the Thames became more animated each moment. The ships, crowded against each other, were loading and unloading merchandise. Several of them were also waiting for the tide in order to gain the high seas.

Jack Adams, Cornillé, Monaghan and Blacton arrived one after the other. Their luggage had, since the day before, been down in the hold or in their cabins. They walked about on the deck, talking or smoking cigars, while awaiting Badger's arrival. As to Green, he was already at his cooking-stove since morning: luncheon was to be taken on board ship on the way down the Thames.

His lordship, his daughter, and the governess, arrived by carriage a few minutes before eleven. Giving his arm to Miss Nelly, Badger rapidly crossed the gangway and stepped on board of his ship. The passengers and sailors were drawn up on the deck to receive them. Miss Nelly was radiant. What a pleasure for her to make so long a voyage! Her traveling costume for the long voyage, a dark blue dress of light material, soft felt hat with turned-up brim, and a veil of the same color as the dress, became her charmingly. Her cheeks, under the influence of her pleasure and excitement, were yet more rosy than usual; her eyes sparkled more and had a more energetic expression. A little too much given to dreaming, she now allowed herself to be swayed by external matters. Besides, she felt herself the queen in this select company; she knew that she would be petted and spoiled by every one. And was she not indeed the fairy in whom all placed their trust, and who would make the hours passed on the sea seem less long? The passengers felt moved when the young girl stepped on the ship, and Miss Nelly's look remained impressed on more than one heart.

His lordship shook hands with all.

"And Flatnose," said he, "why where is he? It seems to me that our journalist fails us."

In truth, Flatnose was absent. Meanwhile, the time advanced and the ship was to sail at eleven o'clock. The English never wait; so much the worse for the late-comers.

A clock in the neighborhood struck eleven. Badger gave the signal for departure. Suddenly, desperate calls were heard on the wharf, and a man appeared, running as quickly as his little legs would permit, red as a lobster, puffing like a locomotive. It was Flatnose, whose *embonpoint* had almost caused him to be left behind.

London Bridge receded gradually in the distance. The *Electricity* passed proudly along the docks which line the left bank of the Thames, between two interminable lines of ships that had come from all quarters of the globe. The monuments of the capital were profiled against a grayish horizon.

Greenwich and its handsome naval hospital were soon passed. They might say good-bye to London. The passengers descended to their cabins in order to put in place such articles as they had taken with them at the last moment. It was also necessary to make some modifications in their toilette: the maritime life was beginning and was to last several weeks.

The ship's bell rang for luncheon and all went up on deck again, where the table was set.

The ship had already made good progress. Woolwich had been passed, with its hulks, the glorious remains of the frigates taken from the French at the battle of Trafalgar. The Thames, with its low banks, flowed through flat meadows. The landscape was monotonous, and but seldom deserved to draw the attention.

Toasts were proposed to the health of Lord Badger and Miss Nelly, and success drunk to the resurrection of Babylon.

After luncheon, they walked about on the deck, smoking and conversing. The ship passed Gravesend and its beautiful gardens, a place of resort for the inhabitants of the capital during the summer. It is at Gravesend that the Thames ends. From here on the *Electricity* sailed on the open sea. In the evening it rounded the headland of North Foreland and entered the channel.

We shall not follow the ship in its rapid passage through the Channel and the Atlantic Ocean. The weather remained fine, with a quiet breeze which did not strain the little vessel. They kept well away from land. There was none in sight but the cliffs of France and England and the granitic rocks of Finisterre when they rounded Brittany.

The time did not pass slowly for those on board, for each one contrived to vary his studies and diversions. Miss Nelly played the piano; Laycock was also a musician, and played the violin. Jack Adams and Cornillé assisted Miss Nelly with their voices. Cornillé especially, a great lover of the opera, knew the principal airs of French, Italian and German music. As to Flatnose, he made puns, composed charades, and told all sorts of anecdotes; he was the wit of the party.

Nor was earnest work neglected. They re-examined the plans; they studied the maps of the country which they were going to visit; they contrived new appliances of electricity. On the latter subject their imagination rose at times to extravagance. Did not jolly Flatnose propose one day to construct electric men with which to people the new Babylon!

Thus the time passed on board. The *Electricity* was a fast vessel, and rapid progress was made. On the evening of the 7th they were already in sight of the coasts of Spain. They sailed close along the coast of Portugal and stopped at Gibraltar to take in coal.

After that they left the Atlantic to enter the Mediterranean. The heat became much greater and the sky more blue. The proximity of the lands and the deserts of Africa made itself felt.

On the 13th they had passed Sicily and the Isle of Malta. The ship was sailing calmly on the wide lake lying between Sicily, Greece and Tripoli, when the sky became suddenly overcast, and a violent wind set in to blow a gale. The furious sea broke over the deck of the ship. The latter lurched and righted again immediately, seeming to defy the elements risen against it. Its hull quivered, its masts shook; but it was able to resist the fury of the waves. The passengers had taken refuge in their cabins. Miss Nelly, not yet sufficiently accustomed to the sea, was rather frightened; she seemed each instant to feel the ship swallowed up by the sea.

Captain Laycock, fortunately, did not lose his head. He had seen much more terrible storms than this one. Clinging to the railing of his bridge, he directed the working of the ship in a firm voice. Land was far off—the Mediterranean deep; there was little to fear.

The storm lasted eight hours. At last it calmed down. The sea became smooth and blue as before. The passengers went on deck again. A good dinner by *chef* Green, washed down with champagne, and lit up by the rays of the setting sun, ended in dispelling the anxieties of the day.

The conversation of course turned on the incidents of the storm. The captain, from his calculations and the height of the sun, concluded that they could not be far from the coast of Africa—towards the promontory of Barca. It was high time that the storm came to an end, or they would have risked being dashed to pieces on a rock.

While they were taking tea by the light of the moon and of the stars which shine so brightly in these dark blue and clear nights of the oriental countries, Miss Nelly asked Cornillé what the cause was of these sudden changes from calm weather to a furious storm, and from storm to a calm such as they were enjoying at the moment. The engineer had begun to explain to the young girl the mechanism of storms and the general theory of the winds, always produced by the sudden cooling of certain atmospheric layers, which acts as a great current of air, when he was suddenly interrupted in his demonstrations by a bright light which illumined the sky. They took it for lightning at the first moment, and thought another storm was coming up; but it was a magnificent bolis. It crossed the firmament in all its length, proceeding slowly, and leaving myriads of sparks behind it. Then it disappeared at the horizon towards the East.

"Father," cried Miss Nelly, "this globe of fire invites us to follow it! It is a messenger which Heaven sends you to encourage you in your project!"

"I accept your augury, my dear Nelly," replied Badger, embracing his daughter. "We are certain of success if Heaven aids us."

As if all the wonders of the earth had agreed on a *rendezvous* on that evening, the sea became phosphorescent. The ship seemed to sail on an ocean of fire. The wake which the prow left far behind it, the foam raised by the screw, the lightest ripples on the surface of the waves were as many jets of fire, which sparkled in the night. The passengers were all collected on the deck, admiring this magnificent spectacle.

Towards midnight the phosphorescence suddenly ceased, and every one sought his cabin, profoundly impressed by the varied events of the day.

The sky remained clear during the rest of the passage. They were, besides, approaching the first port where they were to touch, and the passengers were already making their preparations for disembarking.

One evening the island of Cyprus was at last signaled. In the distance was descried the summit of Mount Troödos, which forms part of the range of Olympus. Then, little by little, the eye discerned the summits of the Adelphi, the peaks of the Macheras, and finally the headland of the Stavrovuni. This promontory, especially, struck the eye by its spiry form. The ship sailed along the foot of the mountain, and by the aid of glasses one could see the temple of the Benedictines, constructed at its summit. The story runs that in the caverns of this mountain the Knight Tannhäuser is awaiting the sound of the last trumpet.

The sun had already set when the *Electricity* let go her anchor before the port of Larnaca, the ancient Citium of the Greeks.

The night was too far advanced to think of landing, for it is impossible for ships of any considerable tonnage to approach the shore. It was therefore necessary to pass one more night on board, notwithstanding the great pleasure every one would have felt in reaching *terra firma*, after passing so long a space of time on the sea.

Next morning the transshipment of the travelers began at daybreak. Boats rowed by natives came to receive the passengers, and brought them to land. The *Electricity* was left in charge of the mate. Captain Laycock, who knew Cyprus, having been there several times, wished to serve as a guide for Badger and his companions.

Since the treaty of 1878 with Turkey the island of Cyprus is governed by England. After sailing for fifteen days, they were once more on English soil. It had been decided to devote a day to the inspection of Larnaca. This is a double city. The Marina is a new quarter, built on the sea-coast. As to the city proper, it is built at about two-thirds of a mile from the shore, in the midst of a large, uncultivated plain, where nothing meets the eye but here and there a few palms with long trunks swaying in the breeze.

What a contrast! To pass abruptly from London to Larnaca—from the mists of the Thames to the azure skies of Asia! At sea, the transition to the difference in the clearness of the sky had been clearly perceived; but the contrast became apparent in all its grandeur when they found themselves on land again.

The city is in reality but a poor village. The houses are low, with flat roofs and walls half crumbled down. Yet this singular medley was pleasant to the eyes and to the imagination. The intense light tinged the walls with reflections unknown in the dull climates of the north of Europe. All objects stood out strongly and in strange relief against the dark blue sky.

And what originality in the varied costumes of the passers-by! Greeks, Turks, Armenians, Jews, Arabs—all the nations of the Orient elbowed each other in the streets, forming the most curious contrasts of color by this intermixture. At the extremity of the city, our travelers climbed a slight elevation, from where the view extended far out to the sea and to the mountains of Cyprus. Sky, earth and sea sparkled under the burning rays of a fiery sun. The eye was dazzled by a light to which it was not yet accustomed. That wonderful charm which all feel who see the Orient for the first time was now felt by Miss Nelly. It was a new world into which she had entered. It seemed to her like a beautiful dream.

The mountain chains which run through the whole length of the island bounded the horizon towards the north and east. Their jagged summits, their sharp peaks, their undulating plateaus—all the details of their form were revealed to the eye with astonishing distinctness. The eye, under the intense light of these regions, must needs be educated anew. Distances are no longer determined with certainty; distant objects seem to draw nearer, for the colors are no longer softened successively by the haze.

Miss Nelly remained a long time leaning on the side of a terrace constructed at the top of this hill. She could not tear herself away from her contemplation. Yet time flew rapidly, and it became necessary to descend again to Larnaca. In the evening every one was once more settled in his cabin, and the *Electricity* was making ready to go to sea again the next morning.

CHAPTER VI.

ON THE BANKS OF THE ORONTES.

The *Electricity* was to land its passengers at Iskanderoon, a small city situated on the Syrian coast, opposite to the island of Cyprus. The passage from Cyprus to Iskanderoon is not long; a mere arm of the sea separates the island from the Asiatic continent. The wind was favorable, the sea hardly ruffled. The disembarcation was effected without any difficulty.

Iskanderoon is situated at the end of the gulf of the same name. It was called Alexandretta before the Arabian conquest. Built on marshy ground, it is very unhealthy during the hot season. Therefore, the rich families are accustomed to leave it during the summer and to resort to Beilan, on the first escarpments of the Amanus.

Only the poorest inhabitants were left in the city. Their sickly aspect, especially that of the women and children, was not designed to delight the eyes of the travelers.

From Iskanderoon, the expedition was to be divided into two bodies, which would reunite, each by different routes, at the place of meeting. One of these two parties, commanded by Captain Laycock, and of which Jack Adams was also a member, would continue by the maritime route. It would sail along the coast of Syria, cross the Red Sea, and go up the Persian Gulf to the mouth of the Euphrates, which the *Electricity* would ascend to Babylon. Lord Badger, his daughter, the governess, Cornillé, Monaghan, Blacton, and Flatnose would form the second group, which would follow the land-route and travel by caravan.

As the caravan is even at the present time almost the only mode of transport by land which exists in Asia, as well for persons as for merchandise, we shall say a few words about that manner of traveling, the organization of which has varied but little since the time when the Midianite merchants, coming from Gilead, crossed the desert to bring balm and myrrh to Egypt, and, between times, bought young boys, whom they sold again as slaves.

The only difference is that to-day, when you wish to go by caravan, you apply to a commercial man of a new class, which probably did not exist in the time of Jacob, and from whom you hire as many horses and mules as are necessary.

This contractor, whom we might compare to our transport and traffic companies, is sometimes the owner of several hundred animals. With his *charvadars* (grooms), he accompanies the caravan, or is represented by a deputy, and holds the responsibility for anything that may occur.

The *charvadars* form a class of men of a certain importance. They represent our railroads and our steamships. From the shores of the Caspian Sea to those of the Persian Gulf, from the frontiers of India to those of China, travelers and merchandise pass under their care. One can but praise their honesty. They lead the mules, pack and unpack them. They occupy themselves in mending saddles, bags and other accessories. They keep pace with the animals in all weather, and often outstrip them. At night they watch by turns over the travelers or the goods.

Lord Badger was directed by the English resident to one of the most favorably known members of this useful corporation, and never was a caravan formed under better conditions. Gentle horses for the ladies, hacks for the men, every animal was the subject of a thorough examination, and was subjected to a preliminary trial.

The military escort was furnished by the authorities of the country, who bowed dutifully to the official orders of the Sultan. On the route which they were to follow to the Euphrates one is not always safe from attacks. But, thanks to the Turkish soldiers and to the excellent arms which had been provided in abundance, there was nothing to fear.

Several days were spent in making preparations for departure. In the Orient, the traveler who leaves the cities inhabited by Europeans must carry everything with him. He takes his meals in the open air and sleeps mostly under his tent. The least neglect, the least omission might prove prejudicial. It is true that a sufficient number of caravansaries are met with on the routes frequented by the caravans. They are the inns of the country. But the only thing that is always to be found ready here—and it is certainly not to be despised—is excellent coffee, served burning hot. Beasts and baggage may be housed here, and a momentary shelter sought. As to the rooms, they consist in small, square alcoves, which the travelers must themselves furnish with all necessary articles, for they are devoid of everything. Some of these caravansaries have a large court-yard, with basin and fountain, shaded by orange and lemon trees; but most of them are very filthy, and it is preferable to camp in the open air.

The last days of September had arrived. The intense heat of summer had given place to the milder temperature of the fair autumn days. The journey was made without great fatigue during the day. The nights only are really to be feared in the Orient; for, by reason of the amount of moisture absorbed during the day by the solar rays, and converted afterward into heavy dew, the nights are always cool and damp, even at the hottest season of the year.

In order to guard against these sudden alternations of cold and heat, our travelers provided themselves plentifully with cloaks, Arabian burnoos and woollen stuffs of the country.

While the caravan is making its final preparations for the journey, we must say a few words in regard to the motive that had determined Lord Badger and his companions to reach the Euphrates by taking this part of the coast of Asia Minor as their starting-point.

Several engineers had conceived the project of constructing a railway which should place the Mediterranean and the Euphrates in communication. Now, it is exactly in the neighborhood of Iskanderoon that it was proposed to place the terminus of the projected railroad. The Euphrates, in fact, after emerging from the mountains of Armenia, turns suddenly towards the west; then, describing another turn, towards the south, it flows for a short time parallel to the Mediterranean Sea, from which it is separated by only about ninety-five miles, opposite Iskanderoon.

It was Badger's intention to take up these projects on his own account. That is why he was desirous of visiting the region in company with Monaghan, in order to see for himself what was the configuration of the ground, what advantages or obstacles it might offer, and what work would have to be performed. Finally, it was also to be determined what place on the coast should be the starting-point of the new line.

It was easy to decide, on the first examination, that Iskanderoon would make an excellent terminus. Drainage works would be executed to render it inhabitable at all seasons. In spite of the violent storms which at times descend from the mountain and rush down into the valley, its harbor is yet the safest on the whole coast. The necessary enlargements and improvements would be made there. Starting from there, the railroad would pass through the high plateaus of the Amanus which separate the sea from the Euphrates, then run along the river, cross at Babylon, and reach the shores of the Persian Gulf. It would thus place England and the Indies in rapid communication. In truth, considerable skilful labor would be necessary to pierce tunnels through the mountains and construct viaducts across the valleys; but these difficulties do not dismay engineers, English, French or American.

On the day before their departure, the travelers had visited one of the ravines over which the railway in question would have to be built. It was called the Devil's Ravine. Lying deep among the rocks, which formed as it were a gigantic notch in the bed of the earth, it owed its origin to one of the earthquakes so frequent in these latitudes. A torrent ran through the bowels of the earth five hundred feet below the spot where the excursionists were standing.

During this walk they were able to ascertain how far the processes of native agriculture are behind our own. In tilling their fields, the husbandmen make use of the primitive plough—used also by the Arabs of Algeria—which consists only of a long wooden beam provided with a share, also of wood, and which hardly penetrates the superficial layer of the soil.

The vegetation was, moreover, very different from that of Western Europe. Miss Nelly saw for the first time the arborescent cotton-tree, the cultivation of which extended over wide spaces, and admired its flowers of a saffron yellow, marbled with bright red. Monaghan picked some specimens of the most curious plants: the *Allium Neapolitanum*, a superb *liliacée*, with white flowers; the *Daphne sericea*, and, especially, the *Arum dioscoridis*, an admirable flower, if it only did not exhale a tainted odor. Miss Nelly's dress was torn on the way by the thorns of a small shrub.

"That is the *Ziziphus spina christi*," replied the geologist to the young girl, who asked its name. "It is called so, I suppose, in remembrance of Christ's crown of thorns."

The next morning at sunrise, after having taken leave of the cap-

tain and of Jack Adams, and having appointed to meet them at Babylon, the travelers forming part of the caravan left Iskanderoon, marching along the sea-coast. The weather was fine, and the little party proceeded quickly and in good order. The following arrangements had been adopted and were to be continued to the end:

First came the mules, with their drivers and the baggage; tents, mattresses, blankets, kitchen utensils, victuals, wood. This little troop was escorted by half a score of Turkish soldiers, in company with whom was Green, the cook. It preceded the main body of the caravan, so that, on arriving at the places where a halt was to be made, everything was found prepared for the meal or for the night's rest.

Badger, his daughter, the governess, Cornillé, Monaghan, Blacton,

Flatnose, a guide, and an interpreter formed a group at the head of the rest of the caravan. A wagon, or, rather, a very large cart, *Tahkt-i-Rāhwān*, followed them, carrying the minor supplies and the instruments which might be needed on the march. *Tahkt-i-Rāhwān* may be translated literally by traveling bed. It is a long litter, flat-bottomed, with glass panels and shafts between which one or more mules are harnessed. The top is closed. The interior is lined with mattresses and cushions. It holds two persons comfortably. This vehicle, peculiar to the country, was to serve as a means of transport for Miss Ross and for the other travelers when they should be fatigued from having remained too long on horseback. Miss Nelly rarely used it; but Flatnose and Miss Ross were oftener in the wagon than in the saddle. Thanks to this circumstance, and probably also to the law of contrasts, a delightful intimacy was soon established between the tall and lean governess and the stout and fat journalist.

At some distance behind Badger and his companions the rest of the Turkish escort brought up the rear. In case of attack our travelers would be quickly aided by the soldiers. Besides they were sufficiently numerous and sufficiently well armed to sustain a first onset and give the troop time to rally.

Thanks to their excellent animals, the travelers advanced rapidly. A halt was made several times during the day. In the morning they were up at sunrise. Badger and Cornillé, who were skilful hunters, beat the bushes and were able to bring down some pieces of game. The small hares of Syria were not to be disdained, especially when they had passed through the skilful hands of *chef* Green.

Monaghan frequently separated from the rest of the party in order to study the nature of the ground and rocks. While applying himself to his favorite researches it occurred also that he discovered some interesting specimens of animals peculiar to the country. Thus, one day, while exploring a small elevation, he had the fortune to capture alive a species of rat which looks very much like a mole. This animal has a thick body, fine and silky hair and large head, with a neck so little developed that one might think it were totally wanting. Add to this very small ears and eyes almost completely sunk into the skin.

That day everybody brought in some specimens of the fauna of the country as trophies. Miss Nelly picked up several small turtles that were sleeping by the side of a pool, and Flatnose had a trial of speed with a big African turtle which fled into the grass. It was our stout journalist who came victorious out of the race and who brought back the animal triumphantly in his arms.

On the evening of the first day the caravan arrived at the ruins of Seleucia, or rather at the site which is believed to have been that of this ancient city. The place of the port is to-day covered by the sands. Only a few shapeless vestiges of the ancient city remain. The tents had been raised on the sea-shore. The moon, then in its full, cast silvery reflections on the blue waves. The coasts of Syria were outlined to the farthest horizon, with their protuding capes and their mountainous edge. It was difficult to imagine a spot better chosen for a first night of camping out. Later on, no doubt, such agreeable ones would not always be found.

On the following day they continued to follow the sea-coast. The road bordered upon a sandy declivity which descended to the level of the waters. At times, however, the uniformity of the plain was broken by a detached branch of the Amanus range, which dwindled away in soft undulations beneath the waves or ended abruptly, jutting out above them. Then there was a rise of several yards and the horizon widened. The Mediterranean sparkled in the distance, and the eye was dazzled by the bright light which the waves reflected in all directions. In the evening they reached the mouth of the Nahr-el-Aasy, which is none other than the ancient Orontes.

The camp was laid near the ruins of an old abandoned khan, outside of the walls of the little village of Suediah, which lies on the very banks of the river and serves as a port for the city of Antioch, formerly so important.

The caravan was to ascend the course of the Orontes quite far inland. Its valley might be an excellent road for the railway. The Orontes flows at first from south to north, following the foot of the Amanus. Then, finding a ravine to give it passage, it runs through narrow defiles and empties into the sea.

From Suediah to Antioch the banks of the Orontes are charming. The landscape changes at each turn of the valley. Fruit-trees cover the slopes with their foliage. White houses, with flat roofs, disappear almost completely amidst the clumps of verdure. Bare rocks jut out over the river now and then, overhanging it at a great height. The sky, the trees, the earth, the waters, form an admirable whole.

Yet these favored regions have been witnesses of the most frightful calamities. At this meeting-point of two worlds the nations of

Europe and of Asia have clashed in fearful conflict. The innumerable armies of the barbarian conquerors—from those of Darius and Xerxes to the hordes of Tamerlane and of Jengis Khan—have overrun and plundered them, and thousands of men have left their bones there.

And as if man had not done enough, nature herself seems to have made it her task to destroy her own works. Incessantly undermined by subterranean fires, the ground has often opened in terrible earthquakes, which have overthrown cities and destroyed entire populations.

What does it signify as to the eternal renewal of universal life? Wherever the earth has drunk human blood in abundance grass grows more thickly, the crops are more plentiful. The lava and ashes of the volcanos, which have devastated entire territories, form, in time, soil of an incomparable fertility, covered with flowers and fruits.

Why wonder that, following the example of nature, man also forgets, and, without a thought of the sudden and terrible awakening, rebuilds his dwellings on this same soil which has swallowed up several of the generations which have preceded him?

At about ten o'clock in the morning the caravan reached the little Turkish city of Antakia, formerly the large and wealthy city of Antioch, the most important of Roman Asia. The ancient capital of Syria rises in the midst of a valley, closed in by mountains and washed by the Orontes, which, before reaching the city, divides into several branches, the waters of which turn a large number of mills and irrigate beautiful gardens.

Like most of the once famous cities of Asia Minor, Antioch has passed through many and varied vicissitudes. The time of its greatest prosperity corresponds to the beginning of the Christian era.

Founded by Seleucus Nicator and peopled first by a colony of Athenians inhabiting the neighboring city of Antigonia, it grew rapidly and became the capital of Syria and the residence of the Seleucidæ, *the queen of the Orient*.

Christianity was brought here a few years after the death of its founder by his immediate disciples. St. Paul lived here over a year, and St. Peter was its first bishop. The Asiatic customs of its inhabitants, their passion for luxury, brilliant festivals and pompous spectacles, the refined and elegant habits of its wealthy merchants, seemed to make it an unpropitious centre for the development of the new doctrine.

Yet it is at Antioch that the followers of the Gospel multiplied most rapidly and that they began to be designated by the name of Christians. To its administrative and commercial importance was then added a great religious notoriety, for it soon became a most celebrated metropolis in the Christian world: ten councils were held here from 252 to 380, and in the sixth century it became the seat of a patriarchate which extended over Syria, Cilicia, and Mesopotamia.

In the year 115 a terrible earthquake destroyed a part of the city and carried off 100,000 of its inhabitants. An idea can thus be formed as to what its entire population was at the time. Yet it had recovered again from its disasters, notably under the reign of the Emperor Justinian. A second earthquake, which took place in 583, began the period of its decadence, accelerated by the conquest of the Saracens, who took possession of it, together with all of Syria, in 635. United in the tenth century to the empire of the East, then recovered by the Saracens, it was taken from them in 1098 by the Crusaders, commanded by Bohemond I., who became prince of Antioch.

Under the Latin empire of Constantinople it regained a certain importance, as ephemeral as the cause which had produced it. Nevertheless the little Christian principality of Antioch existed until 1268, and Baldwin VII. was its last prince. Since then it belonged to the Mussulmans, under whom its decadence was rapid and complete. The earthquakes of 1822 and 1872 have subjected it to great damage. To-day it numbers but 15,000 inhabitants.

Our travelers passed through the city without making a stop there. Its fortifications, furnished with 130 towers, its strong citadel raised by the Crusaders, are now but walls cracked by the upheavals of the ground. They were anxious to get back to the banks of the Orontes and to reach Hamah.

After leaving Antioch the road becomes rough, the Orontes flows in deep gorges difficult of access. They were at times obliged to leave the valley and ascend by steep foot-paths. The horses still managed it; but the litter threatened each moment to be dashed to pieces.

On emerging from the mountain, swamps were met with. The country, pretty well populated until then, became almost deserted. The vegetation itself suffered from the tainted air which renders the country uninhabitable. At last Hamah was reached, the ancient *Epiphania*, situated at the bottom of a deep and narrow valley, on an alluvial bed brought in by the waters of the Orontes. Hamah might be one of the stations of the future railway, which would reach this city by passing the range of the Amanus without rising above an altitude of 1,600 feet, and then proceed towards the Euphrates across the desert. The ladies felt somewhat fatigued by a mode of traveling to which they were not yet accustomed. After some consultation it was decided that Monaghan and Cornillé should go alone as far as the town of Homs, which was about twenty-five miles above Hamah; and also that the rest of the caravan should wait for these two gentlemen in the latter place, where everything could be found that was necessary for recovering from their previous fatigues: fresh water, exquisite fruits, vegetables in abundance, would soon have recruited the strength of the travelers.

Homs, the ancient Emesa, is of considerable importance from a commercial point of view. More than 10,000 camels pass through it after the autumn harvests. It is not only a great market, it is also the centre of a very prosperous industry. It possesses manufactories for silk figured with gold, cotton goods and coarser stuffs. Much madder is raised in the vicinity.

A short stream, the Nahr-el-Kebir, has made a passage for itself through the range of the Amanus; its valley might be used for a railway that would have its starting-point at Tripoli in Syria on the Mediterranean, and reach the Euphrates by the plain.

Thus, three natural roads were open to the railway destined to join the Euphrates to the Mediterranean. At present, it was only a question of making surveys; later, when all the documents had been collected, a definite decision would be jointly made.

While Cornillé and Monaghan devoted themselves to these investigations, the rest of the caravan took advantage of the stoppage by inspecting Hamah and its surroundings.

The stay at Hamah is delightful. Its gardens are the most beautiful to be found in Syria, which possesses such beautiful ones. Lord Badger had rented one of these gardens, situated outside of the city, and had there established his camp.

The high plateaux which surround the city produce corn and wheat in abundance. To raise the water necessary for cultivation up to these high plains, use has been made, following the immemorial usage of the East, of gigantic *norias* or water-wheels placed all along the bluffs, and which impart an unusual movement to that part of the course of the Orontes.

The culture of the cotton-tree has given birth to a prosperous industry in this country; more than 3,000 weavers manufacture common stuffs here for the people of the land.

The manner of weaving is as primitive as the manner of tilling, and the loom, which might figure in the retrospective museum beside the plough, probably dates back to the same antiquity.

In one of her walks, Miss Nelly had an opportunity of seeing one in full operation. On the floor of a little hut, too low to admit of an upright position, and lighted only by the opening serving as a door, a young woman, between sixteen and eighteen years of age, of the purest Arabian type, whose costume recalled that of Horace Vernet's *Rebecca at the Fountain*, was seated in Oriental fashion, that is to say squatting on the ground, before a rough wooden frame on which were stretched the threads destined to form the warp of the cloth. With her slender fingers, which performed the functions of the shuttle, the weaver passed the thread which was to form the weft alternately over and under the threads of the warp. She showed a surprising dexterity in this delicate operation. While continuing her work, she inclined her fine head, from which a rich braid of jet black hair fell down on her uncovered breast, now to the right, now to the left of the wooden frame, and looked curiously at the young Englishwoman with her beautiful childlike eyes, roguish and soft, while a smile of naive astonishment parted her red lips and showed her shining teeth.

These walks, giving rest from the long rides on horseback, this knowledge of the familiar manners and customs of a country which is acquired only by living there and seeing its inhabitants close by; these scenes of a rural beauty which the traveler accustomed to follow standard routes observes so rarely, served to occupy the six days which passed away, until the return of the explorers Monaghan and Cornillé, in an agreeable manner. Nevertheless, they were happy to be united once more, and the interrupted voyage was joyfully resumed.

On leaving Hamah, the valley of the Orontes was abandoned in order to reach Aleppo by ascending towards the north-east.

The road followed by the caravan passed over slightly undulating plateaux, varying in height from 1100 to 1300 feet. Vegetation became scarce. No trees. Now and then some dwarfed and stunted shrubs. They were beginning to enter the immense belt of deserts which extends over vast spaces in Arabia and terminates in a rounded point in that part of Asia Minor through which the travelers were then passing.

This vast plain, stretching farther than the eye can reach, is not level and uniform as one might at first suppose it to be. As you advance, you perceive the ground, now slightly depressed, now slightly swelling, is, on the contrary, very uneven. At a distance this unevenness is not visible to the eye, which sees but an ocean of sands, streaked, like the surface of waters in calm weather, with a multitude of little longitudinal striæ.

The sea of sand is no more sheltered from storms than the other sea. The winds which come from the south blow here with extreme violence, for no serious obstacle is opposed to their action, and, in several places, they have heaped up banks of gravel, downs, or ridges.

Here and there a rock rises above the ground, on the surface of which there appear at great intervals large brown spots which one cannot help comparing to islands: these are the oases.

The analogy between the desert and the sea is, moreover, so striking, that it obtrudes itself upon the most uncultivated natures. There is the same impression of grandeur and infinity; but that given by the desert, when seen for the first time, is perhaps still more startling.

It was about nine o'clock in the morning. The heat began to whiten the sky. They were approaching the oasis of Marrah, where they were to stop and rest for a few hours. The horses, conscious of the proximity of the stopping-place, broke into a trot.

By degrees the oasis grew wider. Palm-trees showed their dark green tops strongly outlined against the pale sky. Other trees soon appeared: the arbutus, the orange, the lemon, the mimosa, mingled their varied foliage. The whole vegetation became more luxurious as they advanced.

When, after a long journey through the dull and silent desert, you behold this human nest, full of verdure and freshness, emerging suddenly from the dry sands, it is difficult not to believe yourself the victim of an illusion. How, indeed, could one imagine that the two extremes of the barest sterility and the most exuberant fertility could be united and exist, so to speak, side by side, without losing any of their absoluteness?

There was, however, no deception; it was, indeed, a reality which they had before them. The white houses of the *Ksour*, the slender spire of the mosque, the square mass of the *Casbah*, stood out among gardens separated by hedges of cactus and watered by innumerable rivulets babbling in the thick grass. The sweet smell of the coffee-trees in bloom, the more penetrating odor of the daturas and the jasmines produced an almost intoxicating perfume. By tacit agreement, the travelers brought their horses to a walk in order to enjoy longer the magical picture which was being unfolded before their eyes.

Since their departure from Hamah, that morning, they experienced the sensation which all have felt who—without even going as far as Syria—have penetrated into the Algerian Sahara by the pass of El-Kantara; that of a new Orient, unknown until then, the Orient of the Bible and of the *Song of Songs*. All that has been previously seen is beautiful without doubt, splendid, marvelous, but it offers nothing of which Southern Europe cannot give an idea. Suddenly, without anything to prepare you for this abrupt transition, at the turn of a valley, on emerging from a narrow passage between two rocks, in the twinkling of an eye the sky, the earth, the light, the relief of the objects, all has changed. The vivid pictures of the Bible are then obtruded on the sense and the imagination, the idea of time vanishes, the sense of the present is lost, you feel yourself living three or four thousand years back among the fields of Gilead or in the gardens of Sharon.

Every one was silent; Miss Nelly seemed absorbed in the contemplation of a vision that she feared would vanish. Cornillé, who rode at her side, and who also saw the Orient for the first time, was no doubt moved by the same feeling, for he said to her in a voice full of emotion:

"Is this not beautiful, *mademoiselle?*"

"Very beautiful," she replied, with a slight start, as if awaking from a dream.

"And do you know of what I was thinking?" she added, smiling. "I was pitying my friends in London, who will never see what we see now."

The sheikh of Marrah, informed of the arrival of his guests, came to meet them at the entrance to his casbah, and conducted Lord Badger and his friends into the building, while his servants attended to the escort.

The casbah was a square, heavy edifice, running around an interior court, like all Arabian dwellings. Around the court extends a gallery on which the doors open that lead to the rooms. Under this gallery servants were grinding wheat and maize in a mill formed of two stones turning on each other.

In the centre of the divan, that is to say, of the apartment which, in every Eastern house, is used for receiving visitors, a table had been set, and a collation of couscous, dates, watermelons, milk and eggs was served.

This divan was a large, square room, with a vaulted ceiling, situated on the ground-floor, about two stories high, looking to the north, and having windows only on that side. Everything here was admirably arranged for protecting one's self from the heat and enjoying the delights of the oriental *farniente*. The skeikh insisted on making his guests smoke chibouks and nargilehs,

and our travelers appreciated highly the sweet and perfumed tobacco which was offered them.

When the repast was ended and the coffee had been drunk, Miss Nelly and the governess repaired to that portion of the palace assigned to the women, which they entered alone. However generous and cordial Oriental hospitality may be, the rule which forbids the women from appearing before men with unveiled faces has remained inflexible. The visitors were received by the wife of the sheikh, and by his daughters, who, both widows and childless, had come back to their father, waiting, no doubt, until it pleased him to choose new husbands for them.

Notwithstanding her age—advanced, for a woman of her race—and the *embonpoint* that was beginning to seize upon her, *my lady* Mohammed was still handsome. Of noble birth, she possessed the graceful ease of a true *grande dame*, and consented with a charming simplicity to satisfy Miss Nelly's curiosity on the subject of manners, customs, and usages.

In taking leave of the female portion of the sheikh's family, and while replying as well as she could to the wishes and compliments which the Orientals always lavish profusely on their guests, Miss Nelly could not suppress a certain emotion. She expressed to the three ladies the hope of seeing them again should she pass through the desert again in returning to England. This wish was sincere. She had enjoyed for the first time the hospitality of a veritable Arabian home, and she had felt the charm of that reception, at once reserved and spontaneous, courteous and grave, so different from the commonplaceness, the *banalité* of European politeness, and which causes the traveler to forget that he is a stranger, even in a city through which he passes for the first time, even among people whom he will never see again.

She rejoined her father and the rest of the party among plantations and delightful gardens, where a network of small canals of running water preserved a coolness during the greatest heat of the day.

Lord Badger conversed with the sheikh and the principal proprietors of the oasis on all matters concerning cultivation and irrigation. What he saw and heard gave him encouragement in pursuing his work.

"You see what can be done with water," said he to his companions, "the desert is transformed into a garden. What can we not accomplish when, thanks to our electrical machines, we shall draw it directly from the Euphrates? The whole of Mesopotamia will become one immense oasis."

It was four o'clock, and they intended to reach Aleppo before night. They therefore resumed their journey again, thanking his Arabian lordship for his cordial hospitality.

Soon after leaving Marrah the caravan met with a *Dowar* of nomad Arabs. A dowar is a village in which tents take the place of houses. When the tribe wishes to change its camp and transport it somewhere else, the skins and stuffs which form the tents are taken down, rolled around the stakes which had served to support them, and packed, together with the furniture, packages, and other luggage, on mules and other beasts of burden. The men ride on horseback. The women and children travel on camels.

At the moment when the caravan passed near to the dowar, fire had been lit to prepare the evening meal, composed principally of rice and curdled milk. Children, quite naked, or covered simply with a burnous fastened around the neck, were playing around the tents, near which large dogs—somewhat similar to those of Kabylia—kept good watch, barking formidably and showing their menacing teeth. Women, frightfully tattooed and hardly covered by a dress of blue stuff, were picking up brushwood. Their appearance, it must be said, was anything but attractive, and it could be easily seen that, had some slight service been demanded of them, their reception would not have been of the kindest.

As to the men, some were gravely smoking their chibouks, quietly seated on the ground; others, seated on horseback, were wheeling about at a little distance. Their immense hats, resembling somewhat those of the French market-porters, their heavy lances, from which hung wreaths of black feathers, showed them to be chiefs of large tents. The oxen and sheep, which these nomads take with them everywhere, were wandering about at random on the plains, searching for the thin blades of grass between the pebbles.

The sun had disappeared below the horizon. Thousands of stars were shining with a soft light, as if through a diaphanous gauze. The phenomenon of diffused light was reproduced in another phase than during the day. The most distant objects were distinctly seen, but under forms which seemed movable, immaterial, intangible.

After traveling for two hours through this luminous obscurity, the gates of Aleppo were reached. For several days the travelers were going to live in European society and find again, momentarily, all the refinements of English comfort.

CHAPTER VII.

FATMA.

ALEPPO, or Haleb in Arabian, is situated on the borders of the desert, on the prolongation of the basin of the Orontes. A depression in the ground continues the valley of this river towards the east. Its main course waters the province of Aleppo; the principal cities of this region are Homs and Hamah.

Aleppo has shared the fate of Antioch, from which city it is distant but a few miles, to the eastward; the earthquake of 1833 destroyed half of the city and took off a part of its population. But, more fortunate than its neighbor, it has arisen from its ruins, and to-day numbers 90,000 inhabitants.

It possesses a fortress built on an eminence in the centre of the city.

The caravans which make the journey from Iskanderoon to the Euphrates stop at Aleppo, which is situated at about an equal distance from the sea and from the river. It might perhaps be possible some day to connect the Mediterranean with the Euphrates by means of a canal, the line of which has been fully indicated by nature.

Aleppo is not by far as finely situated as the other cities of Syria. It wants water; the small river El-Koeik, which runs through it, furnishes sufficient for consumption by the inhabitants, but there is not enough water to produce fertility. By industry the natives, and, especially, the Europeans settled in the city, have succeeded in creating beautiful gardens adjoining the outskirts; still, these gardens, though carefully cultivated, do not approach, in the beauty of the trees and the freshness of the grass, to those of Hamah, of Antioch, and of most of the Arabian villages. Aleppo is a kind of artificial oasis which cannot rival those in which nature has done everything.

On the other hand, its streets are better paved, broader, and cleaner than in most Oriental cities, even the largest. The bazaar has nothing to distinguish it from other establishments of the same kind. There are the same wooden stalls ranged on the sides of narrow, covered passages, into which but little air and light penetrate. Only, this bazaar, where the products of three continents are heaped up and exchanged, is the most considerable one of the region. It alone makes it worth the while to stop several days at Aleppo.

The Europeans are quite numerous at Aleppo. As in the whole Mussulman orient, the Latin element predominates. It is chiefly represented by the Genoese and the Venetians, who form a sort of commercial aristocracy, holding the first rank. These rich merchants form a distinct clan, which not every one can enter. Their houses—unpretentious on the exterior, but containing beautiful furniture, massive silver-plate, valuable *bibelots*, accumulated through several generations—form, in the very precincts of the bazaar, a sort of square which bears the name of *Khan of the Franks*.

The English colony, much less numerous, also occupies a separate quarter, the handsome houses of which—in place of a luxury of ancient date—contain all that is attractive in modern establishments.

It was in one of these elegant dwellings that Lord Badger and his fellow-travelers were to stay during their sojourn at Aleppo.

Monaghan desired to study in a particular manner the depression which unites Aleppo to the Orontes. It was therefore decided to move towards the east as far as Dana.

A few hours after leaving Aleppo they passed through a heap of ruins of a singular aspect. At the bottom of a crevice in the ground, sheltered at the north and at the south by rugged walls of blackish rocks, were seen the ruins of an abandoned village. The walls of the houses—built of large blocks of basalt—were still standing. The roofing alone had been taken down, no doubt to serve for other purposes.

BABYLON ELECTRIFIED.

While approaching to examine these ancient *debris*, Monaghan called the attention of his companions to the crevices which furrowed the walls of some of these houses; in some places even, the walls seemed to have been torn up entirely from the ground and transported vertically to a distance of several yards.

These mute witnesses, no doubt dating back several centuries, indicated clearly enough from what cause this village had been abandoned. The population—Christian, to all appearances—had been compelled to flee from the violence of the earthquakes and seek a refuge somewhere else. It was a representation, on a small scale, of Herculaneum or Pompeii. All this part of Asia is, moreover, essentially volcanic. The conical mountains, like those of Auvergne, in France, are frequently met with here. From their jagged craters—to-day extinct and covered with fruit trees—trachytic and basaltic lava has flowed on the surrounding country. Decomposed by the rains, it has spread on the soil the elements of an incomparable fertility. Under the influence of the iron and the phosphoric acid, the vegetation here acquires a superabundance of vitality. Unfortunately, the subterranean activity still often manifests itself by violent shocks. The subterranean gases, seeking an outlet and no longer finding one through the obstructed passages of the ancient craters, explode;

the earth moves and opens, sometimes engulfing in a few seconds the work of many years.

Dana was reached without accident. After having lunched here and left their animals to cool off, Monaghan and Cornillé set out to make surveys in the valley, while Badger, his daughter, and the governess, accompanied only by a guide, went to visit the celebrated Roman tomb, which is still shown in the environs of the city. It is the best preserved monument of its kind in Syria. It bears the date of the year 324 of the Christian era.

As they approached the tomb, our tourists perceived, not without surprise, a white mass which seemed to lean against a stone separated from the monument. While asking themselves what this could mean, they continued to advance, when suddenly the white form rose up, and a woman—a child, rather—whom the sound of the travelers' footsteps had caused to look around, showed her charming face, bathed in tears. She appeared to be fifteen or sixteen years of age at the most; her dishevelled hair and disordered dress seemed to indicate a precipitate flight. She wore the picturesque costume of the Greek women of Syria, very similar to that of the slaves of the rich Turkish pashas : a short and loose vest, covered with lace ; puffed trousers of flowered silk, fastened around the waist by a sash fringed with gold ; *sheshia* edged with gold, and half-boots of yellow morocco.

When she saw the strangers coming towards her, the child sprang up with a bound and started forward as if disposed to take flight again. But the poor creature's strength no doubt failed her, for she stopped, began to tremble, and fell down again on the stone which had supported her before. Miss Nelly approached, and kindly took her by the hand, trying to make her understand, by her caresses, the interest which she took in her troubles. That soft voice seemed to revive the young girl. She raised her head, and regarded Miss Nelly with confidence, seeming to implore her not to abandon her. At a venture, Miss Nelly asked her in Arabic, of which language she had learned a few words, who she was, and how she came to be there. To her own and her father's great astonishment, the young girl replied in pure English.

This is, in brief, the story that she told : a Greek by birth, she had been—at a very early age—carried off by the Turks and sold to a wealthy English lord who owned considerable land in Asia Minor. That was the only period of her life to which she looked back with pleasure. Brought up like a child of the house, she had lived happily until the war broke out between the Russians and the Turks. Her master had been killed, his house pillaged and sacked; her mistress died from the shock, and, while faithful servants succeeded in escaping with the two children, she herself, fallen into the hands of the pillagers, had been sold to a Turkish pasha.

She would not have had much cause for complaint in regard to her new master, who was not a bad man, and would have treated her quite kindly, were it not for the bad counsels of his wife. She, seeing in his slave a future rival, maltreated and tyrannized her without mercy, and lost no opportunity of accusing her before her husband.

The pasha had settled in Aleppo not long before. She had succeeded in escaping; but, worn out with hunger and fatigue, she had fallen, powerless, at the foot of the tomb where Miss Nelly and her father had just found her.

Badger had listened to the young girl with great emotion.

"What was the name of your English master?" he asked, when she had ended.

"Lord Harrigton," she replied.

"I had guessed it when hearing your story, for I knew already the mournful circumstances of his death and that of his unfortunate wife. Lord Harrigton was my kinsman, and, in trying to better your lot, my poor child, I shall fulfil a two-fold duty, for I shall but be acting in conformity with the wishes of my unfortunate cousin. I shall myself conduct you back to your master, I shall procure without difficulty his pardon for your attempted flight, and cause him to treat you better in the future than in the past."

But, at the bare thought of falling again into the power of her persecutors, Fatma (that was the name which her Turkish master had given the young slave) began crying and sobbing anew. The wife of the pasha was without doubt delighted to be rid of her servant. The latter's return would cause new alarms, and she would not fail to make her pay dearly for them. Rather than face the resentment of her terrible mistress, the fugitive would have chosen death. Throwing herself at Miss Nelly's feet, she entreated her to take her as a slave, swearing to love her always and to follow her everywhere like a faithful dog.

Lord Badger made the young girl rise, and tried to restore a little of her courage.

"I cannot dispose of you, in spite of your master, my child," he said to her; "according to the laws of the country, you belong legitimately to him. To try to conceal you amongst us, or to repulse by force those whom your master will send in your pursuit, if he has not already done so, would be to expose us all to the danger of being massacred, for the people among whom we are will not fail to take the part of your ravishers against us. But be reassured: I hope, in restoring you to your master, to proceed in such a manner that he will consent to my buying you. We shall afterward consider what had best be done."

Fatma thanked Lord Badger effusively and returned to Dana with her new companions. On the way, she related the incidents of Lord Harrigton's death. She had, however, little to say about it. A disordered band of Turkish soldiers had invaded his lordship's house. He had defended himself; but, overwhelmed by numbers, compelled to leave a tower in which he had sought refuge, because the soldiers had set it on fire, he had been killed by a bullet.

The geologist and Cornillé were greatly surprised to see Fatma in company with Badger and his daughter. They were quickly acquainted with the circumstances. They congratulated his lordship on his good action, and approved his plan. As to Flatnose, he declared the occurrence to be a very common one. He observed that in a distant expedition, it always happened that some one was delivered, and that logically, Fatma would infallibly have been met with some day or another.

The horses, which had been cooling off, were quite ready. They hastened to get back into their saddles. Fatma succumbed to fatigue and to the excitement of the day. The guide seated her as well as he could on his animal, which he led by the bridle, walking at her side. The young girl and her guide were placed in the centre of the little cavalcade, which then started off.

They had hardly left Dana, when they perceived a troop of Turkish soldiers on the road. Poorly and loosely dressed, as they often are in this part of the empire, they arrived before the caravan in the most complete disorder.

He who appeared to be the chief of the band had no sooner perceived Fatma, more dead than alive, than he began to utter loud cries, and darted toward the unhappy girl, with the evident intention of strangling her. Quick as lightning Cornillé threw his horse between the young girl and her aggressor. The latter drew his sabre and called on his companions to aid him. Cornillé, revolver in hand, kept the chief at a distance, ready to blow out his brains if he advanced a step. Badger, Monaghan, Flatnose, and even Miss Nelly drew their revolvers. The Turkish soldiers hesitated for a moment before this menacing attitude, then, believing themselves to be the weaker, replaced their sabres in their girdles. The chief alone, furious with rage, continued to wheel about the Europeans, whirling his sabre above his head, and uttering inarticulate cries. But, always finding a revolver pointed at himself, he kept at a respectful distance. Suddenly his horse sank under him, and man and beast disappeared together. They had fallen into a hole dug at the side of the road. The soldiers went to the aid of their chief, who was yelling with pain, for his horse was trampling upon him at the bottom of the hole. After much trouble they succeeded in getting the poor devil out, with a broken leg and arm.

This incident entirely cooled the ardor of the belligerents. The soldiers inclined to the belief that their chief was in the wrong, since he had been so unexpectedly punished by Allah. Some pieces of money, which Badger had adroitly distributed among them, served to convince them fully of this fact, so that they ended by being more disposed to follow Badger's orders than those of their wounded chief. A parley was begun. The soldiers explained that the pasha had sent them in pursuit of his fugitive slave. The guide, translating Badger's words for them, replied that Fatma was, in fact, being taken back to her master, and that, therefore, they had but to join the party and go with it to Aleppo. This they decided to do after having tied the wounded man on a horse. The unhappy wretch uttered cries of pain at each movement of his animal, which did not prevent him, however, from shaking the fist which he could still use at Fatma, who, almost fainting after so much excitement, pressed close against Miss Nelly, as if she were the only power capable of protecting her.

The return to Aleppo was not marked by any further occurrence. Lord Badger waited upon the pasha. The latter, desirous, perhaps, of restoring peace in his household and of quieting his wife's scolding, raised no difficulties in the way of selling his slave to the Englishman. And then, the sum offered was large and the pasha in want of money, not a rare thing in Turkey.

It would be impossible to express the joy which the young girl felt when she learned that she was to have nothing further to do with her oppressors. Lord Badger offered her the means of leaving Turkey and returning to her native land. At this proposition the child's face, but a moment before so joyful, suddenly became sad and troubled. She had no longer any relatives, she would be like a stranger in her own land. Having never known any condition but that of servitude, the idea of being free had for her no precise meaning. Happiness, such as she imagined it, was to have good masters to whom one can be devoted and attached.

"I have been a slave since my childhood," she said, ingenuously, "keep me with you as your slave, I shall serve you devotedly as long as I live."

Nelly's soft eyes, fixed on her father's at that moment, seconded the touching request. Badger decided that the young girl should remain with them and should make one of the expedition.

The new recruit was not the least ornament of the party. Lively, merry, frolicsome, always ready to sing and laugh, she was like a joyous bird, twittering and prattling, in the midst of this company of serious people. Miss Nelly entertained no distrust of her new friend. The sincerest affection continued always to exist between these two amiable persons, born under such different skies. Miss Nelly was the blond incarnation of the mists of the north—Fatma the creation of the burning sun of Asia.

It was decided that the young Greek should keep the somewhat boyish costume, which became her so capitally, at least until they returned to Europe. While they were staying in the cities she would be careful not to go into the streets but strictly veiled and enveloped in her *haik*, as the Mussulmans do not allow a woman in Oriental costume—that is, regarded as belonging, like themselves, to the religion of the Prophet—to show herself out-of-doors with uncovered face.

On the third day after the one marked by the episode which we have just related, the journey began again—more monotonous than that from Hamah to Aleppo.

Aleppo lies on the borders of the desert. From here to the Euphrates the boundless waste extends almost without interruption to the banks of the river; then the desert continues towards the East, to end only on the banks of the Tigris. Jabul is the only station of some importance which the caravan encountered.

On leaving Jabul, where the supply of water was renewed, the sky, which until then had been unchangeably blue, took on a pale color. The temperature suddenly grew cooler. Towards evening the rain began to fall. It threatened to be a bad night. The caravan halted, and not a moment was lost in preparing camp. It was high time. Hardly had they finished their preparations, when the wind arose with extreme violence and threatened every moment to tear away the tents, which were, however, firmly fixed to the ground. The rain fell in torrents. Repose was not to be thought of amid this unloosening of the elements. Badger and his people were collected in the principal tent; the men, standing, forming a group, Miss Nelly and her governess sitting as well as they could on heaps of shawls and cloaks, while Fatma, seized with terror, and cowering at their feet, hid her pretty, frightened head between the arms of her friend at each new gust.

Monaghan admonished everybody to be patient; the rain could not last long in this country and this climate. And, in fact, at the end of two hours, the wind abated and the rain suddenly ceased to fall. Each

5

one went to his tent, and soon the travelers peacefully fell asleep in their hammocks, guarded by sentinels who watched by turns.

Next day the sky was again as clear as on the preceding days. The sun rose in a horizon of fire, as if revivified by the shower of the night before. The caravan set out again on its journey.

In the evening the travelers had an opportunity of viewing one of those spectacles which are to be seen only in this dream-land. From two to three hundred camels were walking in file some miles away from them. The outlines of these animals, and of the Arabs who rode them, stood out sharply against the clear sky. The transparency of the air was such that the eye perceived all the details of the forms, and even the regular undulations of the walk. Were it not for the con-

traction of the perspective, one would have believed them to be but a short distance off, and, in this silence of an Oriental night, the ear was instinctively strained to catch the sound of the steps striking the ground. This denial given to previously acquired habits—this contradiction which seems to exist between the two senses which place us in direct communication with the outer world—certainly contributes much towards producing for every inhabitant of the north, newly transferred to the orient, that sort of enchantment in which everything that is seen seems to partake at the same time of the real and of the visionary.

When the silhouette of the last camel had disappeared, the eyes of the travelers were still fixed on the horizon. Flatnose's jesting voice was the first to break the charm.

"Look," cried the journalist, suddenly seizing Badger's arm, "look

BABYLON ELECTRIFIED.

at that long mass that is moving rapidly through the desert. A lamp precedes the gigantic reptile and lights the way. There, a shrill whistle announces its arrival; it's the railroad of your dreams, my lord, the line which sets London and Calcutta in communication."

"You forget to see something else," replied his lordship, laughing. "Turn a little to the right, my dear Flatnose: what do you say of those long poles which are outlined in the distance?"

"Those!" exclaimed the journalist. "Why they are the electric ships which cross Syria by ascending your canal."

It was decidedly useless to attempt to surprise Flatnose in the act of being enthusiastic or serious. Is this an influence of stoutness on the ideas? I leave it to the physiologists to solve the question.

On the next day, towards noon, certain changes in the nature of the ground, bushes and tufts of green grass, announced the vicinity of the river. And, in fact, the silvery surface of the Euphrates soon appeared between the trees—this Euphrates which they were now to descend as far as Babylon.

The place at which they stopped is Baylis. Of an ancient city there remain but shapeless *debris*, a ruined castle on a hill of chalk, around which are grouped the houses of a miserable Turkish village.

CHAPTER VIII.

THE EUPHRATES.

IT is not so easy to travel on the Euphrates as on the Thames or the Seine. Nevertheless Badger and his companions had resolved to reach Babylon by the water-road. For this they would make use of a raft of a peculiar form—already in use at the time when Herodotus visited these countries—and which is called *kalak*.

The *kalak*, the name alone of which has perhaps varied in the course of centuries, is formed by two rows, crossed, of trunks of trees sawed in two and firmly bound together, so as to form a plane surface. Underneath leather bottles are attached, inflated with air, which keep this stage floating above water.

Two *kalakjis*, boatmen, seated on bags, work the oars, which are simply long, straight poles, thin at the end, which is held in the hand, provided at the other end, by way of paddles, with pieces of reed about eight inches long, cut in two and placed crosswise along about three feet of the pole.

The travelers had to wait at Balis while a large *kalak* was being constructed. Materials were fortunately not wanting. Balis, being the starting-point and landing-place for numerous caravans going from the Euphrates into the interior of Syria, possesses building-yards where timber and leather bottles are stored.

In order to beguile the tedium of these days of enforced rest a hunt was organized on the banks of the river. They set out one morning and followed the course of the Euphrates, going up-stream. A light mist covered the immense plain. Then, as the sun rose above the horizon, the vapors disappeared, and the sky showed itself in all its splendor.

For several hours they walked along the right bank among the reeds. Several shots announced that the hunters had met with game.

Indeed, when a halt was made, Lord Badger, Monaghan and Cornillé deposited ducks, geese, and even a beaver on the grass. The last animal must have been one of a colony settled in the marshes which, in that place, line the course of the Euphrates.

After lunch the ladies rambled off in the direction of the river. They had hardly walked a hundred yards or so when they were heard to utter loud cries and calls for help. On arriving at the spot where they were, the men found them stooping down to the ground and trying to hold back a turtle about three feet long, which was endeavoring to reach the water. A ball, fired point blank, shattered the animal's head. A cord was tied around its carapace, and it was dragged to and hoisted on the wagon which had brought the provisions.

On the way back it was decided to leave the marshy banks of the Euphrates and to continue the hunt on the small chalky cliffs which line the river at a little distance. They hoped to find other kind of game here, especially partridges, quite common in this country. The hunting, which had already been good in the morning, was still more successful on these plateaus. But the best shot was made by Flatnose, so he said, at least. He claimed to have killed a rare bird, unknown in Europe, and which he intended to add to the collection of the British Museum on his return to London. It was in vain that he was pressed to show this bird; he remained inflexible. At last, on arriving at the camp, our excellent journalist majestically drew from his game-bag the prize which was one day to establish his fame. A loud burst of laughter immediately disconcerted the poor man—his bird was only a vulgar magpie!

The supper was exceedingly merry. Partridges, ducks and geese, served with all sauces by skilful *chef* Green, were washed down by generous wines of France and Spain. In the centre of the table, on a bed of leaves, Flatnose's trophy was pompously displayed. The two young girls had been careful thus to honor the magpie killed by their friend.

As to the turtle, it was cut up and taken on the raft, to serve next day for the preparation of an excellent soup and a sumptuous roast.

The kalak was just finished that evening. On the following morning all embarked, and the descent of the Euphrates was quietly begun. The raft was, on the whole, very comfortable. Cabins sheltered the travelers from the rains or the heat of the sun, which was still great despite the late season. They floated with the current, advancing more rapidly in that manner than might have been believed at first. Several rains that had already fallen on the mountains of the upper basin had accelerated the current of the Euphrates.

During the first days of the trip the landscape continued to be monotonous. The river flowed through level plains, sometimes cutting a wide bed for itself through the chalk or its alluvium. At long intervals small, isolated hillocks were discerned on the bluffs. They were the shapeless ruins of ancient Greek cities, which had, however, had their hour of prosperity—Thapsacus, Nikephorion, Leontopolis, Kallinikon—of which we have but a faint record or remembrance to-day.

The vegetation was poor. In certain favored portions of the soil it consisted almost exclusively of the fruit-trees which abound in this country. A little farther south some plantations of olive and cotton-trees began. At the same time the desert gave place to more inhabited regions, for the villages, which had been wanting entirely south of Balis, became more frequent.

Rakka was passed, the ancient capital of Haroun-al-Raschid. But this capital has fallen greatly from its ancient splendor—it is now but a small village. Farther on came Zelibi, on the summit of a rock. Its ancient monuments, constructed of blocks of translucent alabaster, recall those aerial and fantastic palaces spoken of in the *Thousand and One Nights*.

The stay in the kalak was not disagreeable. The coolness of the nights had been uncomfortable during the first stages of the journey; but, in proportion as they descended towards the south, the air became milder. Indeed, the voyagers often, instead of sleeping under the tent, preferred to spend a few good hours in chatting and meditation on the forward part of the raft. Benches and a table had been placed here for the meals.

The air is so clear and the moon shines so brightly on the banks of the Euphrates, that the journey could be continued during the night.

The mild temperature that evening had led all the passengers to repair to the fore part of the kalak. They conversed while smoking and drinking tea. The spectacle before their eyes was pleasing and interesting. Lightly undulating hills followed along the two banks of the river; gardens succeeded each other uninterruptedly, with their white, flat-roofed country houses. They were evidently approaching some important city, a centre of traffic and cultivation. The pilot announced Deir.

"Deir," read Monaghan, opening his guide-book, "remarkable for its rice-fields, its cotton and tobacco plantations and the ruins of its bridge recently carried away by a freshet in the Euphrates."

"There are the ruins," exclaimed Miss Nelly, pointing to a black mass which seemed to bar the river some distance away.

They were, indeed, the ruins spoken of. The kalak approached them rapidly and had soon passed them.

The next day, when they met again at breakfast, the general character of the country had changed. The low banks of the river and the little hillocks had suddenly given place to uneven escarpments. Even the direction of the Euphrates was modified. Instead of descending towards the south, it now flowed towards the west. It was the long mountain-range of the Jebel-Abgad which produced this disturbance. As the ground rose, the vegetation at once became fresh and luxuriant. This phenomenon was due to the increased humidity of the air, which develops rapidly with increase in height. The high summits condense the vapors on their sides and form springs which filter down to the plains and there produce fertility.

The rocks of the mountain, burned by the sun, had a reddish color which contrasted strongly with the indigo blue of the sky and the gray of the sandy desert. The gorges became more and more narrow; the cliffs overhung the river. The progress of the raft became, at the same time, more difficult. This long band of wood had to be steered between the rocks which rose pell-mell out of the water. It was fortunate that the kalak floated on the surface of the river and that it was solidly built. In spite of the precautions of the skilful pilot, it was impossible to avoid several collisions, luckily without serious results. Not one of the leather bottles was damaged.

Suddenly the Euphrates made a turn and resumed its normal direction towards the south. It had opened a passage for itself through one of the ravines of the mountain.

"Look," cried Fatma, suddenly, "there's a second Euphrates down below there."

This new stream was the Khaboor, the largest tributary of the Euphrates, the outlet for the waters which are collected in the mountain-wall of the Jebel-Abgad. The junction of the two rivers is effected at the foot of a huge cliff, the base of which is washed by the waters of the Euphrates.

Night came on, and they had still not passed out of the gorges. As it would be impossible to continue the journey in the dark, in such an irregular course, they were compelled to run the raft against the shore and to wait until daylight appeared.

Next day they emerged from the mountain. The Euphrates flowed once more in a more level plain; its valley broadened.

The succeeding days were less monotonous than those which had elapsed since the departure from Balis.

The river had hollowed a deep bed for itself through calcareous lands. High cliffs lined both banks of the Euphrates without interruption. The country through which they were passing had at one time been the centre of a numerous population. Ruins abounded everywhere on the tops of the cliffs. Here, it was a tower, half crumbled down with cracked walls, the sun shining in through the windows. There, it was some strong castle, of which nothing was left but portions of the walls, blackened by time. The attention of the travelers was attracted most by the castle of Rahaba, near Mayadim, the ruins of which, still grand, rise at the summit of a craggy cliff.

The kalak is steadily advancing. The city of Anah has been reached, the long city, which stretches along the banks of the Euphrates for five miles. Anah is an oasis rather than a city. Its houses, far apart, are built along roads which wind through a forest of cocoa-nut trees; palms, fig-trees, pomegranate-trees and orange-trees. Unfortunately, this oasis is but of small extent. It is comprised within a strip of ground, confined on the one side by the river, and on the other by perpendicular cliffs.

At sight of this tropical vegetation, forming a singular contrast to that which had been met with until then, our travelers could not help reflecting on the brilliant future reserved for Mesopotamia. What might not be expected from a country where the soil becomes so fertile when it is properly tilled, when man takes the trouble to work ? Mesopotamia is a promised land for future generations.

At Anah, the first palm-plantation was met with. From here on, descending towards the south, the palm-trees were to become more and more common. The aspect of the country changed completely through this transformation of its flora. It is the trees, in fact, which give a country its special character. The icy solitudes of the poles, the forests of the lands of the north, the green shores of the Mediterranean, the oases of the Sahara, virgin forests of the tropics, prairies and pampas of America, steppes of Russia, all are characterized by their special flora.

Numerous boats and kalaks, loaded with merchandise, lay along the shores of Anah. This city is the centre of a considerable trade. Immense fields of cotton and sugar cane are cultivated all around it. An excellent wine is also grown here. Our travelers could see the vines, twining around the trees, and passing from one to the other in garlands and festoons, as in Lombardy.

In the projects of Badger and his companions, Anah was later on to acquire still greater importance. They intended to establish several industries here: sugar-factories, cotton-mills, etc., which the local cultivations would render productive.

They landed, and passed the day in visiting the city and its surroundings. The inhabitants are industrious and quiet; they received the strangers with kindness.

South of Anah, the Euphrates continues to flow between two high walls of rock. The villages of Haditah, El Oos, and Jibbah are built on the steep sides of these cliffs. The inhabitants have generally merely hollowed out their dwellings in the rocks. A simple bit of wall constitutes all the masonry. The chimneys, passing through the roof of the cave, discharge the smoke over the sod above or through the trees which cover the sides of the hill.

But that is not yet the greatest curiosity of these villages. Not able to build any more on the cliff, the inhabitants have had to fix their dwellings on the islets of the river. In order to escape the sudden floods of the Euphrates, they have completely surrounded their houses with high and thick walls, which must be scaled and descended again in order to get inside.

"That is a village built at the bottom of a well," said Miss Nelly, aptly, when they passed close to the first.

And here is Hit, with its sources of asphalt. Monaghan desired to show a singular phenomenon to his companions. The raft was therefore run against the shore, and they landed.

Before the voyagers stood a high hill, formed like an inverted funnel, from the top of which a little brook came running down. Monaghan caused them to taste a little of the water; it had a disagreeable taste and an odor of petroleum. It contained, in fact, a small quantity of this substance.

They scaled the hill. On arriving at the top, they found themselves in presence of a kind of kettle, at the bottom of which bubbled the spring which gave rise to the brook. This had hollowed out a subterranean passage for itself, and burst out a little lower down on the side of the hill.

South of Hit, the cliffs suddenly subside, and the Euphrates flows through an absolutely flat country. Pastures extend as far as the eye can reach on both banks of the river. At this moment these green meadows presented a magic spectacle. Thousands of horses and camels were grazing the tender grass which grows at all seasons, thanks to the moisture produced by the river, whose waters filter through the porous soil.

Then, after the pasturages of Saklawiah, came marshes among which the Euphrates seemed about to lose itself. The grass gave place to rushes and numerous aquatic plants. The river, the banks of which were no longer to be seen, diminished rapidly in depth. They now advanced only through a narrow channel between the reeds. Finally, on the 20th of December, the pilot announced that they were approaching Hillah, a small city built on the site of ancient Babylon. The end of the journey had been reached at last.

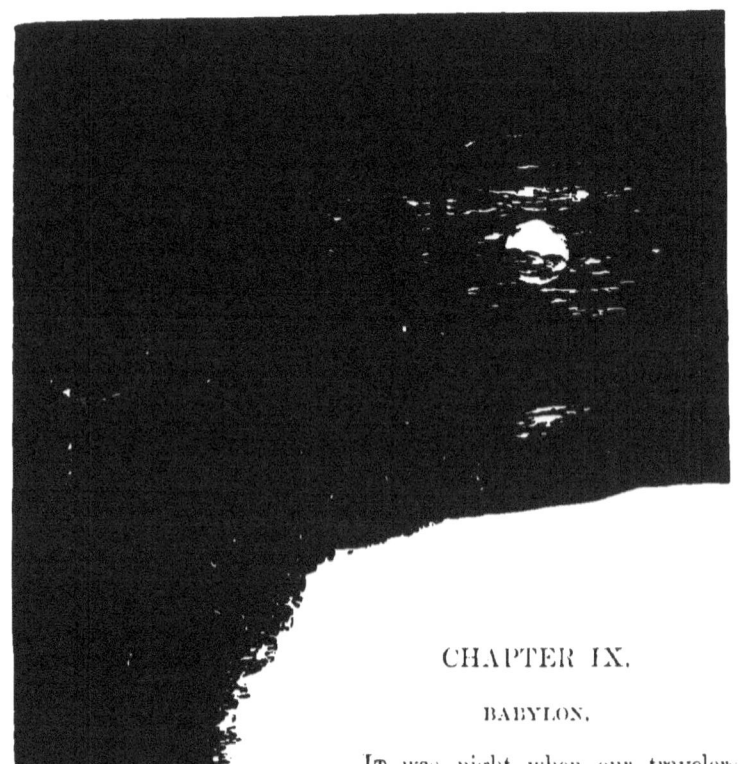

CHAPTER IX.

BABYLON.

It was night when our travelers landed near Hillah, on the left bank of the Euphrates. The evening had been warm, but the air had grown much cooler after the sun had set behind the sands of the desert. This change in the temperature, peculiar to the hot countries, was caused by the proximity of the marshes.

The moon shone brightly in the dark blue sky, and the surrounding objects took on a fantastic appearance under this pale light. Great black masses were distinguished at the far horizon—masses which seemed at times to rise from the ground and float vaguely in the air. The silence was broken only by the melancholy song of some boatmen delayed along the river, or by the far-off voice of the muezzin, who was calling the faithful to prayer.

The tents were raised on the banks of the Euphrates, about a thousand yards from the city. Everybody was fatigued and glad to have at last arrived at the point of destination. Now, all fatigues and privations would soon be forgotten. Were they not at Babylon, on the sacred site of an ancient civilization—on the ground on which it was to appear in renewed splendor—thanks to the application of the discoveries of modern science?

The last part of the journey had appeared longer than all the rest. When approaching the end, one would always like to hurry forward, and the most dispassionate characters are subject to a kind of fever.

Sir James Badger was the first to rise next morning. The stars were beginning to pale before the dawn, and night was disappearing from the east. The banks of the Euphrates were covered with a transparent vapor which was agitated by a light wind.

The others came out of their tents in succession and ranged themselves in silence around his lordship. The moment was solemn—it was like taking possession of the ancient empire of Semiramis.

The light became brighter every moment. On the banks of the river, in the distance, to the farthest horizon, the ground was broken and irregular. The level plain of the desert gave place to hillocks covered with shrubs and thorny bushes.

Each of these knolls was the shapeless ruin of some palace of ancient Babylon. The edifices, constructed entirely of bricks and bitumen, had collapsed under the action of the elements and the agency of man. The bricks, burnt and unburnt, had been again converted into clay, and formed these artificial hills.

Here was all that was left of so marvellous a capital! Where were the palaces, the walls, the temples, the hanging gardens which had made of Babylon the most wonderful and the largest city of the world? Of all these, nothing remains but dust. To-day, only a few tumble-down Arabian houses stand on the site of the city, where so many different nations had met, which had been so often conquered and raised up again from its ruins, which had sheltered the great conquerors of the world—from Cyrus and Alexander to the Arabs.

The city of Hillah obstructed the view towards the south: Hillah-el-Feïdah, that is to say, Hillah the grand, which occupies a portion of ancient Babylon. It is shaded by date-trees and is surrounded by magnificent gardens. They saw the bridge of boats, six hundred and fifty feet long, which places the city, built on the right bank, in communication with the suburbs on the opposite bank.

Not far away from the camp some Arabs had also raised their tents. They were pilgrims going to the holy city of Kerbela.

Badger, armed with a field-glass, was looking anxiously in the direction of the city, behind the bridge of boats. At last he uttered a cry of joy:

"The *Electricity* has at last arrived at Hillah!" said he. "I can

see very distinctly its smoke-stack and the colors of England and my own flying from its mast."

The ladies were left in the camp under the protection of Monaghan,

Blacton and Flatnose. The last was delighted to have arrived at Babylon. From that moment his *rôle* of *reporter* was to begin. He had already settled himself comfortably before a small portable desk, and was covering several sheets of paper with his jovial prose. How many things there were to write to his editor in this first article!

As for Badger and Cornillé, they proceeded towards Hillah. Badger had not been mistaken. It was indeed the *Electricity* which floated on the waters of the Euphrates. Half an hour later they were on board of the little ship effusively shaking Captain Laycock's hands. How happy they were to see each other again, safe and sound, after an absence of six weeks!

Laycock and Jack Adams had arrived without accident at Bassorah with the little fleet. The *Davy* and the *Faraday* had been immediately unloaded, and the working-stock stored in the docks of the port.

This done, the *Electricity* had been loaded and had ascended the Tigris as far as Tekrit, with Jack Adams and the hands for the hydraulic works. Here, as it was impossible for the steamboat to continue on its way, there being not enough water, the machines had been transferred to flat boats, which could go up without difficulty as far as Mosul.

The *Electricity* had descended again to Bassorah. After receiving a new load, it had this time ascended the Euphrates as far as Hillah, where it had lain at anchor for two days, awaiting Badger's arrival. With the working-stock, the ship brought at the same time the hands intended specially for Babylon.

After having listened to this report and having assured himself that all was in good order, Badger, accompanied by Cornillé and Captain Laycock, waited upon the representative of the Turkish government at Hillah. The latter had received official orders from the Sultan through the governor of Bagdad. A hundred soldiers had even been sent from that city, designed to secure the works at Babylon against an armed attack.

All the forenoon had been occupied in this way. Our three friends remained in camp only during the lunch-hour. Then there were renewed handshakings and endless questions regarding the events of the two journeys. If Laycock had many interesting things to relate about his voyage and his trip on the Tigris, Badger and those who accompanied him had also enough to say on their part.

The introduction of Fatma to the captain and of the captain to the young girl was gone through in due English form.

"Charmed with so lovely a recruit," said the old sea-dog, shaking the young girl's hand. "May we always make only equally agreeable ones!"

The repast was very merry. At this moment these men were collected around a table placed on the sands of the desert which surrounded them on all sides. Very small, indeed, did they appear. And yet it was they who were going to transform these deserts into a rich country. With electricity for their arm, they would produce, on this barren ground, a most brilliant manifestation of the creative power of man.

"To work!" said Badger, rising. "We have enough to employ the rest of the day usefully. The first thing that we have to do is to look for the most suitable site on which to establish our electric works. Come, let us go!"

Everybody wished to be one of the party. They had become so rusty in the joints from the long stay on the kalak that every one was very glad to take a long walk. Besides, their curiosity was strongly excited; they wanted to see the ruins of ancient Babylon—that capital which is quasi-legendary to-day.

It was necessary to construct the works on the very banks of the Euphrates. Two advantages were thus gained: that of having the water near at hand and that of being able to unload more easily the goods brought by the ships. It was therefore decided to follow the banks of the river, going up-stream. For it was especially up the Euphrates that they had the most chances of finding a favorable position.

The first impression was not a good one. The banks were low and marshy, formed by a variable soil. The choice of such a situation was not to be thought of, for the buildings would have no solidity whatever here, and they would be exposed each year to disastrous inundations.

Luckily, rising ground was discerned towards the north. They, therefore, directed their steps straight towards that point. After walking half a mile or so, they arrived at the foot of a hillock which the Arabs call *Kasr*, that is to say, castle. The appearance of this hillock caused it to be taken at first sight for one of nature's accidental effects. It was covered with grass and bushes like the commonest of hills. Miss Nelly was, therefore, not a little astonished to learn that they were at the foot of the ruins of an immense monument erected by Nebuchadnezzar.

In climbing up the sides of the kasr, portions of brick walls were indeed discovered.

"Singular mortar," said Monaghan, breaking off one of the bricks. "You see, gentlemen : here, as in Egypt, they used sometimes a mixture of lime and bitumen, sometimes bitumen only."

A little higher up, there was a veritable quarry dug in the very sides of the hillock : an enormous heap of burnt and unburnt bricks. For several centuries the poor inhabitants of Hillah had been getting the materials here to build their houses with.

The view from the top of the kasr extended far into the distance. One could take in at a glance the immense perimeter formerly occupied by Babylon. A multitude of small *tells*, scattered through the plain right and left of the river, marked the sites of the palaces and monuments that had disappeared.

"Can one really believe what is said concerning the enormous extent of Babylon?" asked Miss Nelly, addressing Monaghan. "Was it as large as London, or larger?"

"At least as large, Miss Badger," declared the geologist. "It had the form of a square, fifteen miles on each side, which gives an area of two hundred and twenty-five square miles. But the houses probably did not cover all of this space. The ancients had the custom of leaving, between the city and the encircling walls, quite a broad strip of ground, on which it was forbidden to build."

"Is the reason for this interdiction known?"

"Probably a religious prescription. But I confess to you my profound ignorance in matters of ritual, ancient or modern."

During this little archæological digression, Blacton, who had finished examining the plateau on which they were collected, declared it to be an excellent spot for the future works. Though near to the Euphrates, it yet lay at a sufficiently high level to be safe from the most violent floods. The surface, almost horizontal, was sufficiently large. As to the very irregular base, Cornillé and he estimated it at no less than fifteen hundred yards. It thus filled all the required conditions.

A few hundred yards from the first plateau, a second hillock was perceived, also situated on the banks of the Euphrates, but somewhat less in height. This other ruin bore, in the country, the name of *Babel*—that is to say, completely ruined.

They descended the kasr again and went towards Babel. This hillock, like the first, is an enormous heap of bricks burned or dried in the sun, and joined together with a cement of lime or asphalt: The mass has crumbled down under the repeated action of the elements, forming a rectangular plateau, whose sides measure two hundred and twenty-five feet by five hundred and twenty, with a height of about two hundred feet.

"An excellent place for my thermo-solar pile," exclaimed Cornillé, who was the first to reach the top of the plateau. "Babel is but a few steps from the kasr; my pile will be near to the works."

"In any event," said Laycock, "material will certainly not be wanting for the erection of your buildings. You will have inexhaustible quarries of bricks under your very feet. The Babylonian workmen who fashioned these bricks four thousand years ago, little supposed that they would serve one day to construct electric works."

The walk had been a long one. Since leaving Hillah, they had covered over four miles. It was decided to rest for half an hour on the top of Babel.

"So it is well understood," urged Badger, "that the kasr will serve as site for the works, while the thermo-electric pile will be placed on Babel? I have no objection to make to your choice, gentlemen; you can begin work to-morrow."

"As for me," said Miss Nelly, "there is one thing that is not quite clear to me. Although I have felt the difference that exists between the Oriental sun and our poor sun of London, I yet ask myself how you are going to find a sufficiently large quantity of solar heat here to form numerous works, give motion to electric locomotives, and illuminate and heat cities! Now, what a furnace of heat is the sun?"

"I happen to have something to convince you in my note-book, here," said Cornille; "it is a calculation by Mr. Marcel Desprez, which will give you an idea of the immense quantity of solar heat uselessly lost in certain regions of the globe."

The engineer then read these few lines:

"To evaporate a kilogramme * of water under a pressure of ten atmospheres, it must be furnished with a quantity of heat equal to 650 calories. Now, the apparatus of Monsieur Mouchot permits the evaporation of about a kilogramme of water per hour. Let us see what that represents on a surface equal to that of France, for example. The area of France being about 200,000 square miles, it is easily found that the quantity of water which will be evaporated in an hour, during a fine summer's day, is about 17,700,000,000 cubic feet, or 500,000,000,000 kilogrammes. In order to evaporate a like quantity of water in a good boiler, it would be necessary to burn 60,000,000 tuns of oil, that is to say, one-fifth of the total actual consumption of the whole world. The powerful locomotives which draw the express trains on our railroads, when they are used at full power, evaporate somewhat over 180 cubic feet of water per hour, producing a 500 horse-power on the pistons. It follows from this that the solar radiation, on a surface equal to that of France, could evaporate enough water to feed more than 80,000,000 of locomotives, producing together 40,000,000,000 horse-power. If this quantity of steam, produced under a pressure of ten atmospheres, escaped freely into the air, supposing there is a discharge of 610 kilogrammes per second and per square yard, it would take a funnel with a diameter of over 550 yards, or equal to that of the crater of a volcano."

"I bow before science and before the figures," said Miss Nelly, smiling, "and I make a most humble apology to the sun. I certainly did not suspect that he possessed such power."

"Mesopotamia," resumed the engineer, "enjoys a continually clear sky. The brightness of the sun is rarely dimmed there by clouds.

* 2.2046215 lb. avoirdupois.

Twelve square yards of surface are sufficient to give, by means of the thermo-electric pile, a one-horse power during the whole day. Babel has a surface of about twelve thousand square yards; we shall attain a thousand horsepower for our first trials."

"Let us go, my friends," said Badger; "here we have been resting for half an hour, lunch awaits us, and there is still enough to occupy our time usefully from now until dinner-time."

They all rose. Flatnose yawned, stretched his arms, rubbed his eyes. He had slept during this conversation, too serious for him. The secrets of science had little temptation for him. He was content to admire the results and to make them known; when, in order to satisfy the demands of the modern public, he thought it necessary to adorn his fanciful style with a learned quotation and technical terms, he always had some kind friend at hand to furnish him with the elements of this bit of effect. Thanks to this innocent subterfuge, he added to his reputation as a charming narrator, an incomparable reporter, that of being second to none in encyclopædic knowledge.

CHAPTER X.

THE DISCOVERY OF GRIM-MITSCHOFFER.

NEXT day they set to work. The camp was fixed inland, five hundred yards east of the kasr, on a knoll high enough to afford security from inundations. It was decided to construct in this place the workshops, storehouses, dwellings, and all the buildings necessary for so large an undertaking.

On the evening of the fifth day the camp presented a picturesque and animated appearance. Blacton and Cornillé, comfortably established for a prolonged stay, occupied huts at the top of the eminence; so that they could watch, even at a distance, and notice anything that happened in no matter what part of the work-yards, at any hour of the day or night. Around them, and suitably spaced, were grouped the huts occupied by the foremen and superintendents. More than a hundred tents, intended for the workmen, and near each of which a fire was kindled to prepare a meal for three or four persons, rose on the grassy slopes of the hillock. Beside the workmen brought from England, there were also native workmen hired at Hillah and even at Bagdad. Farther on, the Turkish soldiers, whose sole duty was to protect the work against the attacks of plunderers, were stretched around the fires of their bivouac, silently smoking their long pipes while preparing a frugal supper.

Considerable material had been brought before Badger's arrival, through the care of the English consul. They were but waiting for an order to transport it to the site chosen for the future works. This order had gone off the day before; immediately after the arrival of the timber and iron, the constructions were to be begun.

Jack Adams had returned to the upper valley of the Tigris, where Badger was to join him in a fortnight. Cornillé and Blacton remained to construct the electric works and the thermo-solar pile. Captain Laycock had already gone the day before. He was returning to Bassorah with his little steamer to bring a new load of machinery. It would take him nearly two weeks to reach the Persian Gulf and ascend again to Babylon. The new caravan, composed of Badger and his daughter, Flatnose and Miss Ross, was to await his return before proceeding to Bagdad.

A new life began for Cornillé and Blacton. Since their departure from London they had traveled as amateurs, as tourists; at present, their enormous task claimed their whole attention.

Blacton was glad to resume his familiar occupation. His whole dwelling was converted into a workshop: on every hand were seen plans, drawings of machines, models of all kinds of apparatus. It was he who assigned to each one his work. It was he to whom they applied for orders and instructions. He was the centre towards which everything converged. Silent and always keeping in the background during the whole duration of the voyage, he now displayed an activity which one would never have suspected him capable of showing. Here, in his element, Blacton, rather awkward in a drawing-room, became again the incomparable engineer, around whom everything took life and was transformed.

As for Cornillé, never had a man at the beginning of his career, and filled with a noble and lawful ambition, seen brighter prospects open before him. If the undertaking succeeded—and everything seemed to indicate that it would succeed—not only would his name become famous among those of all contemporary engineers, but wealth would inevitably come to him, and open all its treasures to him. Distinguished, young and rich, what height might he not attain?

And yet, if he had carefully questioned his heart, Cornillé would perhaps have perceived that ambition did not absorb him entirely. Enjoying now since many months the intimacy of Lord Badger, who treated him more as a friend than as a simple collaborator, brought together every moment with Miss Nelly, he could not help feeling for this charming young girl an affection more tender than was to be desired for his peace of mind. But he wished to ignore this love, decided as he was to conceal it in the depths of his heart. Of an essentially proud and upright nature, our friend would have blushed to yield, even in secret, to a sentiment which he could not declare openly to her who was its object. Miss Nelly's social position, the rank which her father occupied in the upper English aristocracy, stood in the way of this avowal, which, on the part of the engineer, would have been an act of indelicacy towards the man who showed him so much confidence and friendship. He was thus firmly resolved to suppress his passion and to find in his work a protection against every weakness unworthy of him.

Badger, accompanied by Monaghan and the two young girls, visited the surroundings of the works during the few days which he had to pass in Babylon. The site of the ancient capital is now nothing but a dismal solitude. A large number of mounds, scattered throughout the plain, are all that remains to mark the spot where stood the ancient palaces. These mounds are formed by the accumulation of bricks, burnt and unburnt, reduced, most of them, to a state of dust. The Babylonians could not employ stone in their constructions, for their city lay too far from the calcareous or granitic lands. With the clay of the Euphrates they made bricks; with reeds and asphalt, which are found in abundance in the neighborhood, they joined these bricks together, and so constructed walls. Time and the elements have produced their effect on such fragile materials. A few centuries more and not a vestige will remain of the city of Nimrod, of Semiramis, and of

Nebuchadnezzar, of the capital which astonished antiquity by its splendor.

The Babylonians had succeeded in transforming this immense plain into a fertile country, which, under the Turkish rule, has again become a desert. They had arrived at this result by a thorough irrigation of Mesopotamia. Wherever there is water the vegetation is marvelous.

The earth is saturated with manure; the trees have their roots in the water and their tops in a burning air. All conditions are thus united for obtaining an extraordinary fruitfulness.

Badger and his companions had an example of this on their first excursion. Coming to the edge of a marshy piece of land, they saw an Arab stooping over the ground, holding a long stick in his hand, with which he drew little furrows in the wet soil. Puzzled by this spectacle, they drew nearer. The Arab had already scratched a large surface. He paid no attention to the presence of the Europeans and continued his work. When he had finished he took a bag and scattered wheat by the handful over the ground which he had turned up; then, with his stick, he roughly covered the seed with a light layer of earth, and went away without saying a word.

After their return to camp, they learned that it was in this way that the Arabs cultivated the ground. And yet, in spite of this rough manner of tilling and sowing, the results obtained surpass all belief. Four months after the sowing—that is to say, about April—the crop is ripe and ready for the harvest. A single grain of wheat has produced thirty or forty fold increase.

Badger acquired the certainty that Babylon would soon become the public granary of Europe. These results need not astonish us, for Mesopotamia is the native land of wheat. What results would not be obtained when the too primitive process of farming, practised by the Arabs, had been replaced by the perfected methods of Europe!

On the day before the one on which Laycock was to return from Bassorah, an expedition was organized for exploring the right bank of the Euphrates. Babylon extended over both banks of the river, which the Queen Nitocris had caused to be spanned by a bridge. Not a trace of this monument remains to-day.

This time the party was complete, excepting Blacton, whom it was now impossible to get away from his work for even an hour. Cornillé desired to visit an important hill—the Birs-Nimrod—which it might, perhaps, be possible to make good use of later on. Perhaps, too, the engineer was inwardly happy to journey once more by the side of Miss Nelly. She was to leave on the second day after. Who knows if he would ever see her again?

Flatnose himself had designed to make one of the party. This would give occasion for a new article for his paper; and, finally, he was fully decided by the fact that they were to be accompanied by the provision wagon, in which vehicle he could be comfortably installed, and in company with the charming Miss Ross.

They started at daybreak, for it would not take less than the whole day to go and return conveniently. The caravan descended along the Euphrates, passing near to the place where they had landed the first time. About a thousand yards farther on they entered the suburbs of Hillah—poor hovels, inhabited by 'half-vagabond Arabs. After having passed along a lane which seemed to be deserted, they reached the bridge of boats which connects the suburbs on the left bank with the city, built on the right bank, then they entered Hillah. This city resembles all those that line the Euphrates—white-washed walls, houses with flat roofs that serve as a place of assembling for all the members of the family during the summer evenings, large gardens where palm-trees wave their tops in the wind, mosque with slender minarets.

They had quickly passed through the city, and were once more in the midst of the solitude. The landscape was the same as that on the left bank, in the neighborhood of Babel and of the kasr—the same monotonous plain, studded with knolls formed by heaps of bitumen and bricks. These tells were, however, less numerous here. The reason of this is that Babylon extended principally on the left bank of the Euphrates; the other part was, properly speaking, nothing but an immense suburb.

In the distance rose a sort of hill which overlooked the plain. They proceeded straight towards it. The eminence of Birs-Nimrod lies about five miles from Hillah and about ten miles from the kasr and from Babel. The caravan, not hurried in its march, had taken nearly four hours to pass over the distance.

The Birs-Nimrod—that is to say, the tower of Nimrod—is one of the rare monuments which have escaped the complete decay of the ancient palaces of Babylon. Constructed on the banks of one of the arms of the Euphrates—the one which takes most of the waters of the river to Lake Nedjef—it was formerly an immense observatory erected to science in the reign of Nebuchadnezzar. It bore the name of *Tower of the Seven Spheres*. The Arabs think they see in it the ruins of the ancient Tower of Babel.

Birs-Nimrod is a striking example of the rapidity with which the monuments of Babylon have disappeared. The dimensions of the mound, quite rectangular, are 630 feet in length by 488 feet in breadth. Its height, above the level of the plain, is at present from 195 to 225 feet. Now, Strabo, in his time, gave it a height of five stadiums, which corresponds to about 600 feet. Since Strabo's time, the tower of Nimrod has, therefore, become about 375 feet lower. If there is no interruption to this rapidity of destruction, not a trace of it will remain a thousand years hence. Why be astonished because the other monuments, less solidly constructed, have already disappeared almost completely?

They ascended the mound, not a very difficult undertaking, on account of the slight declivity of the slope. Arrived at the top, our travelers found themselves face to face with a fine wall, thirty feet in height, which stands about in the centre of the plateau.

"Why, bless me," cried Flatnose, suddenly, looking up at the top of the tower, "an aerial telegraph! Illustrious Chappe, how happy I am to be able to salute here the last specimen of thy admirable invention!"

They all raised their eyes to the spot indicated, and saw, to their stupefaction, a long black machine which made signals by the aid of two enormous arms. At the same time, inarticulate sounds, apparently coming from the same point, struck their ears. They drew nearer; the long machine began to move around the platform, and redoubled its signals.

Badger took his glasses and looked up.

"Why, it's a man," said he. "He is dressed in black, and is as lean and dry as Don Quixotte. What the deuce is he doing up there?"

The man, since it was one, leaned over and cried in Arabic:

"Help me! I am dying of hunger; I have been here for three days!"

Badger knew a little Arabic; he understood what the man was saying.

How deliver him? That did not appear easy at first sight. The tower was solid, without stairs. Some windows, placed at equal intervals, indeed pierced the thickness of the walls; fragments of arches also stood out at one of the corners. But, unless one were a cat or a monkey, climbing the edifice by this means was not to be thought of.

"How can we reach you? How get up there?"

"Raise up the ladder which has fallen at the foot of the wall, on the other side," replied the stranger in French.

They passed around to the other side of the wall, and saw indeed a long ladder lying among the bushes.

It was now easy to understand how our man had been left on the top of the tower: he had reached the top by means of the ladder; but, by some accident, this had slid to the ground, thus leaving the visitor a prisoner.

The ladder was raised against the wall, and the unfortunate captive could at last descend.

Pale, weak, famished, the poor man was in a sad condition. Fortunately, the lunch was served at the bottom of the Birs-Nimrod. The whole party descended the hill again, and quickly sat down to table.

"Do you feel better now?" said Badger, when the unknown had swallowed his first mouthfuls.

"Very much better, thank you," he replied, in pure English. "I was almost dead with hunger when you delivered me from above there."

"Can you tell us now who you are?" said Badger.

"*Ja*," said the unknown, with his mouth full.

"But does this gentleman then know all the languages?" exclaimed Flatnose. "After all, that is not astonishing, since we are at Babylon."

After having recovered his strength somewhat, the man related his adventures. His name was Grimmitschoffer, and he was occupied at the time with archæological researches relative to the ancient empire of Assyria. Since several days he was exploring the ruins of Babylon, and had begun his researches at the monuments on the right bank. Desirous of mounting the tower of the Birs-Nimrod, he had taken two Arabs with him to carry a long ladder. But fancy his stupefaction and his fright when, having reached the top of the building, he saw his two rascally Arabs overturn the ladder and run off at full speed!

For three days he had called for help. Not a human being had appeared near the tower. Determined not to die of hunger, he was about to hurl himself from a height of thirty feet when Badger's caravan had appeared at the horizon.

Through what dreadful anxieties had he not passed during an hour! What if the travelers should turn away from the Birs-Nimrod without seeing his signals or hearing his desperate cries!

Grimmitschoffer knew Badger and his companions by name. He had been informed at Hillah of the arrival of the Europeans and of the end which they pursued. They desired, said the inhabitants, to recover the treasures buried for centuries in the kasr and in Babel.

As to himself, he was, as he modestly declared, a distinguished archæologist. He had published more than a hundred memoirs and had written over a dozen volumes on the monuments of all the countries of the earth. He desired to reconstitute the plan of Babylon, in order to demonstrate to the scholars that ancient Rome was constructed on exactly the same plan as the ancient capital of Assyria, with operations analogous to those of the Assyrian monarchs.

He had already published a number of volumes and written several manuscripts on the subject. "I happen to have here some notes as proof in support of this," said he, drawing a manuscript from his pocket, and he prepared to read them.

"Later on! Later on!" cried the others in chorus. "Eat first; you shall read afterward."

Grimmitschoffer reluctantly replaced his manuscript in his pocket.

"You are too long," remarked Flatnose, a moment later. "I propose to cut you down, Mr. Grimmitschoffer; it takes a minute to pronounce your name. I shall call you simply Grimm."

"Unanimously adopted," said all the others, rising.

A few hours later the excursionists and the learned scholar Grimm were back at Babel.

"By the bye," said Badger, when they met again, "you forgot to tell us before, Mr. Grimm, what your nationality is."

"I have none, my lord," replied the antiquary; "a man like me is above the questions of frontiers and nationality, I am a citizen of the Universe."

"If that is so," put in Flatnose, "your real name is not Grimmitschoffer, but certainly Volapük."

CHAPTER XI.

FROM BAGDAD TO MOSUL.

CAPTAIN LAYCOCK arrived the following day with a fresh cargo of machines and material.

The caravan, as we already know, was to be composed of the following persons: Badger and Miss Nelly, Fatma and Miss Ross, Monaghan and Flatnose. To these must be added Grimmitschoffer, who is no longer called by any name but that of Grimm, and to whom Badger had proposed to travel in company with him, as long as his archæological researches should keep him in these regions. He would thus avoid accidents similar to that to which he had nearly fallen a victim. Grimm, who desired precisely to ascend towards the north, following the banks of the Tigris, to explore the innumerable ruins scattered along the river, eagerly accepted his lordship's kind offer. Thus another new member joined the expedition. It must be said that the adjunction of this other recruit was not received with very great favor. Fatma's arrival had been hailed with joy by every one; Grimm's was not received with so much enthusiasm.

Yet Grimm was an excellent man; but his forty-five years—he looked at least sixty—his bald forehead, his long hair falling in locks on his neck, his large nose and the enormous spectacles which hid half of his face, could not vie either with the fifteen years or with the naive grace of the young Greek.

On the preceding day, after the return to camp, Grimm had again wished to read his manuscript on his comparative study of Rome and Babylon. Unfortunately, on account of the general fatigue, every one had retired to his tent after supper. The following day, another fruitless attempt: the whole day was occupied in preparations for the departure. Our archæologist had to resign himself and put his manuscript away for a more favorable time.

Five days were necessary to finish the complete equipment of the caravan. At last, on the 6th of January, they were ready to start. The *Electricity* had already left again three days before. The little steamer was to descend the Euphrates to its junction with the Tigris, and then ascend the latter river as far as Bagdad, where Badger and his companions would await it. They had preferred to go directly from Babylon to Bagdad by the land-route. The journey would last only three days and would consequently be much quicker than in going by the *Electricity*.

The separation was cordial. Blacton and Cornillé wished their old companions a pleasant journey. Badger gave his last charges, and shook them by the hand, much more deeply moved than he would have wished to show.

When Cornillé bid Miss Nelly adieu, it seemed to him that the young girl's eyes were wet. She answered him in an uncertain voice, that seemed as if contracted by emotion. Then he encountered the look of Fatma, whose mischievous smile seemed to say: I foresaw it long ago.

"Can it be that I am loved," thought the engineer to himself. At the very thought a great joy filled his soul. But, summing up all the energy of his will, he said to himself that, even in the interest of his heart's idol, he must hope that she would forget him.

The distance which separates the Euphrates from the Tigris between Babylon and Bagdad is only about forty-nine miles. The journey can be easily made in two days, especially in the month of January, when the temperature is endurable.

The Arabs have given the name of Jezireh to the region which extends between the two rivers. It is a vast, mountainous plain, solitary and level, whose horizon is bounded only by infinity. The Turkish government has caused modest caravansaries or khans to be erected, which, from distance to distance, offer a shelter and resting-place to the caravans.

Six hours after leaving Babel they arrived at the first of these khans. A halt was made to rest and to take dinner. In the evening the second one was reached. The tents were raised for the night, and they prepared to eat supper near a large fire of dry brushwood.

It was a beautiful star-lit night. The flames of the improvised hearth threw strange lights on the surroundings of the camp. The travelers talked long about the journey they were undertaking; about Jack Adams, of whom they hoped to have news at Bagdad or at Mosul; about the hydraulic machines and the turbines.

Next morning at daybreak the caravan set out again. After going a mile or two they came across one of those canals which served to spread the waters of the Tigris and the Euphrates over the plain. This one, about sixty feet wide, bordered right and left by high embankments, crossed the desert in a straight line and converted it into a fertile plain. It is now half filled up. Large pools of stagnant water covered with green weeds, intersected by long strips of sand, are all that remain of this fine work of the Babylonian engineers. How easy would it not be to restore it to its original state!

They had almost reached the third khan when an accident happened which might have had grave results, but which, fortunately, ended in a comical manner.

Flatnose and Grimm, who, notwithstanding their frequent quarrels, or perhaps because of this, felt at times the irresistible necessity of being together, rode at the head of the party. Suddenly their horses were seen to sway from right to left and fall heavily to the ground. The rest of the caravan immediately hurried to their assistance. Monaghan, who was the first to arrive, had to stop his horse, which was plunging into deep holes. He dismounted and made signs to the others to stop.

In the meantime Grimm rose, felt himself from head to foot and ascertained that no bones were broken. As to stout Flatnose, he had to be lifted on his legs. He groaned as if there was not a bone left whole in his body.

"Try to walk," said Monaghan to him.

He made a few steps in advance, but plunged into another hole and fell heavily again. They succeeded at last in getting him out of this, to him, doubly dangerous spot and bringing him back to *terra firma*.

He was bruised, but not wounded.

The guide explained what had happened. They had passed over the burrows of a colony of jerboas. These animals dig deep underground galleries close to the surface of the ground, which cave in when a heavy body passes over them. He added that accidents like those which had just happened were not rare.

On the evening of the same day they discerned at the horizon the minarets and cupolas of the mosques of Bagdad, in Arabic Dar-es-Salaam, the abode of peace.

Seen thus at a distance of two miles or so the ancient capital of the Abbasside caliphs appears to the surprised and delighted eye of the traveler such as he has been able to picture it to himself in a past which seems to belong as much to fairy-land as to reality.

The city covers almost the same space as in the time when it contained a numerous population, and nothing stands in the way of the imagination which ascribes to it the splendor and magnificence of bygone times. The white houses, on the terraces of which one seems to see the shadows of the women who have come out to breathe the perfumed coolness of the night; the sharply defined spires of the minarets, vying in slenderness and lightness with the slender trunks of the palm-trees; the Tigris, which unfolds like a broad silvery band; the sky, of a clearness unequalled even in the Orient, indicate well the city of the *Thousand and One Nights*, where, in one of the fantastic palaces indistinctly seen by the light of the stars, Scheherazade is perhaps just relating one of her wonderful tales.

Unfortunately the fairy scene disappears as you approach it. When the caravan had passed the walls it found itself in a large waste place, in which, here and there, stood the ruins of some miserable cabins. A

few hundred yards farther on they entered the suburbs on the right bank of the Tigris. At the end of a long street they reached the banks of the river, which was crossed on a bridge of boats and not far from which Badger and his companions took possession of a large building which the English consul had rented for them and caused to be furnished in European style.

Next day Miss Nelly and Fatma, the first to wake up, desired to inspect the house before breakfasting. It was composed, like all the dwellings of the rich Arabs, of one-story buildings arranged around a large square court. The gallery giving access to the apartments on the ground-floor was supported by small, light columns of palm-wood, with graceful corbellings and delicate capitals.

The two young girls descended by a narrow staircase into a sort of cave, or rather a vaulted chamber hollowed out below the level of the court. They were informed that this was the *sirdab*. Here the inhabitants of the house sought refuge during the excessive heat. They found here both coolness and shadow.

There being nothing further to see below, they ascended to the flat roofs by an interior staircase. From here there was a splendid view to be had of the city and the surroundings.

"It's too beautiful!" cried Miss Nelly, after having contemplated this scene for several minutes. "Fatma, do bring my father and our friends."

A few minutes later they were all collected on the terrace. Flat-nose alone was wanting. He snored like an organ-pipe, forgetting in sleep his misfortunes of the day before. They had not had the heart to wake him.

The panorama which was unfolded before their eyes was truly magical. Bagdad, with its masses of houses, its gardens breaking out between the terraces, its cupolas and minarets covered with brightly colored faience, extended on the two banks of the Tigris. The river, broad and sparkling, wound through the plain amidst a forest of palm-trees. To the east, to the north and to the south there was the limitless desert, the waste desert, with a soil of clay and sand. At the east the mountains of Persia raised their snow-covered summits towards the sky. The distance prevented them from seeing the details, but the peaks, the rounded domes, the dentated crests, could be distinguished with exceeding clearness. Below, dark masses detached themselves: they were the smaller mountains, the lateral chains which seem so grand to the traveler standing at their base and which disappear before the enormous mass of the central chain when regarded from a distance.

Leaning on the balcony of the terrace, our friends could not tear themselves away from their contemplation. The dazzling sun, reflected on the gold of the surrounding sands, flooded everything with so bright a light that the city appeared as if enchanted.

Miss Nelly was enraptured to see Bagdad at last, the city isolated in the midst of the deserts which seem to separate it from the rest of the world, a city that is almost fabulous to the inhabitants of the Western countries.

Alas! the reality was not altogether like the fiction. The palaces of Haroun-al-Raschid, the monuments of Zobeidah have crumbled into dust. Everything has contributed towards the destruction of the splendors of the ancient caliphs: the Turks, the Tartars, the tempests, and even the inundations of the Tigris. Bagdad has fallen greatly

from the position which it had formerly occupied. Its walls have grown too wide for its present inhabitants, reduced in number to fifty thousand.

Fortunately the true observers and the true artists are not subject to the same deceptions as the common herd of tourists, for whom the most beautiful things have exactly the value of theatre scenery. For those who know how to see, the reality offers compensations which well replace the dream. If the Bagdad of to-day does not resemble that of the *Thousand and One Nights*, it yet has its blue sky, its beautiful river, its incomparable climate. In its mosques and in its bazars the varied crowds still jostle each other, the throngs belonging to the various nationalities which have divided this part of Asia among themselves. The Turkish rule has not been able to take from it its essentially Arabian character. It remains the most Oriental among the Oriental cities, the ideal capital of a poetic empire that has disappeared.

Yet they could not stay forever on the terrace, sunk in contemplation; they must take advantage of the few days which would elapse before the arrival of Captain Laycock to visit the city and its environs. It was decided that each one should follow his fancy and go where he wished.

Badger, accompanied by his daughter and Fatma, proceeded towards the bridge of boats which serves to connect the suburbs on the right bank with the city, situated on the left bank. The cities of Mesopotamia have always developed principally in the direction of the setting sun.

After having crossed the bridge, our three sight-seers entered a coffee-house composed of a covered gallery serving as a divan, and under which several Turkish merchants, nonchalantly extended on cushions, were smoking their chibouks and drinking pure Mocha.

Opposite to the coffee-house was an abandoned mosque, devoted to certain ruin by the carelessness and unconcern of the natives. The Arabs do not destroy the monuments—as they have wrongfully been accused—but they allow the most beautiful of them to be destroyed by the action of time and the elements, without ever trying to oppose any obstacle.

Since it has allowed itself to be despoiled of the most beautiful countries in the universe, this people, which in times of old founded the most wonderful empire of the world, seems to be prey to a great nostalgia. Become conquering by the spirit of religious proselytism, it awaits, one might think, a new prophet who shall arise and recommence the marvelous legend, the remembrance of which pursues it. Until then, what avails it to be disturbed? Nothing is worth troubling about; such seems to be its motto.

On the Tigris there was a perpetual moving to and fro of craft of all shapes and kinds. Boats with long flexible masts and sails swelled by the wind were descending the stream, taken rapidly along by the current. Ships and kalaks, run aground or made fast near the shore, were bringing timber, cut on the mountains of Persia, to the capital, and were loading and unloading merchandise.

But what diverted the two Londoners most was to see the numerous "guffehs," or coracles, descending or ascending the river, transporting passengers and packages from one shore to the other.

These "quffehs" are a very curious kind of boats, contemporaneous, no doubt, with the kalaks, and also dating back to the Assyrian epoch, for representations of them are seen on the bas-reliefs found in the excavations. They might be compared—excepting the handle—to the oval baskets which the French peasant-women use for taking butter and eggs to market. They are constructed of plaited rushes, and covered with bitumen. They are guided with a single oar, which propels them by turning.

The bridge of boats also presented a very animated appearance. It was being incessantly crossed by a varied procession : Arabs of the desert, mounted on their small and spirited horses; pedestrians or Jewish merchants, pursuing their pleasure and their business, at the slow, even trot of the large white asses mottled with designs in color of hennah; native women, carefully veiled, somewhat resembling walking bundles; Kurdish women, with uncovered faces, accompanied by their husbands, tall fellows, with a hardy and proud air.

Then there were large flocks of sheep, fed in the meadows which line the Tigris, going to the slaughter-houses of the city; camels, heavily loaded with the products of Persia and Arabia.

The next day was devoted to visiting the mosques. The English consul had obtained, not without trouble, the authorization of the military governor of Bagdad, with the express reservation that the visitors should leave their shoes at the door, a condition to which the ladies as well as the men submitted with good grace. One must never uselessly hurt religious feelings. For the thinker and for the sincere believer, every religion is to be respected for the reason alone that it is a religion.

The best preserved mosques are those of Abd-el-Kader, Abd-el-Rahman, and that of the Sheikh Yoosuf. Built of brick, they are lined on the exterior with squares of colored faience, which form exceedingly pretty designs and give the minaret a light and graceful appearance.

On the interior the mosques, by their bareness and simplicity, remind you a little of the Protestant churches. No statues or altars;

no representations of figures of man or beast. Arabian architecture allows of but little ornament other than geometrical designs. On the whitewashed walls are inscribed verses from the Koran; there are no benches or seats of any kind; the faithful pray kneeling on mats or carpets. It cannot be denied that these temples, where the soul feels itself, without help or an intermedium of any kind, face to face with the only God, produce a very thrilling effect.

Bagdad possesses a railway, or rather a tramway, the only one which exists in Mesopotamia, and which serves to connect the city with the pretty and elegant village of Kazmin, composed of fine villas and gardens full of flowers. Our travelers went out after breakfast one day to take a walk there.

Kazmin is the country-seat of the capital, the *rendezvous* of the wealthy Arabs during the heat of summer. It is also a place of pilgrimage venerated by the Persians, who come to pay their devotions at the tomb of the iman Moosa-ibn-Jaffar, a celebrated Shiite martyr.

This tomb lies in a superb mosque covered with blue, black, white, and rose-colored faience. A large crowd of pilgrims had come together there. It was necessary to forego inspecting its interior, for, in the eyes of these fanatical Mussulmans, the mere presence of the Europeans would have profaned the holy place. They had to be content with admiring the exterior of the monument, a large, square edifice, in the midst of a court surrounded by arcades. The platform is surmounted by two gilded cupolas, shaped like mushrooms. At the four corners, there are four minarets with gilded tops. The general effect is rich and beautiful. The tints are delicate and mellow.

Eight days thus passed very quickly, in promenades and excursions, until the arrival of Captain Laycock. They embarked once more on the *Electricity*, to ascend the Tigris to Mosul.

On leaving Bagdad, the river flows through a forest of palm-trees. In the deep shadows of the woods, country-houses with their orchards form bright spots.

To the right and to the left lay the level plain. Towards the *magrab*, that is to say, the west, the desert extended to the extreme limits of the horizon.

Towards the east the country was fertile. Near the ruins of Ctesiphon, a valley, parallel to that of the Tigris, and still more fertile, extends in magnificent carpets of verdure to the foot of the mountains of Persia. It is the valley of the Diyalah, one of the most important tributaries of the Tigris, and which runs into this river a little above Bagdad.

After having passed the pretty village of Mahdhim, half hidden among date-trees, the river makes a turn, and Bagdad and its minarets are lost to view.

A little farther on, the passengers of the *Electricity* could see for the last time the cupolas of Kazmin sparkling in the rays of the noonday sun.

Above Kazmin, the landscape becomes more monotonous. The desert approaches nearer and nearer to the river. The latter makes a wide turn towards the east, then ascends again towards the north.

On the second day they passed Samarrah and its celebrated mosque. Under the caliphs Samarrah was a large and flourishing city. It was the favorite residence of the eighth caliph, Motassem-Billah, who made it his capital in order to punish the inhabitants of Bagdad for their turbulent character. To-day it is nothing but an unimportant village. How many capitals have arisen and have disappeared thus in Mesopotamia!

Yet, if the Shiite tradition is to be believed, a great destiny is yet in store for Samarrah. It is from this city that the Mahdi will come, who will appear like another Messiah.

A little before Samarrah an embankment was remarked, formed by a very high rampart of earth, which began at the Tigris and extended farther than the eye could reach into the desert. The *savant* Grimm declared that they had before them the celebrated wall of Nimrod, which served both as line of defence and boundary line between Mesopotamia and Media.

They were, in fact, ascending rapidly toward the north. In the absence of the Median wall the temperature and the brightness of the sky would have sufficiently informed the travelers of this fact. In the middle of the day it was still warm, but in the morning and evening it became cold enough to oblige them to dress as in winter, and it was well for the party that they were abundantly provided with blankets and furs.

Toward the east the mountains of Persia, becoming more and more visible, showed not only their peaks and summits, but even their slopes covered with snow. The dazzling sheet descended the heights down to the beginnings of the plain.

BABYLON ELECTRIFIED.

Below Tekrit the water of the Tigris suddenly changed color and became yellowish and oily. This phenomenon was produced by the naphtha which flowed on its surface. Monaghan collected a certain quantity of it, which he was able to set on fire.

A little farther on the ship passed over the springs themselves of the inflammable liquid, which bursts out above the water in big, black and fetid ripples, then to spread out over the surface. The geologist explained that the presence f petr leum is not unusual in the neighborhood of the mountain-chain; they were entering an extremely curious volcanic country and would have occasion to study a large number of natural phenomena.

At Tekrit they had to leave the *Electricity* and bid adieu again to Captain Laycock. The latter was to return to Babylon to transport the rest of the material there. He was charged with a thousand compliments to Cornillé and Blacton. Miss Nelly even intrusted him with a friendly line to Cornillé, below which Fatma added a good-day—" *bon-jour* "—in French.

It was easy to procure a large boat at Tekrit for ascending the Tigris to Mosul. They were comfortably installed in it and the journey was continued.

The monotonous desert began again after Tekrit, but it did not last long. The mountain-chain, which always lay on the right, drew perceptibly nearer to the river. Soon it raised its escarpments beside the

Tigris. They entered a narrow ravine, where the river had opened a passage for itself.

This whole region seems deeply disturbed. To the right and to the left of the Tigris rugged walls rise abruptly, from which each year, with the melting of the snow, enormous blocks of stone become detached. The defile is obstructed by huge rocks between which the river rushes and roars.

In the evening, by moonlight, the effect of this chaos is fantastic. It seems as if the mountain would close up and engulf you. The rocks then take on strange forms. One might take them for the genii of the earth, guarding the entrance to these deep gorges and defending it from the approach of daring intruders.

On emerging from the defile of Hamrin a large valley is entered. To the left extends the mountain wall through which you have just passed; to the right arise the steep walls of another mountain-chain. The Lesser Zab, a tributary of the Tigris, here joins with it amidst marshes filled with rushes.

At this point the Tigris ascends at first toward the northwest, then directly toward the north.

Grimm pointed out a high hillock on the right bank. This is the hill of Kalch Shergat, which marks the site of one of the most ancient cities of Assyria, Calah, or Chalach, one of the four primitive cities mentioned in *Genesis*. The three others were: Nineveh, Rehoboth-ir and Resen. All four were founded by Asshur, grandson of Noah, from whom the Assyrians derive their name.

They had, in fact, left Babylonia, that is to say the empire of the south and of the plains, to enter into Assyria, the empire of the north and of the mountains. The ruins became as numerous as in the vicinity of Babylon and of Bagdad. They were in the region which, according to the Bible, has seen the arising of the most ancient empires. The tells continued almost uninterruptedly on both banks of the river. Grimm thus had occasion frequently to give his traveling companions the benefit of his profound knowledge of archæology. It was in truth exceedingly interesting to listen to him.

The high mountains draw nearer rapidly, abruptly closing up on the east the plain through which the Tigris flows. Their glaciers rise to an enormous height. On their blackish sides the fields of snow formed spots of a dazzling whiteness. At sunset these snows and glaciers are tinged with the most varying colors. The whole gamut of tones appears here in a gradation of color the delicacy of which no brush could render.

At the mouth of the Greater Zab the spectacle is truly admirable. You cut through the wall perpendicularly at its axis. Parallel chains and the valleys lying between these chains are seen to defile successively. From this results a variety of points of view which holds the admiration constantly in suspense, for none of these valleys resembles the other.

Yet the farther you advance the more gigantic the landscape becomes. The summits accumulate and eclipse everything with their enormous masses, the snow descends lower continually.

A few miles farther on the two slopes subside again. The river spreads broadly between two verdant and flowery banks. As in all valleys sheltered between high mountains, the air was calm, the temperature warm and penetrating. The flora was that of the southern countries of Europe, while on the various levels of the mountain the zones of vegetation of the temperate and frigid regions are superposed, even to the limit of perpetual ice, where every trace of vegetation disappears.

About a mile and a quarter from the Tigris rise the ruins of Nimrood. In excavating the tell the palace of Asshur-Nazirpal has been discovered, as well as inscriptions which have made possible the reconstruction of a very interesting portion of the history of Assyria.

A few hours later the boat arrived at Mosul, and our travelers left their moving house for a more comfortable dwelling.

Badger's first care was to go to the English consulate at Mosul in quest of news about Jack Adams. He received the very latest. The engineer had almost completed his first hydraulic works near Jezireh-Ibn-Omar in the upper valley of the Tigris; all his men were in good health, and he was impatiently awaiting the arrival of his lordship to inaugurate his first electric station.

At ease on that score, Badger occupied himself with the means of transport for taking himself and his companions first to Jezireh and then to the different valleys of the tributaries of the Tigris. The use of watercourses as a means of communication was, in fact, no longer to be thought of. For two months they were to penetrate into the region of the high mountains that separate Persia from Assyria and from Mesopotamia, climb steep passes and surmount the separating ridges of several deep valleys.

As it would take a week to organize the new caravan, raise beasts and men, and procure the provisions necessary for so long a journey through wild and uninhabited countries, it was decided to devote this waiting-time to visiting the ruins of Nineveh, Khorsabad and Bavian.

The next day but one was fixed upon as the day of departure for this excursion. During these two days Mosul was to be inspected.

Mosul, by its position, is one of the most considerable cities of Mesopotamia. The point of junction of the principal valley tributary to that of the Tigris, it carries on an extensive commerce with Persia, the Caucasus and the Kurdish tribes of the mountain. It has about forty thousand inhabitants; its importance is not due only to its commerce, but also to the manufacture of marvelous stuffs. It is said that Mosul has given its name to the light fabric which we manufacture in Europe under the name of muslin and which has been imported from the East.

Mosul is built in form of an amphitheatre, on the top of a hill which is nothing but an advanced ramification of the range of the Seinjar. The Tigris flows at the foot of this hill and divides into several branches. At this place the river is already navigable for rafts of some size. A fine bridge of boats gives access to the city.

The appearance of Mosul is quite grand. The principal buildings and the houses of some importance are constructed of alabaster, which is called marble of Mosul. One of the two bazaars is very handsome and presents a most animated appearance. The other resembles all the establishments of the kind. At the summit of the hill, in the centre of a magnificent garden, baths have been constructed, fed by a thermal spring. Turks and Arabs come here all the year round to seek remedies for their ills or occasions for amusement.

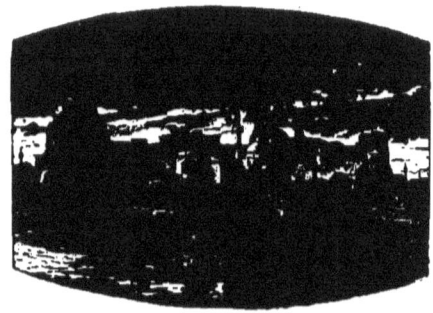

CHAPTER XII.

THE GROTTO OF BAVIAN.

At the hour appointed everybody was ready for the projected expedition to the ruins and to Bavian.

After having crossed the bridge of boats which connects Mosul with the left bank of the Tigris, they followed a road of somewhat over a mile and arrived opposite a high mound, which covers a space of no less than twenty-five acres. It is the Kouyunjik, where ancient Nineveh stood—Nineveh, the great city, "of three days' journey."

As a site for a capital, it was difficult to choose a better spot. Near to the mountains, from whence it could obtain the stones and all the materials of construction; on the bank of a large river, which then had, no doubt, a much more considerable discharge of water than to-day, it opened and closed at its will the road which placed the east and the west in communication. It kept in awe the undisciplined tribes of the mountain as well as the peoples of the flat land.

When the Assyrian empire is solidly founded, Babylon replaces Nineveh. That is the invariable law. Every government which is established by the right of the strongest must think as much of defending itself as of attacking. The first care of the conqueror is to fortify himself in the positions gained. The hordes which he hurls upon unsuspecting populations must be able, when necessary, to seek refuge behind impregnable ramparts.

Later on, there are considerations of another kind which sweep it away. The period of conquest and war is succeeded by the period of development and wealth. Nineveh is the eagle's nest of the Asshurs and Nimrods; Babylon, the brilliant capital of the magnificent empire of Semiramis.

Grimmitschoffer desired very much to make a thorough study of Nineveh. In his system, everything that related to the Assyrian empire had an importance of the first order, for, from the foundation of this mighty empire began, according to him, all the misfortunes of humanity. Nimrod was the first despot, the first to put in practice, if not to formulate, the celebrated axiom: Might is right. The tyrants and the Cæsars who came after him were but his continuators and his plagiarists. But the reign of force, the emblems of which were the winged heads of bulls found in the excavations, was drawing to its close. Right and justice, represented by the lamb and the ram, would reign once more upon earth, and he, Grimm, might perhaps be the Moses destined to lead humanity into this promised land, or, rather, into this recovered paradise.

The Kouyunjik had been excavated in every direction by preceding explorers. Cut open by blows of the pick-axe, it allowed subterranean galleries to be seen at several points, extending in all directions.

Grimm, bearing a lantern in his hand, and followed by two men also provided each with a lantern and a pick-axe, entered the largest of these galleries.

"Above all," cried Flatnose, as the archæologist disappeared in the darkness, "above all, do not forget to bring us back a Ninevite, living or dead."

"And select a handsome one," cried Nelly in turn, laughing, "I shall give him as a husband to Fatma."

While Grimm, in search of some precious find, was thus entering into the depths of the earth, the others, led by Monaghan, were examining the uncovered ruins and débris. It could be ascertained that the interior apartments of the ancient palaces were lined all around, to about two-thirds of their height, with slabs of marble and of sculptured stones. The sculptures represented combats or hunts. Fragments of sphinx were found, of lions, and of immense winged bulls such as those which have been sent to the *Louvre* and to the *British Museum*. There were numerous enameled bricks. The prettiest were laid aside to be brought away.

Meanwhile the time passed and the antiquarian did not reappear. They went to visit the village of Nebbi-Yunus, on one side of the mound of Kouyunjik, and also situated on a small hill, where, it is said, the prophet Jonah lies buried. God had commanded him to go and preach penitence to the Ninevites. The irascible prophet, who would, perhaps, not have been sorry to have seen with his own eyes the destruction of the evil-doers, took good care not to obey, and fled on a ship. It was only after the adventures of which we know that he decided to fill the *rôle* of a messenger of peace, the grandeur of

which he understood so little. The fig-tree is still shown under which, his sermon finished, he went to sleep, not without still raging inwardly against the divine mildness.

They were returning to the mound, when the two men who had accompanied Grimm to aid him in his researches, came running towards them at the top of their speed. They told them that an accident had just happened to the poor *savant*. He had advanced into a narrow cleft in the ground, when it had caved in and he had been buried under a heap of rubbish.

A rescuing party was quickly organized. Monaghan, at the head of a dozen men armed with pick-axes, advanced to the spot where the accident had taken place, and set about to deliver the victim of archæology.

We shall say at once that, this time again, Grimm was to escape with his fright. He being protected by an angle in the wall, the crush had not reached him; but his position was a most uncomfortable one, for he could not make a single movement. At the end of an hour's work, he was delivered, without a scratch, and brought out in triumph among his companions.

But the poor man was confused. Nothing could be more comical than his disturbed face.

"Ill fortune pursues me everywhere," said he, sadly. "She does not want me to connect my name with immortal discoveries."

"She will requite you later on," said Badger, gravely, while the others could not refrain from bursting out laughing at sight of the piteous appearance of this knight of the sorrowful countenance; "do not lose courage so easily."

Cheered up by these kind words, Grimm was able to remount his horse, and they took up at last the journey to Khorsabad, lying about fifteen miles north-east of Mosul. After a pleasant ride through a hilly country, already covered with a luxuriant vegetation, they found themselves, at about eleven o'clock, opposite to the ruins. The end of January, in these regions, is equivalent to our month of April in Europe; the fruit-trees in full bloom gave a holiday appearance to the whole country.

The ancient palace of Khorsabad was the summer residence, the *Versailles* or *Compiègne*, of the kings of Nineveh; its situation in a pleasant valley, at the foot of a chain of mountains, high enough, yet without being craggy and wild, shows that these cruel tyrants, these capricious and sanguinary despots had a very strong feeling for nature.

There is nothing new under the sun: some forty centuries ago, as in our day, the sovereigns and the wealthy people left their sumptuous palaces and opulent residences, to dwell in pleasant villas like those whose ruins are so frequently found on the hills and mounts in the vicinity of Nineveh. And at that time, like to-day, it would no doubt have been very bad form to exempt oneself from this custom, imposed as much by fashion as by a real attraction.

The ruins of Khorsabad extend over a surface of nearly two square miles. They are well enough preserved to have permitted the reconstruction of the geometrical plan of the buildings. Around the palace and its outbuildings rose a small village, where resided the courtiers and noblemen who did not wish to remove from the court.

The palace, according to some, was built in the reign of Sargon, the

Salmanazar of the Bible. By excavations there have been uncovered, for a distance of over a mile, walls of seventy-eight feet in breadth by over ninety-seven in height. On this immense display of surface a multitude of bas-reliefs represent the principal events in the reign of Sargon.

Khorsabad possessed also an observatory, consisting of a tower, four stories high, in a quite good state of preservation. Built of stones—very abundant in the mountains—the cities and monuments of Assyria, properly speaking, have been much better preserved than those of Mesopotamia, for which only very destructible materials have been employed. The ruins of Khorsabad have enabled scholars to restore in part the history of the ancient empire.

Grimmitschoffer was beside himself with joy at sight of these treasures. His misadventure of the morning was completely forgotten. But what threw him altogether into an ecstasy of which antiquarians only have the gift, was the visit to a large cellar which had served as a warehouse for an iron-merchant. More than 160 tons of iron implements of all shapes had been dug out here, which had served for the daily uses of life.

With the aid of these authentic documents, it would have been easy to write a chapter on the private life of the ancients, and to see them acting like real beings, and not like fantastic shadows.

Having caused a few blows with the pick-axe to be made in one corner, Grimm had the joy of seeing several new specimens come to light. It was necessary to restrain his ardor. If they had listened to him, a whole week would have been occupied in digging up the

8

ground, and they would have taken back several tons of rusty iron with them to Mosul.

Flatnose approached him and, with the greatest coolness imaginable: "Your excavations displease Lord Badger," he said to him in a low tone. "He is afraid that you might find a dynamo-electric machine or a thermo-solar pile amongst this heap of iron, and then, good-bye to his ardor and enthusiasm. For if the ancient Ninevites or Babylonians made use of these machines, he would be nothing but a vile plagiarist, and his pride would not permit him to continue his work."

On hearing these words, which he was far from taking for a joke, Grimm gave a violent start. One might have said that he had just been struck by lightning. His eyes, fixed on Flatnose, seemed to say: "How has he been able to fathom my secret?" The truth is, that the comparative study of Rome and Babylon was but the least of the claims which Grimm believed he had to immortality. The principal one was the discovery of the *rôle* which electricity played with the ancients. Of that secret Grimm spoke to nobody. He would even have feared to commit it to paper, so long as he had not collected all the elements of an irrefutable demonstration.

It will therefore be understood what a blow good Flatnose's innocent sally of wit had dealt him. Yet he composed himself, notwithstanding, and, in an instant, had recovered all his *sang-froid*.

The night was passed under the tents, opposite the ruins. Everybody was gay and in high spirits, except Miss Ross, on whom these perpetual changes of place began to tell; she was becoming peevish. She was no longer in her first youth, nor even, perhaps, in her second. It was evident that a comfortable little home—the vision of which haunted her more and more—would have much better been her object than the position which she occupied with a man, twenty times a millionaire, who lived like a prince, and that the mists of the Thames would have seemed to her preferable to the most beautiful sunrise on the mountains of Assyria. Faithful to her duty, she followed the caravan without complaining too much, but also without the least enthusiasm. She seldom left the wagon while they were on the march, or the tent while they were in camp.

Next day, at dawn, they set out for Bavian. It was necessary to cross the mountain chain which separates Khorsabad from the latter locality.

The ascent was difficult enough. Miss Ross had been seated on a mule. The poor woman clung desperately to the beast. At every movement of the animal she expected to fall into the ravines or over the precipices. At the summit of the Makloub they had a splendid view of the valley of the Tigris and the adjoining mountains.

The descent was rapidly accomplished, and they had soon reached the deep gorges in which Bavian is situated.

The travelers followed a narrow valley overhung on the right and left by parallel escarpments. One would not believe oneself to be any longer in the Orient, but in a valley of Switzerland or Tyrol. The vegetation, completely different from that of the Euphrates, is identical with that of the northern countries. The oak, the walnut, and, especially, the fir, grow here as in a valley of the Alps.

Suddenly they find themselves opposite to a high wall of limestone, on which colossal figures were cut out in relief, still perfectly preserved. The various inscriptions which accompany these figures permit them to be attributed with certainty to the epoch of Sennacherib. As to their intent, it is probable that they were destined to perpetuate, throughout the centuries, the fame of the Ninevite monarchs.

At a later period caves have been dug in these rocks and have served as dwellings for human beings. These troglodytes were probably Christians of the first centuries, who sought a refuge from persecution, or joined to lead a cenobitic life in common. Without respect for these ancient monuments, they have perforated the heads, the bodies, the emblems. It would be useless to ask whether this mutilation excited Grimm's indignation. He delivered an eloquent philippic against these ignorant Christians, who had never understood anything of the ancient myths and symbols, and saw everywhere idolatrous images to destroy. He sent them to the devil, these poor people who perhaps had acted thus only in the hope of meriting heaven.

But this immense bas-relief was not the greatest curiosity of the valley. The guide conducted the party a few hundred steps farther, to the bottom of a narrow defile, dark and damp, where, a short time before, the entrance to a still unexplored grotto had been discovered. What a godsend for an archæologist! What might he not discover in the bowels of the earth!

It was the English consul at Mosul who had informed Badger of this recent discovery, and if the latter had eagerly welcomed the project of an excursion to Bavian, it was especially with a view to being the first to explore this cavern. The Englishman has with him always and everywhere the preoccupation of asserting—on no matter what soil—the supremacy of England. As he had the good fortune to have just at hand a true *savant*—in spite of all his eccentricities and faults, this title could not be denied Grimmitschoffer—Lord Badger had decided to profit by this in order to learn whether there was really occasion for undertaking serious excavations in the grotto, in which case he would not have failed to inform his government, and thus secure for it an initiatory part in this kind of discovery in which to-day all the civilized nations of Europe are strongly interested.

They had therefore provided themselves with torches and with the implements necessary in such cases, and it had been decided that they all should enter into the grotto, and that every one should take part in the researches. The entrance to the cave was narrow. But, after a few steps of rapid descent on an inclined and muddy ground, the gallery became higher and wider. A sharp current of air met the face, and confused noises were heard in the distance.

The unknown attracts us irresistibly, and the vague awe which it inspires has something to do with this attraction. It was unanimously decided that the grotto should be explored in every direction. Miss Ross did not share the general opinion; she stopped suddenly and declared flatly that she would not go another step forward.

"Very well," said Badger to her, "you can go back to the entrance of the grotto and await our return. We shall return in two hours at the most; you will be better off up there than with us."

Miss Ross did not wait to be told this twice; she turned back and had soon regained the mouth of the cave.

The exploration continued; the passages succeeded each other without interruption. They then directed their steps in the direction whence the sounds seemed to come, which they continued to hear. They thus came to a large hall, from the roof of which hung magnificent stalactites, assuming the most varying and strange forms. Long colonnades, massive pillars, fonts, statues, could be perceived in an endless depth. The light of the torches, reflected on the facet of every crystal, caused thousands of sparkling jets to flash from it. You might have fancied yourself transported, as in some marvelous fairy-scene, into subterranean palaces inhabited by the genii of the planet.

"How beautiful it is!" was the simultaneous exclamation of the two young girls, who were holding each other by the hand.

As to Grimm, he admired nothing of that which won the admiration of the others. To tell the truth, the beauties of nature had but little fascination for him; the only thing which seriously interested him was to investigate what humanity had done, believed and thought in the most remote epochs of its existence on this earth. His eye scrutinized all nooks and corners; his hand, armed now with a pike, now with a pickaxe, examined all the fissures in the walls, all the swellings of the ground.

"What!" cried he, "not an inscription—not a tomb—no trace whatever of the passage and the voice of man! Was this grotto then unknown to the ancient inhabitants of these regions as well as to the present ones?"

After having searched the immense hall in all directions, they entered a new series of galleries. They passed through several more halls, smaller than the first, each offering some new natural curiosity, but no indication of human industry.

As they advanced, the air grew damper, the noises more distinct, and it became easy to discover that the cause which produced them was the fall of a cascade. In fact, on issuing from a passage which was so low that it was almost necessary to crawl in order to reach its end, the explorers found themselves before a kind of abyss, at the farther end of which an impetuous torrent rushed furiously down. They advanced cautiously, clinging to the arms of the guides, along a wet and slippery bank which led close to the waterfall. The current of air was so strong as to almost extinguish the torches.

Monaghan took a Bengal light from his pocket and set fire to it. In the brilliant light of this piece of firework it was possible to take a survey of the whole of the cavern. During the few minutes that the illumination lasted, every one was in raptures. When everything was once more enveloped in comparative darkness under the dim light which the torches threw out, a sepulchral voice was heard to murmur in a disconsolate tone:

"Nothing! still nothing!"

Nothing further remained to do but to retrace their steps and regain the entrance of the grotto. If the exploration had not been fortunate from an archæological standpoint, from a picturesque point of view it had been wanting neither in interest nor in unforeseen views. In order to perpetuate its remembrance, and to secure for the antiquaries of the fortieth or the fiftieth century the pleasure of deciphering at least one inscription, they cut on one of the interior walls, with the point of a knife, the names of the visitors who, on such a day of the month, in the year of grace 18—, had been the first to explore the grotto to the falls, and had given it the name of Victoria.

Three hours after having penetrated into the cave, our tourists were assembled again at its entrance. Miss Ross was no longer there. They called for her several times, but in vain.

They thought that she had found herself inconvenienced by the dampness, and that they should certainly meet her, in ascending the valley, near to the wall with the bas-reliefs. Miss Ross was not there, however.

They now began to be very uneasy as to the fate of the good miss. What could have happened to her? Wild beasts? There were none in that region. Thieves, brigands? Perhaps she had lost her way—taken a wrong road. All the surrounding thickets were scoured; every corner of the rocks was searched. The rest of the day was employed in the search, but in vain; night came on, and Miss Ross was still not found.

They rejoined the rest of the escort where they had left it the day before, and camped again in the open air, but they were on their guard. The disappearance of the governess showed that the country was not safe. They might be attacked unawares. No new incident, however, arrived to trouble the rest of the travelers, and the night passed quietly.

At daybreak, the search began anew, with no more success than on the preceding day. Everybody was really distressed. The disappearance of Miss Ross was the first tragic event that had happened to the expedition. Misfortunes never come singly, says the proverb. Flatnose, more afflicted even than the others, concluded from this that they were about to enter upon a series of misfortunes.

It was now useless to prolong the search. It became evident that Miss Ross was no longer in the neighborhood. The only expedient was therefore to return to Mosul and inform the English consul, so that, in concert with the native authorities, he might take all necessary measures to find the unfortunate governess again.

The stay at Mosul could be no longer extended, however. The caravan was ready. Badger decided to start two days later and join Jack Adams. As they had to come back to Mosul in a few weeks, Miss Ross was to await the return of the caravan at the English consulate.

CHAPTER XIII.

THE HYDRAULIC WORKS.

On leaving Mosul the caravan followed an uneven road over hills, soon to descend again into deep valleys. They were quite far from the Tigris, for the ravines ough which it rushed were too narrow and too steep to leave free passage.

They penetrated deeper and deeper into a mountainous country. The peaks became sharper, the summits steeper and they were approaching the limit of perpetual snow. At times, while passing over a high neck, the cold was felt. Fields of snow were crossed in which beasts and men sank to the knees.

On the second evening they encamped on a furrowed and creviced plateau. At a little distance the Tigris roared at the bottom of a precipice. Grimm announced that they were on the site of Eski-Mosul, that is to say old Mosul.

After leaving the plateau of Eski-Mosul, the road descends rapidly. At the horizon an immense plain is seen, through which the Tigris winds, escaped from the long series of defiles.

A few hours after they reached the river again and followed its banks. The temperature had become spring-like again; the grass and the flowers reappeared.

In the distance, in the mists of the evening, a city seemed to rise from the bosom of the waters; it was Jezireh-Ibn-Omer, built on an island, or rather on an isolated rock, in the middle of the Tigris.

The city lies at the foot of an old fortress, which rises proudly on the summit of a mount formed by regular layers of black basalt and white marble. An old bridge in ruins adds to the picturesqueness of the landscape.

The caravan encamped on the banks of the Tigris, opposite to the city already sunk in sleep. Everybody was cheerful; they had arrived at the site of the first works. Next day they would certainly meet Jack Adams again, from whom they had been separated for so long a time.

At the first glimmer of dawn next day the caravan set off again in order to reach the works before noon. The mountains drew nearer again rapidly from the north, the plain was transformed into more undulating ground. Finally, at about eleven o'clock, at the bottom of a charming valley, delightfully shaded by fruit-trees and coniferous trees, they perceived a structure of European appearance—it was the hydraulic works.

The approach of the caravan must have been announced by the workmen at the works, for Jack Adams came running at full speed to meet them; the arrival of Lord Badger transported him with joy.

They all dismounted, and, handing the reins to the men of the escort, pressed around the engineer.

Yes, they felt a very great joy in seeing him again, brave and courageous Jack Adams. He had had to battle against men and against the elements; but he had emerged victorious from the conflict. He possessed the tenacity which makes men of action. Badger had bid him to succeed, and he had succeeded.

The first hydraulic works were completed. Next day they could make the turbines turn and transform the power of the water into electricity.

As they walked along, Jack Adams told of his battles, his labors, his hopes. They had also many events to tell him of. He had been struck at once by the absence of Miss Ross; her disappearance seemed to him inexplicable. He knew already through the letters of his friends all that concerned Fatma, but he was ignorant of the discovery of Grimm.

They approached the European house which served as a dwelling for the hands at the works. Built at the foot of a gently sloping mamelon, it was sheltered by a kind of copse. A fine lawn of an emerald green extended to the banks of the Tigris, whose torrent-like waters rolled along at a little distance.

To the branches of some trees whitish balls were fixed, which were found to be cocoons.

"So you raise silk-worms, too?" Miss Nelly asked the engineer.

"They raise themselves," replied the latter. "These are wild silk-worms, which live on a kind of evergreen. The silk which they produce is not by far as fine and as soft as that of their domesticated congeners. Nevertheless, the women of the country use it for weaving very strong stuffs. It is an indication which might perhaps be turned to account. By planting a large number of evergreens the number of silkworms which live on these trees would likewise be multiplied, and a textile material would be produced which would cost but the labor of manufacturing it."

They entered the house. The construction was extremely simple, the furniture of wood. The utensils necessary for a household of six men, books, maps, tools and instruments, that is all that met the eyes of the newcomers. But each object was in its place; there was nothing that did not present a picture of order and neatness.

Every one had made efforts to receive Lord Badger and his party in a worthy manner. The pleasantest room in the house, as might have been expected, had been reserved for the ladies. In the absence of sumptuous ornaments, this chamber, which Miss Nelly was to share with Fatma, was profusely decorated with garlands of leaves and flowers. A delicate attention by which his lordship's daughter was visibly touched.

Jack Adams had given up his room to Badger; the others and he himself were to sleep on camp-beds in the only room which remained available, or in the store-rooms, in the annexes of the hydraulic works.

The luncheon was short; they were anxious to inspect the placing of the turbines and of the electric machines. Immediately after they had taken their coffee, they rose from the table and declared to the engineer that they were ready to follow him. Grimm himself showed almost as much eagerness as if the most improbable of ruins had been in question.

They took a small shaded path through the woods. Five hundred steps farther on, they arrived at the banks of a kind of mill-race formed by the river, which, a hundred yards farther to the right, descended in a cascade along a narrow gorge—an excavation, rather—cutting the mountain throughout its whole breadth.

At the entrance of the defile, every one stopped to admire the waterfall. The Tigris fell in cascades, white with foam, and filling the air with a deafening roar.

On raising the eyes, a building was perceived constructed above the abyss, and suspended over the raging waters. It was the works.

It must be acknowledged that Jack Adams had known how to choose a favorable spot. The damming of the Tigris had been easily accomplished, and they were certain of having a considerable power at their disposal.

Nothing could be more picturesque than these works, perched above the torrent, disappearing almost amid the masses which overhung it. Jack Adams did the honors of his establishment. The arrangement of the work and of the machines was admired. On the following day, moreover, they were to see the whole in motion, and would be able to judge of the perfection of the work.

"Until to-morrow, then," said Badger. "We shall return to admire your establishment. Works are beautiful only in motion. When at rest, they seem like a dead body, and inspire only sadness."

Jack Adams proposed that they should continue the promenade a little farther and go up the defile for a thousand yards or so. They could not go higher, for the path ended completely. The proposition was, however, accepted with enthusiasm.

The road which they followed had a slight but continued ascent. They walked along the torrent, which roared loudly and rolled its waters through a chaos of fallen rocks, sinking deeper and deeper into the bowels of the earth.

All along the path the young girls picked a large number of small flowers, quite new to them, and the names of which Monaghan told them directly. Nothing could be more delicate than their serrated leaves—nothing more fragrant than their perfume.

By an acoustical phenomenon somewhat difficult to explain, the ear, in spite of the uproar of the cascades, could distinctly hear the slightest noises, even to the song of the birds, even to the humming of the insects, as if, in the grand action of nature, the most humble lives were to preserve their individuality.

The landscape was sublime. On all sides there were steep walls, entirely covered with long black firs, clinging to the rough rock and thrusting their roots into the smallest fissures. The distance made them appear smaller and smaller, and those which covered the summit seemed no longer any more than a few inches in height.

As to the walls, they rose to prodigious heights, reaching at least from a thousand to twelve hundred feet. Over the abyss, the awed eye beheld still higher peaks, which were lost in the clouds. This spectacle is so grand, that no one who has not seen it can have any adequate conception of it, even with the most faithful description. Only a painter—and what a painter must he be!—would be able to reproduce these tints of so tender a green, these plays of light, these fantastic shadows which fill the bottom of the gorge. The sun, still brilliant, but very much inclined towards the horizon, lit up the summits with its intense light, and projected broad shadows at the base of the peaks. At the farther end of the defile, an enormous mountain, entirely white, appeared in the majesty of its slender forms.

If the gaze, instead of being directed upwards, was lowered towards the ground, the spectacle was no less sublime. From the pathway to the Tigris there was an immense accumulation of rocks, above which the firs spread their sombre foliage.

They had arrived at the end of the path. There, the rocks drawing closer together and overhanging the abyss, they had to retrace their steps. It was, besides, time to return to the house. Night comes on quickly in the gorges of the mountain; and, with night, the chilly air of the summits invades the depths. Our travelers were able to avoid night and cold; they arrived at the dwelling, actually famished. A good dinner awaited them, and they did it credit.

The next day was to be an important one for the members of the association. The inauguration of the works was the first tangible result, the first step towards the completion of the whole work.

At eight o'clock they took again the road already followed the day before. The morning was splendid; the sun shone in a cloudless sky. The mild temperature promised a fine spring day. In these high mountain gorges the climate approached that of southern Europe.

The workmen were already at their posts. When Badger and his companions were collected in the machine-room, Jack Adams gave a signal. The sluices were immediately opened;

the water, now falling with its full weight on the turbines, set the whole mechanism in motion. The wheels turned with an astonishing rapidity, the leather belts whistled in passing from one pulley to another; the rings of the dynamo-electric machines, turning with a fearful rapidity between the arms of the electro-magnets, gave their peculiar humming sound.

But it was not these details, surprising for the common run of people, which at this moment held the attention of those present. Collected in a corner of the room, they all followed anxiously with their eyes a small instrument hung against the wall. For this instrument was a dynamometer, intended to give the measure of the electric force produced by the machines.

Now, according to the calculation, it was necessary that this electric force should reach a fixed minimum in order that the current might be transmitted from the works at Jezireh to the central works at Babylon. It can therefore be imagined what must have been the anxiety of all the spectators. If the minimum was not reached, if Jack Adams had erred in his calculations, this important part of the enterprise would have to be abandoned. They would have to give up the idea of transporting the power of the waterfalls in the mountains to Babylon.

They did not have long to wait. At the end of a few minutes, during which the turbine took on a uniform movement and the dynamo-electric machine became surcharged by magnetization, the dynamometer, after a few oscillations, stopped at a fixed point.

"Forty-eight," cried Jack Adams, in a voice which showed his inner emotion.

"Won!" replied Badger. It was sufficient to reach forty.

And, his face showing no outward sign of the least emotion, but with a fervor which showed his joy, he shook Jack Adams vigorously by the hand.

They were delighted with the brilliant success gained by the engineer. Indeed, during the whole duration of the meal, at which Badger, his companions and the employés of the works were united around the same table, the experiments of the morning formed the sole topic of the general conversation.

Green, the famous, the model cook, had surpassed himself for the occasion. He had made a trip to Jezireh the day before, and had bought exquisite poultry and the most savory fruits of the country.

For money, everything that is desired can be had in any part of the world; and we know that money was least wanting in his lordship's party.

At the end of the meal toasts succeeded each other without interruption. They were brought to Badger, to Jack Adams, to Monaghan. Even Flatnose and Grimmitschoffer were not forgotten; the first, on account of the admirable account which he had written on the spot, at the foot of the electric machine, and which was destined to bring joy or consternation to the admirers of Lord Badger's attempt or to those jealous of him; the second, because of his extraordinary adventures, which would one day cover his name with glory.

The series of toasts was ended, when Badger rose and said:

"To the health of Cornillé! We must not forget the absent one. Like Jack Adams, Cornillé will succeed and will also have his hour of victory."

Miss Nelly raised her glass like all the rest, which did not prevent Fatma from noticing that her young friend had blushed slightly when her father uttered the name of the Frenchman.

"My dear Mr. Adams," said Badger, addressing the engineer, "will you please to tell us now where you have located your other works? Is the work advanced, and do you expect soon to inaugurate them?"

"My lord," replied the engineer, "I have ascended the Tigris to its sources, and have found suitable sites for three new works. The first is situated at the confluent Botan-Soo, near a village called Schebleh; the second is at Bodia, on the Batman-Soo. As to the third, it stands higher up, at Egil, on the Tigris itself. The constructions are far advanced, for they were begun shortly after that of these works. The results obtained here this morning prove to me that the three other works will give still better results, for the turbines employed are more powerful. I wanted first to try the least powerful machine, certain, after that, of success with better apparatus."

"It is well," said Badger, "and I congratulate you on your courage and your intrepidity in overcoming all obstacles. Well, gentlemen," added his lordship, rising from the table, "I see that there are still bright times in store for science!"

A few days of rest were necessary before facing new hardships, in a hilly and still little known country. It was decided, therefore, to remain for a further part of the week at the hydraulic works.

The happiest of all during this halt was Grimmitschoffer. One evening the celebrated archæologist was at last able to read his manuscript. While Flatnose was sleeping in a corner of the common room, Badger thinking of his projects, Miss Nelly and Fatma chatting softly of that which young girls talk about, Grimmitschoffer slowly and reverently read his manuscript. His reading lasted over an hour. When it was ended at last, Badger congratulated him and assured him that this work would be the delight of all the scientific societies of Europe and America.

"My dear sir," added his lordship, "you will be honored by the academies and named a corresponding member on your return to Europe."

Grimm was consequently under the influence of the deepest joy. His fairest dreams were to be realized, and he beheld himself finally arrived at the pinnacle of glory.

Badger and the two young girls loved to watch Jack Adams' work.

They often passed whole hours sitting on the banks of the Tigris, of which they heard the distant roaring among the rocks. Nothing charms the imagination like this music of the waters. One can dream on the banks of torrents as well as on the shores of the sea.

Jack Adams was often questioned by his lordship's curious daughter. She absolutely desired to know what kind of a turbine had been placed in the works.

"But, Miss Badger," replied the engineer, "that cannot interest you."

"On the contrary," said she, "you cannot believe how much I admire these *chefs-d'œuvre* of mechanism. You cannot imagine, Mr. Engineer, that a young girl should be fond of science? In the opinion of men, a miss thinks only of her toilette and of frivolous things. That is a mistake, you see. Young girls are also able to take a lively interest in that which is grand and beautiful. My father has undertaken a gigantic work. He is surrounded by courageous men. I admire you and delight in your conflicts with matter."

"How handsome she is," said Jack Adams to himself, bewitched by the inspired air of the young girl.

Her eyes had grown brighter since her sojourn in the Orient. Her pale cheeks were tinged with a deeper carmine. The life in the open air had developed her supple body; far from injuring her, the wanderings in the desert and in the mountains had added a new charm to her attractiveness, already so great before.

CHAPTER XIV.

ACROSS THE HIGH MOUNTAINS.

THE caravan is again at Mosul, and is preparing to leave for the mountains of Kurdistan. Sadness is depicted on every countenance.

What can have happened? The fact is that at the moment when we find our travelers again, Badger has brought them bad news. He has returned from the English consulate, and it has been impossible to find any trace of Miss Ross. Yet the most active search was instituted. The surroundings of the grotto were searched; the few inhabitants of the neighboring villages were questioned. Useless labor: it had been impossible to find her, living or dead; nobody has heard anything of her.

They had to resign themselves, therefore, and give up the poor governess as lost. She was the first innocent victim of the enterprise.

They lamented her sincerely. Good and obliging, in spite of her peevish manner, she left a void difficult to fill.

Miss Nelly lost in her a devoted friend, who had replaced her mother as to cares and attentions. Badger was moved more deeply than he wished to have appear. But the most afflicted was Flatnose. We have not forgotten that Miss Ross shared the bottom of the large provision wagon with the journalist. There, a little romance had begun, which, if not as dramatic as that of Romeo and Juliet, would nevertheless have been concluded in London by a happy marriage.

Some good news had in a certain measure counterbalanced the bad. Badger had brought with him from the consulate a long letter from Babylon. There was excellent news; everything was going on as one could wish. Cornillé announced that the buildings of the works on the Kasr and on Babel were rising up visibly. Captain Laycock had been seen again, with a load of machines. He had immediately left again for the Tigris, which he was going to ascend as far as possible, to bring the last turbines intended for the hydraulic works erected by Jack Adams.

Cornillé had added a few pleasant words for Miss Nelly and her little friend Fatma. This good news, and Cornillé's remembrance, caused Miss Nelly to forget somewhat the disappearance of her governess.

Badger and his companions were now going to travel through wild countries, even more mountainous than those of the upper Tigris. Few Europeans had been able to penetrate among the unsubjected hordes of the Kurds. This people, similar to the Montenegrins, have contrived to live in an almost complete independence in the midst of the most terrible emigrations and of the invasions of the Asiatic or European conquerors. Isolated within their mountain walls and on high plateaux, the waves of the inundations have dashed powerlessly against the granite rocks which formed their dwellings.

It was necessary to visit these countries, for it was there that they were to find the most powerful water-falls. The snowy summits of the mountains send innumerable impetuous torrents down into the plain. There could as yet be no question of constructing hydraulic works amidst this hostile population. But, in the near future, Badger hoped to remove the difficulties and to place his turbines there in all security.

A twofold object was thus pursued by visiting the mountains of

Kurdistan. They were going to explore an unknown country, visit the torrents and water-falls, and prepare the placing of the future works. As to the second aim, it was to open negotiations with the chiefs of the tribes and to obtain their authorization to place turbines in their country.

Badger was almost certain of gaining this latter object with facility. He counted for that on the instinct of these primitive races, which impels them to accept with enthusiasm everything that is capable of ameliorating their material condition. Besides, would they not behold these wonders of science with a superstitious terror? When, with electricity, torrents of water drawn at the springs would be sent through their kanots;* when, with this fluid, they would be lighted and warmed, would they not bow before the power of Allah?

But we are leaving the caravan to penetrate among the Zebari Kurds and quietly ascend the Greater Zab. At Amadiah, Badger had a long interview with the patriarch of the Chaldeans, in the famous monastery of Raban-Ormuz. The patriarch promised his protection, and that he would use all his influence in the country for furthering his lordship's projects. From there they went to Julamerk, a populous centre, where Badger had a very important conference with the principal chiefs of the country. Finally, descending the same river again, the caravan proceeded to Rowandiz, where we now find them.

Rowandiz occupies an immense surface on a deeply cleft soil. Its numerous flat-roofed houses, assuming a cubic form, descend to the bottom of the ravines in a curious confusion, to rise higher again on the opposite slope. One might fancy that one were beholding the remains of a gigantic avalanche of blocks of stone, tumbled down from the summits of the neighboring mountains. The heat makes itself strongly felt here in summer. The inhabitants then retire to the roofs, which are sheltered against the rays of the sun by thick curtains of foliage.

When the caravan entered into the city, it was market day. The bazaars were crowded by a busy throng. Rowandiz is a thoroughfare for the caravans which go from Mesopotamia to Persia; therefore this place is of great importance from a commercial point of view. Much tobacco of a good quality is also raised here, which is sold powdered,

---

* The kanots are underground conduits which serve to transport to a distance the water drawn from the springs of the mountain.

and from the oaks in the vicinity gall-nuts are gathered, which are exported to Europe.

On leaving Rowandiz, they were going to enter a series of wild ravines, of difficult and even perilous access. The guide affirmed that they would yet meet with immense masses of snow. No matter, they must advance and descend into the valley of the Lesser Zab, from which they were separated only by a ridge that could be crossed in two days.

During the whole morning the path offered no serious difficulty. They wound around the base of broad conical layers, produced by the centenary accumulation of the detritus descended from the surrounding summits. These cones were covered with a rich vegetation of oaks, of birches, and, especially, of coniferous trees. The pines and firs attained a height and a thickness that were at times extraordinary.

Water was abundant. They frequently met with brooks running down the slopes, murmuring among the trees of the forest, which crossed the path and were then lost in the unknown depths of the ravines.

At about eleven o'clock, as they were proceeding comfortably on level ground, well shaded with trees, they came across a cool spring which gushed out from the base of a rock. It was decided to make a halt at that spot and to take luncheon.

While Green, assisted by the scullions, was starting a good fire, intended for roasting a rib of mutton, Badger and the other travelers were resting, seated on a row of flat stones.

The conversation turned on the electric wires, destined to connect the various works with the central works of Babylon. In fact, similar to an immense spider-web, which was to extend over Mesopotamia, a large number of wires were to start from the mountains of the north and of the east to concentrate all the electricity of the hydraulic works on the summit of the kasr.

"Our wires," said Jack Adams at this point, "will be underground. If we should stretch them on posts, they would be too much exposed to the inclemencies of the weather, to the storms, and, above all, to the vandalism of some excited fanatics! Buried beneath the ground, they will be completely protected from these causes of destruction."

"It will be a long job," observed Monaghan.

"With time and money," replied Badger, "everything is accomplished."

"That is true, my lord," replied the geologist.

"The work must be already begun," resumed the engineer. "In six months or more Babylon will be connected with the works at Jezireh. The *Davy* and the *Faraday* have returned to England to bring their cargo of wires and machines. They must be back by this time, and the workmen are at work at Babylon."

"Admirable! admirable!" cried Grimmitschoffer, enraptured by the last words of Jack Adams. "Electricity is certainly the most beautiful of all the sciences!"

"After archæology, however," said Flatnose, patting the *savant* on the shoulder.

The latter turned around furiously, but his wrath was quickly appeased; he had too great a disdain for so ignorant a journalist as Flatnose. The others burst out laughing, and Grimm thought that this laughter was intended for Flatnose, and not for him.

When the meal was finished, the guide informed the travelers that they were in the neighborhood of rich lead and copper mines. That was Monaghan's affair. It was immediately decided that all who were willing should go in search of these mines. When the little party was formed, it ascended the path for about two hundred yards, to a half dried-up torrent, the pebbly bed of which they had to follow for several minutes.

Monaghan, Jack Adams, Miss Nelly, and Fatma, the only persons of which the little troupe of geologists was composed, not including the guide, each held a little hammer in the hand for breaking the rocks and ascertaining their nature.

At last they stopped. The guide made them climb the steep slopes of the right bank of the torrent. Clinging to the trees and to the projecting points of rock, the first aiding those who followed, they were soon collected at the foot of a high grayish wall.

Detaching a fragment by a smart blow of his hammer, Monaghan showed his companions a heavy mass, with a bright glitter as of lead lately cut. They could not make a mistake in view of these distinctive characteristics. They had before them an enormous vein of galena, very easy to extract.

They descended again, and the guide caused the travelers once more to enter the bed of the torrent. Jumping from stone to stone, two hundred yards farther on they reached a clayey bank, which they had much trouble in climbing. The slippery ground gave no support.

The guide, more agile, was the first to reach the top of the slope, and held out his staff to Monaghan. The latter, in turn, assisted the young girls to get up. As to Jack Adams, who was the last, he wanted to climb the bank alone. But he came to grief; for, his foot slipping from under him, he slipped and drenched his legs in the water of the brook. They laughed heartily at his little mishap. Accepting now the aid of the staff which Monaghan held out to him, the engineer had quickly rejoined his companions.

Entering a copse, the guide conducted the party towards an escarpment of a reddish color. This was an iron mine, composed of red hematite. Monaghan broke off a specimen which he put in his bag with that of the galena. The spot in which they were formed a sort of clearing. Jack Adams proposed that they should rest for ten minutes before returning to join Badger. There happened to be here some large stones on which they could sit down. The ten minutes past, Fatma was the first to rise, and, laughing merrily, the little madcap cried:

"I'm going to break my seat with my hammer!"

Then, giving a blow with the instrument on the stone which had served her as a seat, she caused a large piece to fly off. It fell at Monaghan's feet. He quickly picked up this fragment. After having examined it for an instant, he cried:

"Why, this is copper ore! It's malachite!"

In truth, Fatma had just broken that precious and rare stone which is used for manufacturing vases, clock-stands, ornaments of every kind.

The geologist was struck by the idea of breaking his seat also. A general amazement: this was also a block of malachite. Then there was a frenzy for destruction. All, armed with their hammers, began to break, not only their seats of a minute before, but also all the surrounding stones. They had to submit to the evidence: it was always the same copper ore.

Monaghan, desiring to conceal the value of the discovery before the guide, said that this ore was poor and without value. The trouble was unnecessary, however, for the Kurds had no inclination to work these metalliferous deposits. These treasures were awaiting the arrival of the Europeans to be converted into iron, lead, copper, or ornamental stones.

"To horse, gentlemen!" cried Badger, as soon as our geologist had rejoined the rest of the caravan. "The way is long, and we must not lose time if we wish to arrive at a camping-ground to-night."

The ravine which they left on their left hand grew deeper at every step, while the sides of the rocks rose on the right to a dizzy height. Their progress was impeded by the presence of pebbles which rolled under the feet of men and horses.

For two hours they thus passed around the base of a lesser chain; then they entered a deep hollow which had to be ascended in order to reach the highest point of the axis of the mountain. Several torrents rushed from the top of the mountains, through this furrow, down into the lower valleys. Swollen by the recent rains, the waters were overflowing and tumultuous. The passage of these torrents could not be effected without some difficulty, and even danger. At one of them it was necessary to dismount. The men of the escort pulled up big stones on the banks of the torrent and arranged them dexterously in the midst of the foaming waters.

The men passed over easily. As to the horses and mules, half in the water, half on the stones, they also succeeded in crossing the difficult passage.

At five o'clock, the roar of a cascade was heard quite near by. A quarter of an hour later the caravan passed out on a sort of bare promontory. The forest ceased suddenly at this spot. On the opposite side a gigantic jet of water rebounded from rock to rock and was swallowed up in a deep basin three hundred feet below the promontory. The cascade might have been some nine hundred feet in height, which would place the beginning of the falls at about six hundred feet above the heads of the spectators.

The scene was truly wonderful. To the left of the cascade, the mountain rose perpendicularly to a height of from fifteen hundred to eighteen hundred feet. The cliffs, of a reddish tint, were entirely bare, without the least trace of verdure. To the right, the horizon became somewhat enlarged, at a greater height. A sort of gorge was seen, hemmed in by two walls of a greenish tint. These variations in color gave the place a strange appearance. It was conjectured that, at the time when the mountain had taken origin in consequence of a frightful commotion of the earth, this spot had been the centre of some subterranean irruption. And in fact, Monaghan picked up some stones and declared that these cliffs were in a great measure composed of amphibole. Now, amphibole characterizes the rocks of lower origin, issued from the interior of the earth's crust.

When they turned their backs on the cascade, which made a deafening uproar, the view extended into the distance over the mountains and the plains through which wound the Greater Zab. What a panorama! The eye looked down over an immense expanse. The sun, already standing very low in the west, left the plain in comparative shadow, while the distant mountains and the surrounding summits were tinged with the brightest of colors.

The guide regarded the horizon with an anxious eye.

"There is going to be a storm this evening," said he.

This announcement was received with an incredulous air. The sky seemed clear; no cloud could be seen in the distance. Yet the sagacity of the mountaineers is well known : they are but rarely mistaken in prognostics of this kind. The color of the rocks, the temperature of the air, the intensity of the light, a thousand nothings which the stranger does not notice, are for them infallible signs.

"From what do you know that there will be a storm?" asked Jack Adams.

"The base of the mountains, at the level of the plain," replied the guide, "is clouded in vapors."

"Which proves," said Monaghan immediately, "that there is a layer of cold air above the warmer air of the plain. We shall therefore have rain, it is to be feared."

"Let us ascend," resumed the guide. "In twenty minutes we shall have reached the top of the cascade. There we shall be sheltered from the wind in a charming valley, and you can raise your tents in all security."

The caravan therefore continued its ascent, which was difficult during these twenty minutes. The path turned back several times on itself, overhanging the sides of the cascade at a perilous height. The horses slipped and did not know where to set their feet. A fall would have been fatal. They were obliged to ascend on foot, leading the animals by the bridle.

But what a delight when they arrived on top! They trod on a tender and bright green grass, dotted with innumerable small flowers of the most varied colors. It was paradise after the infernal regions. A brook wound luxuriously through this turf, not suspecting what fate awaited it a few yards lower down. It was this brook, in fact, which gave rise to the cascade.

Right and left of the grass-land the mountains rose perpendicularly. They followed the brook; ten minutes later they reached the farther end of the little plain. There, sheltered from the wind, they raised the tents and made preparations for passing the night.

The guide's prognostication was already being realized. The air grew gradually darker, and the rumbling of thunder was soon heard in the distance. In spite of the threatening sky, Badger, the young girls, Monaghan and Jack Adams went back to the edge of the grass-land, to the place where the brook fell in a cascade. They wished to see once more the sublime spectacle of the plain of the Greater Zab. But everything was now dimmed by the mist. The storm was passing below them, following the course of the valley.

Retracing their steps, therefore, they slowly returned to the camping-place. What a delight in taking a walk in such a place! Suddenly the farther end of the pass was lit up by a bright red light, and fantastic shadows ran along the sides of the rocks. It was *chef* Green who was lighting his kitchen-range, that is to say, who was cooking the supper on a wood fire.

The storm drew off. Only a few drops of rain fell on the heights. The night passed quietly; they slept to the rumbling noise of the cascade.

The next morning at daybreak the ascension of the mountain was continued. The highest point of the ridge had to be gained by about noon. The descent would then be made rapidly to the valley of the Lesser Zab.

The path began at the foot of the escarpment to the right and rose in long zig-zags across the fallen rocks of a former torrent. The ascent was not excessive; yet progress was made difficult by the want of firmness in the ground on which they trod. Finally, at the end of an hour, the caravan reached a kind of platform a few yards in width. Little flowers grew out through the clefts in the rock. A hundred steps farther on they turned suddenly to the right, to enter a deeply sunk pass. The cold was intense, for they were approaching the snow. Already they saw some large white patches at the back of the defile, in the places sheltered from the sun.

It is impossible to imagine a wilder and more solitary spot. The ravine was bound on the right and on the left by almost perpendicular rocks of an olive-colored black. Not a blade of grass, not even moss on these stones as hard as granite. Before them they saw the defile which rose rapidly, obstructed at its upper part by gigantic heaps of rocks.

"That looks like the entrance to the infernal regions," said Miss Nelly.

"You are nearer right than you think," replied Monaghan. "I very much suspect fire of being the author of these sublime horrors. We must be near to the centre of a volcanic eruption."

"Look," cried the young girl, stopping before a rock. "What can this queer plant be that is crawling over the surface of this stone?"

"You know it well, notwithstanding, Miss Badger," replied the geologist. "It is this which forms the forest through which we had to pass in order to get here."

"What!" exclaimed Miss Nelly. "Is that a fir? It has but little resemblance to those vigorous trees, so straight and proud, which I perceive some two or three hundred yards below us."

"These are nevertheless common firs," said Monaghan. "The mountain is full of surprises for the traveler, and this is not among the least of them. This defile is very cold and avalanches and freezing storms are passing through it continually. The firs have, therefore, had to modify their conditions of vitality in order to resist the inclemency of the air. Here they crawl along the stones like ivy, pressing their attenuated branches against the surface which protects them. We are again passing through a forest of firs, as we did farther below. But what a change in the constitution of the trees! They are hardly visible, dwindling down to a few thin stems, similar to ivy."

"It is strange, indeed," said Miss Nelly.

They had arrived at the foot of the barrier which ended the ravine. At that point there was no longer a regular path. They had to climb over the boulders, heaped up in the most fearful confusion. Everybody dismounted again; the horses had to be led by the bridle. The most difficult part of the passage had been reached. Finally, after much exertion and many falls, fortunately none of them serious, the caravan arrived safely on a long surface, covered with a fine grass, like down. The journey now became an agreeable promenade. They arrived at the edge of a lake with blue and limpid waters. But, in striking contrast, the basin of this lake and the surrounding rocks were of an opaque black.

Monaghan stopped, picked up some specimens of the rock, examined them minutely, and said:

"Gentlemen, we have arrived on the crater of a former volcano. This lake has filled the orifice through which the lava passed which we have climbed since passing the cascade. I can now understand the cause of the dismal color of these mountains and their complete barrenness. The rocks on which we tread are diallage and serpentine. Their hardness has resisted the attacks of water and air; no plant can find subsistence in so sterile a soil."

The caravan passed around the lake. They stopped for an instant to rest and to take some nourishment. Only a short stay was made, for it was extremely cold.

An ascent of about a thousand feet remained to be climbed. This was an easy task, for the path was broad and the slope comparatively gentle. In three-quarters of an hour they had reached the highest point of the mountainous ridge which separates the valley of the Greater Zab from that of the Lesser Zab. The view from these heights was admirable. The eye looked down on an endless horizon of snowy summits, lofty peaks, domes sparkling in the sun and deeply lying valleys.

Notwithstanding all the attractions of this marvelous panorama, it soon became necessary to descend. A cold wind blew on this side, more exposed to the west than the other. The snow, rarely met with during the ascent, covered the side of the mountain for a slope of several hundred yards in length. The guides enjoined them to advance with caution. The path was narrow and slippery; a false step might bring about a catastrophe. For the first hundred yards all went well. Suddenly Flatnose was seen to lose his balance, fall from his horse onto the edge of the path and roll towards the abyss on the sides of the mountain.

There was a cry of alarm. Every one stopped, regarding with terror the journalist's fall. But, strange to say, Flatnose's body disappeared from the view of the astonished spectators. After he had rolled for several seconds, a ball of snow was seen to form, which grew larger visibly, going down the declivity with a frightful velocity, bounding over the rocks, continually increasing in size. The ball of snow was transformed into a gigantic avalanche. Finally, arriving at the bottom of the slope, it struck violently against a rock which barred its way, and scattered in all directions.

What a surprise! from the midst of the ball a black spot was seen to shoot out and sink into a bed of snow thirty yards farther on.

"It's Flatnose!" cried Badger. "He is not dead. I see his legs struggling in the air. There! see him sit up and feel himself! Poor fellow!"

The black spot was, indeed, seen to move. The caravan descended the path as quickly as possible. A quarter of an hour later they were close by Flatnose, still bewildered by his miraculous fall, but without the least wound. They caused him to drink a cordial. It was long before the poor journalist, strongly agitated, regained his speech. He did not understand his situation at all. They had to explain to him how, his body having formed the nucleus of a ball of snow, he had come to be drawn along in the centre of the avalanche; how he had been preserved by just this covering of snow; how at last the final collision had broken his prison, where he ran the risk of being suffocated.

In the evening the caravan, hardly yet recovered from the excitement, encamped in the valley of the Lower Zab.

CHAPTER XV.

A SAD EVENT.

The camp had hardly been fixed, when the sky suddenly became overcast, and a fearful storm broke loose in the mountain. The tents, shaken by a raging wind, threatened every instant to fly away. They had to be folded up again in all haste, and a better shelter sought in some miserable huts which stood not far from there. This hamlet is called Khoi-Sanjak.

The storm lasted for two long hours. At last the sky began to clear up. They availed themselves of the opportunity for leaving the smoky and evil-smelling place in which they were cooped up. The spectacle which our travelers then had before their eyes cannot be depicted. No description could give any idea of it. No brush even would be capable of reproducing such a combination of wonderful colors.

While the gorge below was still wrapped in darkness, farther above

(143)

the sun shone in all his brightness. The snow, the nevés, and the glaciers of the high summits were tinged with colors of the most intense purple. At the base the most dazzling white reflected sheaves of golden light. Surprising contrast of nature! After the furious battle of the elements, the day appeared again as clear and fine as before.

This fair weather lasted but a quarter of an hour; the sky became clouded again. A gray hue spread over the valley; a fine and cold rain continued to fall for the rest of the evening.

The inhabitants of the hut in which our travelers had sought refuge said that the valley was not very safe just then. A band of marauders had passed a few days before and must be keeping the field in the neighborhood.

Next day the sun shone in all his brightness. The caravan resumed the journey, redoubling its caution. It was forbidden to separate; the guns and revolvers were carefully examined.

The morning passed quietly; the country seemed deserted. After the noon-day meal, they entered a series of narrow defiles. Suddenly, the scouts of the advance guard pointed out a group of ten Kurds of suspicious appearance. Badger immediately gave the order to halt. The whole of the caravan concealed itself behind a large rock which obstructed the gorge. Badger resolved to send some scouts forward. It was necessary to get information as to the intentions of these men. The caravan was numerous enough and sufficiently well armed to resist an attack of ten marauders; but his lordship desired before all to avoid shedding blood. A fight, even with brigands, might compromise the success of his future enterprises. He had entered these mountains as an advocate of peace and of civilization, and did not wish to fire a useless shot. Four resolute men were chosen to move forward. Jack Adams placed himself at their head. Flatnose, excited by his adventure of the preceding day, declared that he also would join the band of scouts. They all tried to dissuade him from doing so.

"I have nothing to fear," said he in a jesting tone. "There are no more robbers in these mountains than there are Krumen in Tunis. You will see that these people are peaceful shepherds, who come to play pastorals in this poetic spot."

Our six scouts advanced slowly, hiding behind the rocks and bushes. Ten minutes later, they were hardly a hundred yards away from the Kurds. The latter, seated in a circle around a fire, were just taking their meal. They had tied their horses to the trunks of some trees near by. Their guns, lying on the ground beside them, were within reach of their hands.

Jack Adams and his companions remained motionless for a moment, trying to divine the intentions of these Kurds. But there could be no mistake about it. These were neither traveling merchants nor shepherds leading their flocks; they were nothing else but highway robbers.

One of these men was suddenly seen to rise and disappear behind a copse. He reappeared an instant later, dragging two prisoners after him, with their hands bound behind their backs. He was evidently bringing them to take their share of the meal. One of these prisoners was a woman, with torn garments and half-naked. The other was a man.

Flatnose took out his glasses and examined the new arrivals. Suddenly he drew his revolver from its case. Then, darting forward, he cried with a harsh voice:

"It's Miss Ross!"

At the cry uttered by Flatnose, the brigands sprang up with a single bound and darted toward their guns. Flatnose, wild with rage, was running forward like one possessed. Jack Adams and the four scouts tried to overtake him, but it was too late. They heard the brave journalist cry: "No, it shall not be said that I will not save Miss Ross from the hands of these brigands!" At the same time, he fired off the six shots of his revolver in the direction of the robbers. The latter immediately replied with their guns. Poor Flatnose, struck in the centre of the forehead by a bullet, fell to the ground without moving again. He had been killed instantly.

At the sound of these reports, Badger and his companions hastened at a gallop towards the place of the fight. On seeing so numerous a party coming up, the brigands became afraid. They untied their horses, were in their saddles in the twinkling of an eye, and fled, abandoning their two prisoners. Jack Adams, rendered furious by Flatnose's death, fired the two shots of his gun after the brigands; the four men who accompanied him immediately followed his example. Two of the brigands were then seen to sway on their horses and fall to the ground, while the animals continued their wild flight. The rest of the fugitives were soon out of gun-shot.

Jack Adams rushed to the aid of Flatnose. Badger, Monaghan, and the rest of the caravan, came up at the same moment. There was a general amazement. Except Jack Adams and the four scouts, the new-comers did not know of the catastrophe. Flatnose was raised up. Monaghan, who was somewhat of a doctor, examined the wound.

All care would be useless; the bullet had entered through the forehead, shattered the brain, and passed out again at the back.

The body was laid on the grass. For some moments there was a complete silence. What! Flatnose, their jolly companion, was now dead! They would never see him again! And yet everything before them remained unchanged in appearance. The sky was blue as before; the torrent murmured merrily among the pebbles.

Miss Nelly was the first to break the silence:

"Poor Flatnose," said she, drying her tears, "he was an honest fellow."

"He was only a journalist," said Grimmitschoffer, on whose heart the episode in the cellar at Khorsabad still weighed.

"Yes, sir," replied Badger, irritated by this, to say the least, untimely reflection; "but he was also a brave soul. His death has shown it."

"You misconstrue my meaning, my lord," replied the *savant*. "I am as pained as you are by the death of your friend. I simply meant to say that, for the success of your enterprise, his loss is less irreparable than if it were Mr. Jack Adams, for example, who had been killed."

"Before a corpse, and above all the corpse of a companion, of one who has shared our joys and our sorrows, interest is a thought which cannot enter into our hearts," replied Badger.

A renewed silence followed upon these curt words. All regarded with sadness the body of their friend. Death had been so instantaneous that no feature of the face was altered. The half-closed eyes had the same expression of jolly good humor; the lips seemed still to smile after a final pun.

This time it was Jack Adams who was the first to speak:

"Gentlemen," said he, "I think it is time that we should look after the prisoners."

"Are there any prisoners?" cried those who stood around him.

"True, gentlemen, I have forgotten to tell you that it was while trying to save Miss Ross that Flatnose met his death."

"Miss Ross," cried Badger, "Miss Ross is here!"

His lordship, conducted by Jack Adams, proceeded towards the spot where Miss Ross and her companion were waiting to be released. They had seen the brigands take flight; they understood that the Europeans had remained masters of the field. Miss Ross had no doubt but that the caravan that was attacked was that of Badger; she saw the end of all her sufferings coming at last. She little suspected that a new and irreparable misfortune was the price of her liberty.

When Badger and the engineer had approached near enough to her to be recognized, the poor woman started forward to meet them. She could only express her happiness at first by tears and disconnected words.

Badger, whose heart was pained at sight of this joy, did not know what means to employ in order to prepare her for the sad news.

"Who is this man who is with you?" asked he.

"He calls himself Cahuzac. He is a photographer, a Frenchman, whom the brigands had made a prisoner with me."

His lordship made a few steps towards the photographer, and held out his hand to him, telling him that he was welcome among them.

The events which we have just related had followed each other so rapidly that the prisoner did not understand his situation as yet. He had some persons before him of whose intentions he was ignorant. All that he knew was that a fight had taken place, that some men had been killed or wounded, and that he was free.

"Please to come with us, *monsieur*," said Badger to him in French.

Miss Ross, however, seemed to have a sort of presentiment of some catastrophe.

"Your companions are all alive and well?" she asked, hesitatingly.

"We have a terrible misfortune to deplore."

The four arrived at the group which surrounded Flatnose's body. With a movement, the instructress pushed aside those who stood in her way, and, without a cry, without a tear, she knelt down beside the inanimate remains of her faithful companion, whose hand she held between her own for a long time. The poor woman's grief was all the more touching, as she believed it to be her duty to repress it. Faithful, even when she beheld her hopes falling away, to principles of austerity, exaggerated perhaps, but respectable, she feared to set her pupil a bad example by giving way to all the feelings which weighed down her heart.

Yet a heroism too long sustained is beyond the power of human nature. The unfortunate woman soon became convulsed with violent sobs. Miss Nelly comprehended that it was time to put an end to this painful scene, and, partly by gentle force, partly by persuasion, she succeeded in bringing away Miss Ross, who could at last weep with no other witnesses but the two young girls.

For the first time the true character of her instructress had been revealed to Miss Nelly. Youth is at times cruel without wishing to be so, and through ignorance. In spite of her kindness of heart and the true affection which she felt for her governess, the young English girl had not refrained at times from laughing at what she called Miss Ross's romance. That one should have one's little romance at twenty was very natural in her eyes; but that a woman who was more than twice as old as herself should also want to have her own, seemed to her a most unlikely thing. She now understood that, on the threshold of old age, the love founded on real sympathies and on mutual esteem can hold as high a place in life as, at twenty years, a more romantic and tender sentiment. The affection which circumstances had caused to arise between Miss Ross and Flatnose, and which was to have ended in the marriage of the old maid and the old bachelor, deserved to be respected, and not to be made the subject of jests.

Miss Nelly resolved to atone for her faults and to assuage the grief of the poor afflicted girl by causing her to feel that she understood her. Fatma, who, for her part, had not a few roguish tricks on her conscience with regard to the instructress, showed her an unaffected sympathy. Her heart was also very full at the thought that she would never see her good friend Flatnose again, and, without analyzing Miss Ross's feelings, she wept with her.

In the meantime, the two wounded bandits were lying on the road. Some soldiers were sent to bring information as to their condition. A few minutes after, they were brought before Badger, their hands tightly bound behind their backs. The one had a broken leg, the other a shattered shoulder. In spite of their sufferings, which must have been intolerable, no complaint escaped from their tightly closed lips, and they looked insolently around on all of those present. Badger gave the order to bind up their wounds and to tie them fast to horses. He intended to deliver them over to Turkish justice.

Before continuing the journey, a painful duty remained to be performed: to commit the body of their unfortunate companion to the earth. Every one came up to bid the journalist a last farewell. Miss Ross also desired to perform this pious duty.

"Are we, then, going to leave him thus?" exclaimed she, amid heart-rending sobs.

Badger understood the poor girl's meaning.

"No, Miss Ross," he said to her, pressing her hand with a warm grasp, "trust to me. We shall lay the remains of our friend in a place where they will be secure from the attacks of men and animals, and, on my return to London, I promise to do all that will be necessary to have them transported over there."

This promise seemed to allay Miss Ross's grief a little. Of her dream of modest happiness there now remained but the hope of praying over a tomb.

Badger and Jack Adams alone remained to perform the last melancholy duties. Monaghan, offering his arm to the governess, who wept no more and seemed as if petrified, descended again with the two young girls, who were weeping bitterly. A large stone was laid on the grave; it would serve to identify the place by later on, when they would be able to transfer Flatnose's remains.

The sun was about to set when the caravan took up its march again. Badger would at no price encamp on the scene of the sinister event. They would make but a few miles, but at least they would flee from this melancholy spot.

For two hours they journeyed along, sadly and silently. Each one was absorbed in his thoughts. The sun had set an hour before when Badger gave the signal to halt. The tents were raised and the camp fixed for the night. Thousands of stars sparkled in the firmament. They could perceive that they were again approaching the sandy plain. The wind from the west brought warm gusts with it.

"That is the air of Babylon, my friends," said Badger, when they were all united at supper. "May the grandeur of our work cause us to forget our sadness. If man desires to conquer, it is necessary that he should learn to rise above the miseries of humanity."

These words raised their spirits. Yes, the future was there, and, however sad the present might be, they should not look backwards, but always ahead. One star shone with a greater brilliancy than the others: it was the star of science, of progress, of civilization. Guided by it they would all advance together, hand in hand. Very few of them, perhaps, would see the goal of their labors. Perhaps, too, the end was too far off, and none would be able to reach it.

In order to give Miss Ross some diversion from her grief, Badger asked her to relate her adventures.

She had wandered a little from the entrance of the grotto, when she suddenly saw three horsemen coming towards her at a gallop. She attempted to flee and to get back to the cave, but the brigands seized her in an instant; her cries were smothered by the aid of a handkerchief, which was placed over her mouth. One of the bandits tied her to the crupper of his horse; then she became unconscious, remaining so for quite a long time, without doubt.

When she regained consciousness, she was confined alone in a room with ruined walls. She endeavored to escape, but doors and windows were firmly barred. At the side of a filthy rug stood a jugful of water, a thick piece of galette, and some slices of dried meat. This was her whole nourishment for three days. On the fourth day the door opened; a man entered, who made signs to her to follow him. She was again tied to the crupper of a horse, and the journey was resumed.

For a whole day they followed ravines and hardly traceable paths among the mountains. Finally, at nightfall, they arrived at a village. The man unbound her and brought her into a house of better appearance than the first. An old woman received her, and made her understand by signs what she would have to do to help in the care of the house. In short, she had become the slave of the Kurds.

She always hoped that a favorable opportunity might present itself for letting Badger know what had become of her.

Her master, who was one of the prisoners—the one with the broken shoulder—had shown himself comparatively mild towards her; she begged Badger to be merciful with him.

Cahuzac's story was much simpler—at least with regard to his captors—for, if he was to be believed, it was only after a long series of extraordinary events that he had ended by foundering among the wild tribes of Kurdistan. Passionately fond of voyages and adventures, but with no resource other than his profession as a photographer, he had traveled over a good part of the globe with his apparatus.

Soon wearied by the monotony of the large European cities, he had not feared to brave the most barbarous countries, relying, no doubt, on the civilizing properties of the object-glass and of collodion. Kaffirs and Patagonians, Laplanders and Kanakas, all the types of the universe had heard the formal "Don't move now, please!" which, he affirmed, he knew how to say in all known and unknown languages.

If he had not amassed a fortune by this profession, he had at least risked his life more than once. Every manifestation of astonishment on the part of his listeners he cut short with an "Oh, I've had many other experiences like this," which seemed to indicate a man not easy to disconcert.

After a rapid recital of his earlier adventures, a recital accompanied by a wholly Gascon mimicry, which did not fail to astonish his English hearers a little, but which caused Fatma's eyes to open wide in amazement, Cahuzac told how he had been made prisoner by the Kurds. Well received at the beginning, he had finished by observing no precautions whatever when passing from one village to another. He was

walking peaceably along the torrent of the Lesser Zab, humming a walse in *Madame Angot*, when he found himself surrounded by a band of marauders. He was bound and loaded, together with his instrument, on a horse, behind the back of a fierce Kurd. This occurrence had not ruffled his good humor. He had finished the walse interrupted by his capture. Then, he had sung into the ears of his astounded companion the air of the *Dispute*, finally that of the *Conspirators*. He was at the second verse of this when the troop halted at the place where he had been saved. Cahuzac, however, felt no uneasiness as to his fate, and gave proofs of the most jovial tranquillity. He intended to exhibit his talents as a photographer to his captors, and expected quickly to regain his libery. What would they have done with a poor wretch like himself?

"The fools have freedom of the city everywhere, as well in the dominions of the king as in the country of the most savage nations," he said, by way of conclusion.

The photographer's narrative offered some diversion from the sadness of the party that evening. In fact, there was nothing in the way of their gaining a new companion, who, moreover, seemed to be full of good humor. Badger therefore proposed to Cahuzac that he should stay with him as far as Bagdad. The latter did not wait to be pressed, but gladly accepted the offer.

Two days later the caravan arrived without accident at Altyn-Kopri, and encamped in the vicinity of the city.

CHAPTER XVI.

THE VALLEY OF THE DYALAH.

BADGER, who had at first intended to deliver the two wounded Kurds over to Turkish justice, had changed his mind.

In short, although plunderers and robbers, they were not murderers. In reality, Flatnose had been the aggressor. It is more than probable that if, instead of firing on them, an attempt had been made to enter into negotiations, they would have been very willing to give up their prisoners in return for a ransom.

Bandits the Kurds are by nature. Would Turkish justice find the crime sufficiently great to merit a severe punishment? If the two prisoners were set at liberty, it would be all up with Badger's influence over the tribes of Kurdistan, while, if he himself took the initiative in pardoning, that act of clemency on his part would produce the best effect.

His lordship, therefore, went to the two wounded men, to whom he caused to be explained that he gave them back their liberty. At the same time, he gave orders to conduct them to Altyn-Kopri, where they would be taken care of.

When the litter passed near to the Europeans, the captor of Miss Ross shook his fist at Badger while uttering some words which they could not understand.

"What did he say?" Badger asked of the guide.

"I do not dare to repeat it to you."

"Speak on, I wish it," ordered Badger.

He said: "Dog of a Christian, I shall be revenged."

"He will be dead to-morrow," was Badger's only answer.

This scene took place on the morning of the day which saw the arrival of the expedition near the walls of Altyn-Kopri. A few hours later Badger and his companions resumed their journey.

The caravan continued to follow the banks of the Lesser Zab and passed before the city. Altyn-Kopri is built on an island, with banks worn away by the waters of the torrent. The houses rise picturesquely above each other on a succession of broad terraces, the first of which begins above the cliffs which fall perpendicularly into the Lesser Zab. An oviform bridge passes majestically over the torrent. Below, the rapid waters roar at a great depth between two rows of calcareous walls.

From this bridge on, the caravan ceased to follow the course of the Lesser Zab. It entered a road perpendicular to the river, advancing towards the south. Progress now became less difficult. The mountains grew less steep, the valleys less uneven, and offered a more comfortable passage for men and animals.

Two days later, they arrived without accident at Kerkook, situated at the sources of the Adhem, one of the tributaries of the Tigris. Jack Adams recognized the possibility of placing works over the torrent. Water was plentiful, and there was a sufficient inclination of the ground.

Kerkook had another attraction for the caravan. Naphtha springs are found there in plenty. Badger and his companions repaired to the most famous of these springs. Monaghan desired greatly to study these repositories on the spot. It would be possible later on to make use of these natural riches, to win which no attempt has as yet been made in that part of Mesopotamia.

"Isn't naphtha the same thing as petroleum?" Miss Nelly asked the geologist, when they had arrived before the spring.

"Pretty much the same, Miss Badger," replied the geologist. "When it is a slimy liquid, with a strong smell, it is called petroleum, and when it is a transparent liquid, with an almost agreeable odor, we call it naphtha. . . ."

Thus speaking, Monaghan took up in a glass a small quantity of the liquid which flowed at the bottom of the spring. He poured the contents on a hollow stone and put a lighted match to it. A large flame immediately sprang up.

"You see, gentlemen," said the geologist, "that this is in truth a naphtha spring."

"This country must be full of naphtha, then," said Cahuzac. "I have already gone over this region in all directions, and I have everywhere met with springs similar to this. Since you pass to Kifri in order to gain the valley of the Dyalah, I shall conduct you to springs much richer than these."

"Willingly," replied Monaghan. "What you tell me there does not surprise me. Numerous petroleum springs are found near here in the Caucasus and in Persia. Springs of this kind abound in the neighborhood of Baku and in the peninsula of Apsheron, in the Shervan, so famous for their perpetual fires."

Three days after the conversation which we have just recounted, we find our travelers at Tuz-Khurmali. Here they were to stop for several days in order to give Jack Adams and Monaghan time to reconnoitre the country. Several torrent-like affluents of the Adhem take their rise in these parts. It was probable that a favorable site would be found for large hydraulic works.

Between Tuz-Khurmali and Kifri, Monaghan made a most important discovery. While ascending the course of a deeply embanked brook, he found a bed of coal. The people of the country had no knowledge of the existence of this mine, so well was it hidden from all eyes.

Yet it was not accident only that had aided the men in this discovery. In studying the rocks of the country, Monaghan had recognized the presence of carboniferous layers. By degrees, following the inclination of the strata composing the soil, he had been led to ascend the course of the torrent, the waters of which, by laying bare the rocks, had enabled him to observe the transformations of the strata in the soil. Finally, to his great joy, Monaghan arrived at a place where large black bands showing level with the soil left no further doubt as to the existence there of coal. The lodes appeared numerous and thick; their slight depth would permit them to be easily worked.

Monaghan returned to camp with his pockets full of specimens. Badger experienced an intense satisfaction at this discovery. Coal was an auxiliary on which they had not counted, but which would nevertheless render important services. Although, it is true, the solar rays could be utilized by transforming them into forces for the service of man, yet this was no reason for despising the natural resources which, as it were, offered themselves.

Badger sent for Adams in order to tell him of the good news. He enjoined the engineer and the geologist to observe the strictest silence on this repository of coal. If the discovery was noised abroad it was to be feared that adventurers, as they are found everywhere in such large numbers, might come to make excavations in this country. The benefit of Monaghan's discovery would thus be lost, and it was but just that they should reserve the monopoly of this, so precious combustible for themselves.

"The consumption of coal must be enormous," said Miss Nelly to Monaghan. "Much is already burned for heating purposes, but still more must be consumed by the gas-works and steam-engines."

"Certainly, Miss Badger," replied the geologist. "Do you know how many steam-engines there are existing on the surface of the earth?"

"I have no idea."

"There are one hundred and fifty thousand locomotives, the total power of which is thirty millions horse-power. As to the number of stationary engines, that is still larger, and their power exceeds forty-six millions horse-power."

"These numbers are appalling," said the young girl.

"Now," resumed the geologist, "if, as is obviously true, thirty men are equal to one-horse power, we arrive at the enormous number of a thousand million men replaced by the steam-engines which are distributed among the civilized nations. This number of a milliard of laborers, created by the genius of man, is there not something gigantic about it? Does it not by itself explain all the superiority of the civilized nations over the mass of nations still sunk in barbarism? The savage force of the barbarians can no longer encroach upon our civilization as at the end of the Roman empire. To the brutal force of man we can oppose a still more brutal force, that of our iron machines. We have now the advantage of numbers, for the milliard of workmen whom we have created will always keep in awe the barbarians who might still want to precipitate themselves on our countries. The world is to-day invaded by the Europeans; the inferior races recede and disappear before the superior and intelligent races, submitting to the natural law of the weaker. But let us not forget that we can conquer only with the aid of our machines, with our workmen of iron. In order to make the grape-shot which annihilates all resistance, steam-engines are necessary. Steam-engines are necessary again for boring the cannons, making powder, transporting men and engines of war to the ports and taking the ships from there to the country of the enemy."

"The steam-engines are also instruments of progress, my dear Monaghan," interrupted Badger. "It is the railroads which have given so great a scope to commerce. It is likewise the steam-engines which produce the thousand and one objects necessary for the existence of man. I think that, far from being only agents of destruction, the steam-engines are, on the contrary, and above all, useful, peaceful and civilizing objects."

"You are right, my lord," replied the geologist. "I had considered but a portion of their usefulness, but I am the first to recognize that they are, before all, instruments of peace and of labor."

A few days later the caravan proceeded to Kifri, and then reached the valley of the Dyalah, the most important tributary of the Tigris. A large number of naphtha springs were met with all along the way, as Cahuzac had foretold.

The photographer was decidedly an agreeable and jolly companion. This man, with his restless and intelligent look, had always a smile on his lips and a song ready to float off on the air. Of a simplicity which often bordered on unreserve, he was yet never obtrusive. Amiable, frank, obliging, he succeeded quickly in winning every one's sympathy.

"A good acquisition," said Badger one day to Jack Adams.

"These Frenchmen are all the same," replied the engineer, with a touch of bitterness.

It took twelve days to descend the valley of the Dyalah. Jack Adams found an excellent site for hydraulic works near Kizil-Robat, in the gorges of the Hamrin.

The caravan was now again in a land of plains; the mountains had been finally left. They passed through a veritable garden, intersected by myriads of brooks which spread coolness and fertility round about them. The frosts of winter had hardly been left, when, suddenly, our travelers found themselves amid the splendors of summer, with a burning sun over their heads. This sudden transition was not without its inconveniences. The two young girls had some trouble in standing it. It became necessary to travel more slowly and by short stages.

After leaving Bakuba they ceased to follow the stream, in order to take the shortest cut to Bagdad. The ruins of Dastaghad, as yet unexplored, won Grimmitschoffer's attention for a whole day. The *savant* discovered a colossal head of stone there—weighing at least fifty pounds—which he packed up with the greatest precautions, so as to be able to study it at leisure after his return to Babylon, for, according to him, this find was of a nature to throw a light upon a large section of the country.

"No more brains in one than in the other," murmured Jack Adams between his teeth.

A singular contrast between these two men—the one always looking ahead, hoping everything from the future; the other constantly turned towards the past, seeking there the secret of the destinies of humanity.

On the 19th of April the caravan was back at Bagdad. Every one was very glad to be once more in a known place.

Next day, before lunch, Lord Badger took Miss Rose aside.

"These continual journeys weary you," said he to her, kindly. "It has been so for some time; it would be worse at present, when you would find sad memories everywhere. Return to England. I have taken the necessary measures to secure an honorable existence for you over there. The governess of my daughter can always count on me."

Miss Rose thanked his lordship for his kindness. It would be a trial for her to be separated from her pupil; but, after all, she saw that Badger was right. An instructress since the age of eighteen, the time had come when rest became indispensable for her; the last ordeal that she had just undergone had overwhelmed her.

She was therefore left with the English consul, who was commissioned to send her back to her native country. The parting was painful; they promised each other to write and to meet again in London.

The expedition, reduced by a third, resumed its journey across the desert. This time it was proceeding towards the final resting-place, towards Babylon.

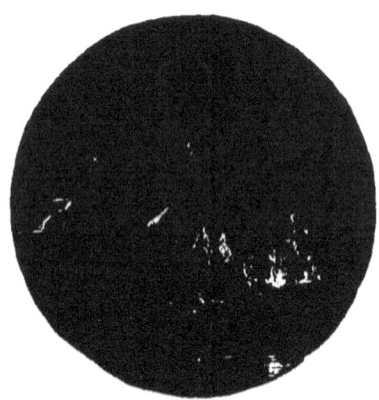

PART SECOND.

THE ELECTRIC WORKS.

CHAPTER I.

LIBERTY.

So here our travelers are once more following the road that leads through the desert from Bagdad to Babylon. This time, on arriving at the latter city, they felt the agreeable sensation that the most determined explorers, the most inveterate tourists feel on returning home. They were no longer to camp under tents or lodge in precarious shelters; they would be at home, in their own dwellings, provided with all European comforts. They were going to find their home again, the *sweet home* which the English know so well how to take with them everywhere.

With Miss Nelly a greater and deeper joy was joined to this impression of comfort—she was to meet Cornillé again. And, admitting that she had not as yet told herself that she loved the French engineer, a separation of three months had caused her to see what a large place he would henceforth hold in her life. Careful of her dignity, proud of her father's name, which she would not have wished to exchange but for an equally honorable and illustrious one, she did not

11 (161)

abandon herself quietly to the sentiment which she felt arising in her, but wished before all to assure herself that he who inspired it was worthy of it. This daughter of the north had never thought that reason and duty had nothing to do with passion, and that love, blind love, is its own law in itself. Between Cornillé and Miss Nelly there was, as it were, a sort of secret agreement, a tacit understanding to deserve each other's love before receiving it.

This had not hindered Miss Nelly from thinking her horse's gait decidedly slow, nor Cornillé from ascending more than twenty times to the top of the Kasr in order to scan all points of the horizon in the hope of seeing the caravan.

On account of the heat, which began to be excessive on the plain, he supposed that they would travel during a part of the night and rest during the day. He was, therefore, since before dawn at his post of observation, when a cloud of dust, seen in the distance, announced to him the approach of the so earnestly longed-for party.

The whole works were immediately in confusion. Every one made preparations to receive his principal in a proper manner. Blacton and Cornillé mounted their horses and went to meet Badger.

The meeting took place two miles from the works. They shook hands cordially with each other. Cornillé ascertained at a glance how much Miss Nelly had gained in beauty.

"I find you always the same, Miss Nelly," he said to her; "this long voyage has not wearied you; aside from your complexion, which is slightly darkened by the sun of the Orient, one would say that you had never left London."

"The fact is," declared Badger, "that my daughter has never looked so well as to-day. What sparkling eyes, what a fresh and rosy complexion!"

Meanwhile Cornillé ran his eye over the party and remarked the absence of two of his old companions and the presence of a new-comer.

"Why, where is our stout Flatnose, and grave Miss Ross?" asked he.

"Flatnose is dead," replied Badger, sadly. "As to Miss Ross, she must be at this moment on her way to England." And he recounted in a few words the events of which we know already.

"Poor Flatnose," said the engineer, deeply moved, "he had a tender heart under his rough exterior."

"We have been deeply grieved by his tragic end," resumed Badger; "yet we have had a diversion from our sorrow by meeting with a new companion, whom I have yet to introduce to you—*Monsieur* Cahuzac, a photographer and a Frenchman."

Then, turning to Cahuzac: "Permit me to introduce you to *Monsieur* Cornillé, the French engineer, of whom you have so often heard us speak."

The two compatriots shook hands vigorously.

The caravan resumed its journey towards the works, which appeared for the first time before the eyes of the travelers.

The sight was a glorious one and well calculated to fill Badger's heart with joy and pride. The two mounts of the Kasr and of Babel rose majestically at the horizon. Their inclined slopes, furrowed by the waters of heaven, had been replaced for a large part of their circumference by thick vertical walls of brick. Counterforts in the form of towers served as supports. The Kasr and Babel now had a striking resemblance to mediæval fortresses. Badger was the first to observe it.

"Your works, my dear Cornillé, resemble a stronghold."

"That is what they are, in fact, my lord," replied the engineer. "Who knows whether we may not have to stand a siege some day? One must never trust the Arabs. From up there we shall be able to resist a whole army."

"You will be victorious," interrupted Cahuzac, "for have you not lightning at your disposition for pulverizing the barbarians?"

"It would not be the first time that electricity had filled this *role*," said Grimm, in an undertone, as if speaking to himself.

As they approached nearer to the works, or rather to the fortresses, for never had works presented themselves under such an aspect, they could see the details more clearly. The upper part of Babel had the form of a large terrace. It will be remembered that the mount—now on the right hand of the travelers—bore Cornillé's thermo-electric piles. Now, to allow the rays of the sun all their force of action, it was necessary to have no elevated obstacle on the upper surface of the plateau. It was not thus on the Kasr, where the works properly speaking were located, that is to say, a large number of buildings intended for various uses. Whence arose a multiplicity of forms, of pointed roofs, of towers, and of chimneys, offering to the eye an appearance which, though most strange, was yet highly picturesque.

"Why is not Captain Laycock here?" exclaimed Badger; "he would see the realization of his work. And what a gigantic work! Honor to those who have contributed towards the erection of this temple of science and progress. Honor to you, my dear Cornillé, my dear Adams, my excellent Blacton; honor to all, for all have done their duty."

Badger had hardly ended these words when another horseman was seen to hurry towards them at full speed. A few minutes later Captain Laycock dismounted from his horse and rushed into Badger's arms.

"Now the feast is complete," said Badger; "I had just made the remark that only you were wanting, and I expressed my regrets."

"I knew the day of your return," replied Laycock. "I would not have been absent for anything in the world. My ship has been at Babylon since an hour. I have just taken the time to put everything on board in order and to get here at full speed."

"Thank you, my good friend," replied Badger, strongly moved by these repeated marks of sympathy.

"This is my last voyage until the return of the ships which have gone to England for a new cargo. Everything is now in its place. I am entitled to a few weeks' rest."

"They will not be grudged you, be assured of that; but I know you—before three days have passed, you modern Nimrod, you will have caused all the echoes of the neighborhood to resound with your exploits as a hunter. Did Captain Laycock ever take a rest?"

A rise in the ground had until then prevented the base of the two hillocks from being seen. When the caravan reached the top of a high dune of sand, a city, a veritable city, appeared before the astonished eyes of the travelers. More than three hundred houses with flat roofs and surrounded by small gardens stood in the space comprised between the Kasr and Babel.

At this sight their enthusiasm reached its height. By the hurrahs, by the repeated cries of admiration uttered by the newcomers, by the way in which Miss Nelly and Fatma clapped their hands, Cornillé and Blacton could judge that their triumph was complete.

"What is the name of this city?" asked Miss Nelly, smiling.

"Badger City," replied Cornillé.

"No, my friends," said Badger; "I cannot accept this honor, however pleasing it may be to my vanity. If you will follow my advice, in fact, none of us will connect his name with any part of the work which we have carried on together. Science is our only master, and must always remain the only one."

"Nevertheless," interrupted Cornillé, "it would be but just to give your name to that part of the city which will serve as the beginning of new Babylon. You are our chief, and this honor is yours by right."

"That is true," exclaimed all of those present.

"No," resumed Badger, "but since you are kind enough to grant me a privilege, I claim that of choosing the name of the new city myself. I wish to have it called Liberty, so as to indicate that it is to be the starting point of a new civilization, developing freely by work, peace, and the union of all."

"Unanimously adopted," replied Cornillé.

"Plus my vote," added the photographer, while Grimmitschoffer shook his head with a sad and doubtful air.

Ten minutes later, the caravan made its entry into Liberty, since that was now to be the name of the city which had arisen, as if by enchantment, in the midst of an arid desert.

All the workmen, headed by the engineers and superintendents, were collected to welcome Badger and his friends, and made the air resound with their enthusiastic and oft-repeated cheers. His lordship dismounted, shook the principals cordially by the hand, and thanked the workmen in a few words full of sympathy.

They then proceeded to the centre of the city, where the dwelling-houses intended for Badger and the members of the expedition were situated. Liberty had a wholly original character: the regularity of the plan, the arrangement of the streets, the care expended on the smallest details of everything that might insure cleanliness and health to the town, proclaimed the European city. But all the arrangements required by the climate, and which the builders had had the good sense and the good taste to retain, the terrace-like roofs, the numerous gardens irrigated by brooks of running water, the covered galleries, the squares adorned with fountains, over which immense awnings of canvas were spread, giving the shade which could not yet be looked for in the new plantations, all this preserved for it its characteristics of an oriental town. In the interior of the houses was again found—in all the details of arrangement and furnishing—the same intelligent application of local usages to the requirements of civilized life.

A large number of European and native merchants had already established themselves in the new town, where all branches of commerce and industry were found represented. The most amusing variety resulted. Miss Nelly and Fatma could hardly believe their eyes. What! This ground, which they had left three months before in a desert-like state, was transformed to this extent? It was a new tale of the *Thousand and One Nights* to be added to those of the Arabian poet. The most amazing wonders dreamed of by the imagination in the time when it reigned wholly over a young humanity, can be realized to-day by science, when it is placed at the service of a grand idea.

It was hardly seven o'clock in the morning. Each of the travelers directed his steps to the dwelling intended for him, in order to enjoy a few hours of sleep. What a pleasure to lie down at last on real beds, between sheets of fine cloth; to resume the gentle habits, the existence full of comfort, of the rich Europeans! Miss Nelly was impatient to see her new abode. An agreeable surprise, which she was far from expecting, awaited her there. Her father had wished that she should here find again her chamber, her little working-room, her piano, her crayons, her books, and all her familiar nick-nacks and *bibelots*. It seemed to her like a delusion at first. But no, there were really her pretty rosewood bureau, her library, her wardrobe, her arm-chair, her chairs, down to even her ink-stand and paper. On the walls her pictures were hanging, and among them the dearest of all, the portrait of her mother.

With a bound she was beside her father, who had remained on the threshold, smiling and as happy as his daughter. And, putting her arms around Badger's neck:

"Really, dear father," she said to him, "I begin to think that you spoil me too much, you treat me like the little princesses of the fairy tales."

"And whom then could I love too much, if not yourself, my dear Nelly? Are you not my only joy, my only happiness? You are the charming fairy who leaves her mark on everything, and whose mere presence beautifies everything which she approaches."

Fatma's chamber was situated near that of her mistress. It was more modest, but still furnished with taste. Without wishing to make the young Greek the equal of his daughter, Badger desired that she should be regarded as her companion and not as an inferior.

It had been agreed upon that every one should be up at noon for lunch. But, long before the hour set, they were all collected in the large parlor. Nobody had been able to close an eye. The minds were too excited by the expectation of the unknown. The contemplated visit to the electric works was the great attraction of the day.

These imposing masses of the Kasr and of Babel, which threw the town into the shade, and bounded the horizon, what did they contain within their steep walls? What were they going to see?

At the stroke of twelve, the heavy cloth curtains, which in the East form the only partitions between the different rooms of a suite of apartments, slid on their rods, and an Arab servant, acting as steward, came to announce that lunch was served. Badger had informed his companions that they would continue to have their meals together at Liberty, just as they had on the *Electricity* and in the desert. If each one had his house, they all would meet together at least at meal-times. It was the surest means for preserving that precious intimacy which, since the departure from London, had as yet remained unbroken.

Cornillé made Cahuzac sit beside him. He wanted to talk of his native land—of dear France. It turned out that they were born in the same province, and that they had a host of mutual acquaintances.

Perhaps they were even cousins—"after the fashion of Brittany," as the photographer said laughingly. At least, if they were not cousins, they knew persons distantly related to both of their families. Unfortunately, Cornillé was given but little rest at this meal. He was the hero of the day; they overwhelmed him with questions, and wanted to know everything.

"You will see presently," replied the engineer.

"At least tell us how your work stands."

"As to that, yes! I assure you that good Blacton has worked well. What spirit! What an absorbing activity! The large works of the Kasr are almost completed; the dynamo-electric machines and the accumulators are all placed in position. As to my thermo-electric pile at Babel, it is in a fair way to advance. You know that we have been able to take with us only a very small part of the immense amount of material necessary for a complete establishment. What I have of it even now has already given me excellent results. I await, without very much impatience, the arrival of the ships which in two or three months from now will bring me the rest of my pile. Its complete setting up will require at least four months. The unfavorable days will have set in again; the sun will not be hot enough. The thermo-electric pile will, therefore, not be in really good working order until a year from now."

After they had taken coffee, all rose hurriedly from the table. Every one hastened to dress in such a way as to be able to brave the hot stinging of the sun of Asia with impunity, then all proceeded to the Kasr. The heat was intense; but nobody felt it, so great was their impatience to see the buildings. The hats of elder-pith, the thick veils, the large parasols, were to give protection against sunstroke.

CHAPTER II.

THE KASR AND BABEL.

IN a few minutes the merry party had reached the foot of the Kasr. The original hill was no longer recognizable. Its grassy slopes had given place to a long series of terraces, intended to hold the ground and the bricks, and, above all, to increase the surface of the works.

It was impossible to overlook the whole plan at the first glance. Therefore Cornillé, so as to give his companions some idea of his work as a whole, conducted them at once to the summit of the Kasr. They reached it by a long inclined ascent which allowed wagons to get to the upper plateau.

The view extended into the distance. The horizon widened in proportion as they advanced on this circular road. Liberty appeared, with its streets crossing each other at right angles and its uniform houses. Then, on the other side, the Euphrates, with its broad bed and clear waters; farther away the Arabian city of Hillah, over which the palm-trees threw patches of dark green, contrasting strongly with the whiteness of the buildings. Finally, at the extreme horizon, the hill of Birs-Nimrod, the scene of poor Grimmitschoffer's misfortune. Fatma, the little rogue—that age knows no pity—called out to him:

"I say! Mr. Grimm, don't you see the tower down there in which you were lodged like an owl?"

Alas! Grimm saw it but too well, this tower of misfortune, which had so nearly become the tower of hunger for him. He pretended not to hear and went in another direction.

"The *savants* are not fond of jesting," whispered Cornillé to Cahuzac, who did not know through what circumstances Grimm had come to be one of the expedition; and, in a few words, he acquainted the photographer with the incidents which had brought about the discovery of the illustrious archæologist.

The party reached the upper plateau of the Kasr, at a height of about one hundred and fifty feet above the plain. Successively narrowed by the receding terraces which flanked its four sides, the mount had at its summit but a rectangular surface of three hundred feet in breadth by four hundred and fifty in length.

A tower of about fifty feet in height rose in the centre of the plateau. It was to serve eventually for the establishment of a gigantic light-house destined to illumine the works and the city. Just now it was as yet but an observatory.

When all were assembled on the platform of this tower Cornillé addressed them:

"Now, ladies and gentlemen, you can oversee the whole of the buildings."

"Does it not look like Mont Saint-Michel?" observed Miss Nelly, who had visited the celebrated abbey on the coasts of Normandy.

"That is perfectly exact, Miss Badger," resumed the engineer. "In short, you see that the plan is very simple—an upper plateau and all around a broad belt of terraces at levels but little elevated above each other. On the upper plateau we have placed the accumulators. They will collect the electricity furnished by the piles at Babel and by the hydraulic works which my friend Jack Adams has constructed on the streams and torrents of the basin of the upper Tigris and of the mountain-chain bordering Persia. As to the lower rows, they hold the dynamo-electric motors. These are of two kinds—the motors destined to act by the combustion of coal and of petroleum are contained in the buildings which you see at your right; at your left we have placed those which will receive their movement through the electricity drawn directly from the accumulators and which are much more numerous."

"It is perfect," said Jack Adams.

"Admirable," said Badger, delighted at the skill of his engineers. "Receive my heartiest congratulations, my dear Cornillé."

"Pardon me, my lord," resumed the latter; "that this work is not all my own, you know. Jack Adams and I laid out the plans together before leaving London. As to the buildings of the works, it is to modest Blacton, who is hidden over there behind the others, that the principal credit is due. Come, my worthy collaborator, come forward, then, to receive the praise due to your labors."

"My friends," said Badger, "everybody has done his duty and is keeping his promises. I thank all in the name of all."

It was decided that they should begin by visiting the buildings set apart for the dynamo-electric machines. They descended from the platform of the tower to the lower terraces by a stair-case more rapidly than by the broad road running on an inclined plane.

Cornillé opened a door, and the visitors found themselves in a large hall constructed half of wood, half of bricks. Floods of sunshine entered through widely opened windows.

"Here we are in the large hall of the dynamo-electric motors," said the engineer.

"Which?" asked Laycock.

"Those which work by the aid of steam-engines."

"And where are these steam-engines?" asked Captain Laycock, in his turn. "I don't see any."

"They are in a building parallel to this. You see that horizontal shaft that runs through the centre of the hall from one end to the other?"

"Yes."

"Well, this shaft receives its rotary movement by a series of wheel-works which are themselves set in motion by the steam-engines in the other building."

"And the dynamo-electric motors themselves are set in action by the horizontal shaft?" said Monaghan.

"Just so."

"Perhaps these gentlemen would rather see the buildings of the steam-engines first," said Jack Adams, in his turn.

"Oh, yes!" exclaimed Miss Nelly, "it is curious to see these great iron monsters work."

The attraction exerted by the steam-engines is easily understood. They seem endowed with life, and what a life! No living being, no marine monster possesses so powerful a breath. What a regularity in the action of their enormous muscles! The powerful rods which the cylinders cause to move backwards and forwards, the beams which rise and descend, give a terrifying idea of their power. And when they spit fire and belch forth clouds of smoke, as if ready to pulverize everything in their way, man, though the creator of these terrible engines, begins to fear them. He dreads the effects of the formidable forces which he has himself set to work.

The building with the machinery was much less spacious than the first. It contained but two steam-engines. But how powerful they appeared!

"These two engines will be sufficient for our first experiments," said the engineer. "The boilers of the one will be heated with coal, the other with petroleum. And neither the one nor the other will be wanting, according to the information which Monaghan has already given me concerning the beds discovered by him in the course of your journey."

They examined the boilers, the steam-engines. Everything was placed in the best condition. They then returned to the first building, that of the electric motors.

"*Monsieur* Cornillé," said Miss Nelly, "could you be kind enough to give me a few explanations concerning these electric motors?"

"With great pleasure, Miss Badger," said Cornillé, happy to seize this opportunity of being brought together with his idol.

"What interests me most," continued Miss Nelly, "is electricity. Steam is already well known. At Jezireh I have seen the motor of the hydraulic works in action. Mr. Adams has taught me the first rudiments; you see, therefore, that I am a *savant!*"

While the rest of the party continued to inspect the machines Cornillé remained behind with Miss Nelly and Fatma, who was as desirous of being instructed as her mistress. They stopped before a first group of five motors.

"These are five Gramme machines, called after their celebrated inventor," said the engineer to the two young girls.

"One of your compatriots, I suppose?" asked Miss Nelly.

"Yes, a Frenchman. This machine is composed of two big electromagnets, placed horizontally one above the other. The two centres form magnetized poles of a considerable power. A ring turns between the two poles in a plane perpendicular to that of the two electromagnets."

"This ring is curious," interrupted the young girl. "I would like very much to know how it is made."

"It is an iron disk which bears a large number of little bobbins. This particular arrangement forms the really new part of the Gramme machines."

"I understand," said Miss Nelly. "I see perfectly the various rollings of the little bobbins. But, dear me! how complicated an electric machine is!"

"As for me," declared Fatma, "I do not understand it at all."

"That is not my fault," said Cornillé, laughing; "to understand anything of it one must first be a *savant*, like Miss Nelly."

"These five motors," continued the engineer, "serve to produce the electric light. This evening you will see our workshops lit up as in broad daylight. The lamps will receive their electricity from the machines which are before you."

"We shall come to see them work," said Miss Nelly.

"Oh, yes!" cried Fatma, overjoyed at the thought of seeing an illumination.

At this moment Badger's voice was heard at the end of the room:

"We are going to visit the second machinery hall; you will find us there presently."

"We will rejoin you in five minutes," replied Cornillé.

The engineer conducted the two young girls before another series of motors.

"These machines," said he, "have been invented by Hefner von Alteneck, and are most frequently designated by the name of Siemens machines, after the name of their constructor. This motor, like the Gramme machine, is composed of two electro-magnets formed by several bars of soft iron. These bars are bent into semi-circles in their centre, leaving a space between each of them and encompassing as tightly as possible a drum-shaped ring. If you will pass to the other side, Miss Badger, I shall describe this drum to you. It is formed by round wooden plates, pierced by the axis of revolution. Metal wires are first rolled around this drum, so as to cover it with an armature of soft iron. Then this first covering is covered with oiled silk, serving as an *insulator*. Lastly, on this so prepared cylinder copper wire is rolled."

Cornillé stopped short in his explanations. Miss Nelly, who had passed to the other side of the machine, was opposite to the engineer. Leaning forward, she was attentively regarding what Cornillé showed her, when, raising her little head, it almost brushed that of the young man, and by an accident their hands touched.

The two lovers nearly betrayed themselves. Thanks to the control which women have over themselves, it was Miss Nelly who was the first to recover herself.

"Let us go and see the other machines," said she, with a perfectly calm air, and proceeding towards the door through which her father had gone out.

"Let us go and see the other machines!" exclaimed Fatma, in her turn, parodying her mistress in her most mischievous manner.

When the latter had rejoined the rest of the company she had recovered her composure, and no one would have suspected what emotion she had just felt.

"What a power of will in so young a head," said the engineer to himself; "does she really love me?"

The new machinery hall which the two young girls, followed by their cicerone, had just entered, was much larger than the first. It extended over two sides of the parallelogram formed by the Kasr.

In this hall had been placed a specimen of every dynamo-electric motor constructed up to this day. And they were not few in number! These motors have nothing really new as to their principle. They are simply more or less ingenious combinations of the motors of Gramme and Siemens. Yet, as nothing in matters of improvement must ever be neglected, even the apparently most futile details, Cornillé and Jack Adams had decided to submit the principal machines of recent innovation to a strict inspection. Thanks to this wise manner of proceeding, they would certainly be enabled to employ only the most improved engines when the time should come to construct the final works.

"This motor," Jack Adams was saying at this moment, pointing out one of the machines, "this motor will serve to light up our apartments with incandescent lamps. It is that of Maxim."

A little farther on another motor attracted notice by its considerable proportions. It was the giant of the place.

"What you see there," continued the engineer, "is the Edison motor. Its weight is fifty thousand pounds. It will be able to feed a thousand lamps."

"With which to light up the whole of Liberty," said Monaghan.

"It will serve for the light-house which overlooks the Kasr," replied Adams.

"A pretty gas-light, that," observed Cahuzac. "You could light up Bagdad from Babylon."

"No," said Cornillé, recovered from his recent agitation. "But, at least, our light-house will be visible at Bagdad."

"Is there not another hall?" asked Badger, as they passed out of the building.

"Yes," said Cornillé, "we have another, smaller hall which occupies the fourth side of the Kasr. But it is empty at present."

"For what do you intend it?" asked Monaghan.

"It will contain electro-motors, that is to say, machines which, inversely from the preceding, will receive their movement through an electric current. The machines which you have just seen will transform movement into electricity; those which we await will, on the contrary, transform electricity into movement."

"Well, then, until later on," said the geologist.

They repaired again to the staircase which led to the upper platform; then they entered an immense quadrangular hall, covering alone three-quarters of the terrace.

Here there were no more machines, no more motors. Only a multitude of cubical glass vessels. On each of these vessels there was a plate of wood, painted black; on each side of these plates two immense knobs of brass. These accumulators—for the glass vessels were nothing else than accumulators—were divided into six series of six different models. All facilities would thus be offered for making comparisons and deciding which of these models was to be adopted in the final experiments.

The hall, which had the form of a long rectangle, had, therefore, been divided into six compartments. A broad passage enabled one to move easily around each one of them.

Cornillé and Jack Adams gave many explanations. They showed in what the difference in each system of accumulators consisted.

Nothing now remained to be seen in the halls, where the concentrated heat became suffocating. Miss Nelly proposed that they should ascend again to the platform, where refreshments and seats had been brought, and to rest a few moments in the shadow of the tower before proceeding to Babel.

The proposition was accepted with enthusiasm, and a few minutes later the whole party was collected around the improvised lunch.

"Mr. Adams," said Miss Nelly, who was doing credit to the collation, "I would like very much to know now how you are going to make use of the immense material which we have just seen. For me, who am not so learned as these gentlemen, that which is most important for me to know is the results."

"You are right, Miss Badger," replied the engineer, "and I can satisfy you immediately. The accumulators are intended to receive electricity from several sources and to condense it. When they are charged it will be possible for us to adapt the electricity to a large

number of uses. Now, which will be the sources which are to charge the accumulators? They will have four quite distinct origins: Firstly, the hydraulic works which I have established on the upper Tigris and those which I shall establish later on its affluents. The electric fluid will arrive from these distant regions by underground wires which will traverse the sandy plains, as I have already had the privilege of explaining to you during our voyage."

"All your explanations are yet before my mind."

"Secondly," resumed Jack Adams, "the motors which we visited but a moment ago. For this end we shall utilize the coal and petroleum, which we possess in great quantity. For, although we shall seek after this to create new forces, we do not intend to deprive ourselves of those which nature gives us so liberally at the present time. Thirdly, the powerful thermo-electric pile constructed by my friend Cornillé at the summit of Babel."

"And which we are going to visit presently," said Miss Nelly, casting a stealthy glance at Cornillé, who, a little apart from the group formed by Miss Nelly, Jack Adams, and Fatma, appeared serious and preoccupied.

"The thermo-electric pile will transform the solar rays directly into electricity. In conclusion, fourthly, hydraulic apparatus, which I shall establish on the borders of the Persian Gulf in a few weeks, will also be placed in communication with the accumulators by means of an underground wire."

"Why these new apparatus, will those of the Tigris not be sufficient?"

"Those of the Tigris will utilize only the waterfalls of the rivers, while those of the Persian Gulf will utilize the waves of the sea, the tides, and the winds."

"Astonishing!" said Cahuzac, who had listened to the engineer's words, "these people no longer doubt anything. They will finish by taking down the moon, the sun and the stars, to make electricity of them."

Everybody began to laugh. This gave the signal for departure, and they set out for Babel.

Seen from a little distance, Babel differed in appearance from the Kasr. Here there were no more constructions by different rows—no more buildings of various and strange forms. The exterior facing was the same; but as it would have been too difficult and would have taken too long to construct walls of one hundred and twenty-five feet in height, the enclosing wall began only mid-way on the slope, which reduced the height to sixty feet. All the space comprised between the encircling wall and the upper plateau had been filled up with earth and bricks. But then it had been necessary to strengthen the wall with powerful counterforts; in default of which, the thrust of the materials would speedily have shaken it.

If the Kasr resembled a strong castle, Babel offered a most striking similarity with a citadel. The large terrace which formed its top was reached by a broad stairway of a hundred steps.

"I intend, later on," said Cornillé at the moment when the little party was walking along the balustrade which led to the first steps of the stairway, "to cover the rubbish which forms the slope with vegetable mould and to plant trees there. Babel will thus be surrounded by a belt of vegetation."

"An excellent idea," said Badger; "one will no longer be exposed, as we are at this moment, to receiving the full reflection of the sun from the bricks."

The ascent was in truth arduous, especially for Miss Nelly and Fatma.

"A little more courage, ladies," said Cornillé; "you will have shade above there. I have had a tent set up on purpose."

"It is to be believed," said Cahuzac, "that the sun wishes to show us that we are entering his domain. What a heat there is here! If you convert all that into electricity, there will be enough to light up the whole earth."

"Not as much as you think," replied the engineer, laughing.

At last all arrived at the upper terrace. They quickly sought shelter under the tent, where it was comparatively cool.

It is, in fact, noticeable that in the countries where the sun darts forth its rays with the greatest intensity, it is cool wherever one is out of their reach; while, in the damp climates, the difference between the sunny places and the shady spots is hardly perceptible.

A few minutes after their arrival, the visitors proceeded towards the portions of the thermo-solar pile that had already been set up. What there was of it was of little importance in comparison with the rest. Hardly fifty elements of the ten thousand of which the total pile was to be composed were here collected. It was thus as yet nothing but a simple experiment, sufficient, however, to permit of judging the final result.

These elements of the thermo-solar pile had a singular appearance. They were long, blackish, metallic plates, presenting their surfaces to the rays of the sun. All these plates communicated one with the other by means of copper wires.

But what was the strangest of all was the long vat which extended below this metallic covering.

"This is petroleum in here," said Cahuzac, after having dipped his finger into the liquid contained in the vat.

"Yes," replied Cornillé. "I use that liquid for insulating the elements of my thermo-electric pile, and, at the same time, for cooling the pole opposite to that which receives the heat of the sun."

Cornillé's pile was examined a long time. This agent was new. From it the most considerable results were expected. No one had the right to ascend to the summit of Babel but the members of the association and a few workmen on whose silence they could absolutely depend. In order to be admitted here, Cahuzac and Grimmitschoffer had been obliged to take oath, just like the others, never to reveal anything of what they were about to see.

"Now, what are those immense cones of tin that I see glittering in the sun over there," Cahuzac suddenly asked; "is that another thermo-electric pile?"

"No," said Cornillé. "You will be enlightened on this point in a moment, my dear Cahuzac. I am just about to take you all over there."

They proceeded towards these large cones which the photographer had pointed out. They shone in the sun like beacons, and some of the reflections were so strong as to be borne with difficulty by the eye. There were three similar apparatus in a row.

"I introduce to you the solar apparatus of Messrs. Mouchot and Pifre," said Cornillé.

"For what do they serve?" asked Miss Nelly.

"To boil water in a boiler. With this boiling water a steam-engine can be put in motion."

"I was in Paris," said Cahuzac, "on the day when *Monsieur* Pifre set up one of these apparatus in the gardens of the Tuileries. The boiler served to feed a small steam-engine, which in turn set a small Marinoni press in motion. The press worked regularly from one o'clock to five o'clock in the evening."

"I have seen these interesting experiments myself," resumed the engineer. "Here, with the sun of Mesopotamia, we shall arrive at much better results."

"What advantages do you think will be drawn one day from these apparatus, more improved?" asked Laycock. "When coal shall be wanting, will it be possible to replace it by the Mouchot apparatus?"

"In the first place, there will be the thermo-solar piles," replied Cornillé. "But, besides, the Mouchot apparatus will be able to render signal service in a large number of cases. The solar receivers will admit of being used otherwise than for bringing water in a boiler to ebullition. Salomon de Caux, in 1615, constructed a thermic machine working with the aid of the sun. Bélidor also invented a pump of the same class. *Monsieur* Mouchot has succeeded in producing a large number of chemical reactions. You see, therefore, that it is possible to obtain an infinite number of industrial operations with the sun."

CHAPTER III.

THE SAM.

LORD BADGER had been right in predicting that Captain Laycock would not be able to remain long at rest. For two weeks they were leading the agreeably and intelligently occupied life which we have just described, when one evening, at dinner, the intrepid mariner made the proposition to have a hunting-party the next day.

This motion was received with joy by those present. It was decided that every one should take part in the sport, as the work would not suffer by a few hours' absence of the superiors. Grimm was the only one to declare that it would be impossible for him to take part in the hunt, on account of the excavations which he could not leave for a single day. No one asked him to alter his mind.

Next day, at the first faint gleam of dawn, everybody was in the saddle. The morning appeared superb, although the atmosphere was a little close. The heat had been oppressive during the preceding days.

It had been decided to proceed towards the north, ascending the left bank of the Euphrates. Here there lay broad spaces, covered with high grasses, where the captain had discovered the presence of a large number of animals. At six o'clock the little party had cleared over six miles. A halt was made. The horses were tied to the trunks of some stunted palms, grown there by accident, and the chase began.

Ten minutes later the shooting began on all sides. From the rapidity with which the shots succeeded each other it was easy to conjecture that game abounded. In fact, the game-bags filled up visibly. No pity was shown, and the number of victims was considerable.

At ten o'clock, as had been agreed upon, every one came to the place of *rendezvous*—a palm-tree a little better furnished with foliage than the others. Contrary to expectation, the sun was less hot than had been feared. Its reddish disk seemed obscured by an invisible vapor. Monaghan showed a certain inquietude.

"This is not natural," said he to the hunters; "some storm is brewing that will not be long in breaking loose. Let us be on our guard; these atmospheric phenomena are to be feared in these regions."

Captain Laycock, on the contrary, insisted that the interrupted hunt should be resumed.

"We have time," said he; "the sun has been gracious enough to veil itself for us; let us take advantage of it. When we see the storm approaching we shall take up the road to Babylon again. With our horses we shall travel faster than it."

The hunt was, therefore, begun again with renewed ardor.

During this time Green was preparing one of those excellent dinners of which he knew the secret. The wines of Burgundy and of the Rhine would not be wanting and would give renewed strength for the exploits of the afternoon.

On their return the hunters found the table set. The horseback ride in the morning and four hours of hunting in the meadows had sharpened their appetites. They ate ravenously, and little was spoken during the first part of the repast.

Little by little the tongues became loosened. Cornillé and Cahuzac, like true Frenchmen, led all the conversation, yet without monopolizing it to themselves. Every one could have his say, give out his ideas. The conversation was charming and lively, dazzling and full of *esprit*. On this ground they were no longer in England, but rather in France, in Paris! Monaghan alone was absorbed and seemed preoccupied. Two or three times he rose in order to examine the state of the sky in the direction of the horizon.

The repast, however, had passed without accident and was nearing its end, when a sudden change occurred in the state of the atmosphere. Puffs of hot air succeeded each other at short intervals. Little whirlwinds raised columns of dust. It seemed as if the day were suddenly waning.

"It's the storm," said Monaghan. "We have not a moment to lose. Quick, to horse, and let us regain Liberty at full gallop."

They rose precipitately. The coffee, brought immediately, was swallowed burning hot. Five minutes later the baggage was loaded again and everybody in the saddle, ready to leave. But at the moment when Badger gave the spurs to his horse the latter, instead of advancing, began to turn around itself, showing signs of a great terror. Everything was in vain, caresses and threats, blows with the whip and pricks with the spur. The other horses followed the example of Badger's steed and refused to advance. Miss Nelly and Fatma would have been unhorsed if they had been less skilful riders. They had to resign themselves and dismount.

But what was to be done? The sky was becoming covered with a yellow mist. At the zenith it was yet free from clouds; but the transparent vapor observed in the morning was taking on the opacity of a great black cloud, increasing visibly, and behind which the sun appeared but as a pale, round spot, fading away rapidly. The air became suffocating; squalls of hot wind whirled up clouds of sand each minute. It was urgent to come to a decision.

It was impossible to think of remaining in the plain, where no shelter whatever offered itself and where no obstacle would check the violence of the tempest.

Monaghan proposed that they should take a direction perpendicular to that of the river and to go inland. Some tells were seen half a mile away. It would perhaps be possible to find a shelter there against the wind.

There was no time for deliberation; Monaghan's advice seemed good and they set out, turning their backs on the Euphrates.

The horses, drawn by their bridles, advanced slowly.

"They are looking towards the west," said the geologist, "the storm will come from there."

In truth, the poor animals, with downcast and dejected look and evidently under the influence of an insurmountable terror, were turning their heads in the direction indicated. A broad, scarlet-red band was beginning to appear at the horizon.

A quarter of an hour, which seemed a century, elapsed before they were able to reach the border of the meadow. The tempests of the sea are as nothing in comparison with these frightful storms of impalpable, burning and suffocating dust. Who has not heard of caravans buried in the sands stirred up by the *simoon* in the midst of the African Sahara? Now, it was precisely the simoon which was advancing, sweeping away everything in its passage, wrenching up everything; the terrible simoon, known under the name of *Sam* in Mesopotamia.

"Let us make haste," cried Monaghan; "see the cyclone coming; do not let us lose a second!"

Unfortunately they advanced only with extreme difficulty.

"I am going to run ahead to look for shelter," cried Cornillé, "and I shall come back to fetch you."

And he darted forward. He was seen to disappear behind a hillock, then to reappear shortly afterward, beckoning to them to advance. But the horses absolutely refused to do so.

"Let us abandon them," said Badger.

"Try to bind up their eyes," said Caluzac.

This course succeeded as well as could be desired, and they were able to rejoin Cornillé in a few minutes.

" What have you found?" asked Miss Nelly, who, in spite of all her energy, began to be agitated by fear.

" Let us give thanks to Grimmitschoffer," replied Cornillé. " For once in his life he will have been useful to his poor contemporaries. Thanks to his mania for making excavations everywhere, he has pre-

pared a large grotto for us, where we can be sheltered as long as the storm lasts."

Indeed, after having wound around a series of tells of greater or less height, they arrived at a large excavation dug at the base of one of them. It was high time. The red band had enlarged considerably; resembling an immense circle, it rose rapidly above the horizon and was about to reach the zenith. Behind it the sky took on a livid color, which took on a deeper and deeper hue, to become entirely black. There was something terrible, almost infernal, in the spectacle. It seemed as though the day was about to end and all nature to fall back into chaos.

They entered the cavity. The roof appeared to be solid. It must have been a half-ruined ancient gallery which the excavations had brought to light.

"What luck!" remarked Jack Adams. "This cavity is set exactly towards the east. We shall therefore have the wind at our backs."

"Provided it does not fall down on our heads," said Miss Nelly, looking uneasily at a deep crack which gaped in the roof.

"You need have no fear, Miss Badger," replied Cornillé. "These walls have been in this state for centuries, and they will yet resist to-day the storm which is soon going to rage."

"And the horses," said Badger, "we cannot have them come in here with us."

"They do not run any further danger," said Laycock; "we shall tie them together, a superfluous precaution, however, for they little think of running away at this moment. Just look at them."

In fact, these animals, absolutely terrified, had lain down on the sand, trembling, pressing one against the other; each hid its head under the belly of its neighbor.

"No matter; we must fasten them notwithstanding," continued the captain, "for they might very likely run off when the storm is allayed."

At the same instant the sun disappeared entirely behind the dark cloud and obscurity reigned. Laycock, Jack Adams and Cornillé hastened to fasten the horses by their bridles. They had hardly re-entered the excavation, when the storm began to roar, terrifying, horrible. The squalls succeeded each other without interruption. The air, become irrespirable, had sulphurous emanations; it seemed as if tainted by an unknown matter.

In the interior of the grotto there was complete silence. These fearless companions, accustomed to struggle cheerfully with danger and to brave it, felt in this hour the inanity of their efforts.

In the presence of the awful convulsions of nature, man feels his impotency and his feebleness; disarmed in the conflict with the unconscious forces which crush him, he can only oppose to them an impassive brow and a stoical resignation. Badger and his companions, standing up, their heads raised, accepted beforehand the decree of fate. Fatma, half fainted from fright, had crouched against her mistress, who, seated on a block of stone, her two hands clasped on the pretty head of the child, seemed to invoke the intervention of a higher and benevolent power.

In the distance the bushes, torn from the sides of the hillocks, were seen to fly about in all directions; immense columns of sand, brought over from the deserts of Arabia, passed by with a dizzy rapidity, smashing on the ground with a crash and scattering far and wide. An impalpable dust penetrated everywhere. In spite of the veils, the handkerchiefs held over the mouth and nose, it entered the lungs and became suffocating. Ears and eyes were filled with it, the hair was powdered with it.

The storm lasted thus a full hour. Then the squalls diminished in violence; the day reappeared slowly, less livid. The air became less hot and less irrespirable.

"That is the end," said Monaghan in a voice made hoarse by the sand.

Every one then awoke from his torpor. Miss Nelly and Fatma went to the entrance of the grotto to witness the last ragings of the

hurricane. Cahuzac made his way by crawling around the horses and came back pushing a hamper before him which still contained several bottles of wine with their seals intact. They could drink something limpid and allay the intolerable uncomfortableness caused by thirst and by the sand.

At once everybody recovered his speech. They congratulated each other on having escaped from danger and from a death that would have been almost inevitable if, instead of being able to seek shelter in the bottom of an excavation, they had been obliged to breast the storm in the open country. Perhaps they would now have been buried under a thick layer of sand.

At five o'clock the sky had recovered its clearness and transparency. They mounted their horses again, and an hour later they were at Liberty. Each one was in haste to get to his room, in order to divest himself of his clothes, which had become veritable haircloth, and to plunge into a cool bath.

When they were united again for dinner some one was wanting—it was Grimmitschoffer. Inquiry concerning him was held among the servants; nobody had seen him return. There was no longer any doubt; he also had been surprised by the storm. They must go to his assistance.

By a lucky accident, and contrary to his custom, Grimm had mentioned the day before in what place he intended to conduct his researches. It was a tell situated at about two miles from Liberty. Laycock, Jack Adams, Cornillé and Cahuzac, each provided with a lantern, proceeded with all haste in that direction. For greater precaution they had also taken a litter with them.

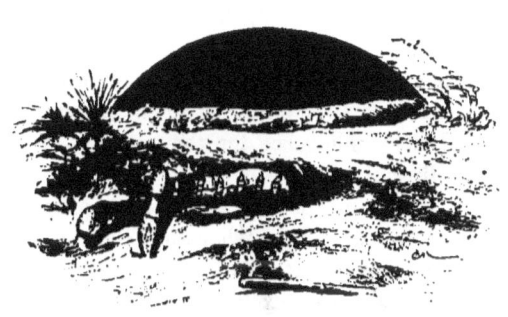

On arriving at the spot indicated, our rescuers began their search at once. Several tells arose in the same place and formed a sort of labyrinth. Each one took a different direction. A quarter of an hour elapsed without any other sound being heard but that of the settling of the sand under the feet of the searchers. At last Jack Adams' voice resounded in the distance:

"This way! Come this way!"

They all directed their steps towards the quarter whence these calls came, and soon perceived Jack Adams bending over a body stretched out at full length and no longer giving any sign of life.

"Does he live?" they asked as they came up.

"Yes," replied the engineer; "but the beatings of his heart are feeble."

Cornillé raised up the dying man's head and succeeded in introducing a few drops of brandy into his mouth. At the contact with the burning liquid Grimm made a movement, a light afflux of blood mounted to his cheeks, he breathed several times with difficulty. Cornillé made him swallow another mouthful. The respiration then became more regular. A few seconds later Grimm opened his eyes. He looked about him with stupefaction; then, closing his eyes again, he fell back heavily on the ground and fainted away.

The case was grave without being hopeless. Before all, it was necessary to transport Grimm to Liberty. He was placed on the litter —still unconscious—and the road to the city was slowly retraced.

On arriving, Grimm was laid on his bed and bled.• This energetic treatment soon produced its effect. Next morning he had completely recovered his senses and was able to get up. But he was very weak and had to be nursed carefully for several days.

Apart from the accident which happened to the antiquary, the sam made no other victims. The damage at Liberty had been insignificant. The centre of the cyclone had passed quite far away, exactly in the place to which the hunters had gone. The Ksar and Babel had not suffered.

Grimmitschoffer, from this day on, showed a deep gratitude towards his friends. But for them he would be lying dead amid the sands. He had more indulgence for the weakness of their minds, narrowed by the illiberal processes of modern criticism. He held their work in higher esteem, in spite of all its incompleteness, and acknowledged that modern man, on the whole, had some good qualities. At bottom Grimm was much better than he appeared to be. A maniac, like all those who make a too exclusive study of antiquity, expressing disdain for the things of the present time, because he had lived too much in the dust of libraries and in the company of old books, his heart had remained confiding and good like that of a child. Finally, he possessed a virtue that has probably been rare at all times—gratitude for services rendered him.

CHAPTER IV.

FROM BABYLON TO THE PERSIAN GULF.

It had been decided that, while awaiting the end of the labors, they would go to the shores of the Persian Gulf in order to study the setting-up of the new works, intended, if the necessity for doing so made itself felt, to transform into electricity the force of the tides, of the waves of the sea and of the winds.

Jack Adams and Monaghan could have undertaken these investigations alone; but Lord Badger and Miss Nelly were particularly anxious to descend the Euphrates, or, more properly speaking, the Shat-el-Arab, to its mouth at the sea. Their journey in the Orient would have seemed incomplete to them if it were not continued to the celebrated gulf which has played so important a rôle in all the international relations of the ancient world and on the shores of which high scientific authorities place the true origin of Arabic civilization.

As to Caluzac, he preferred to stay with his friend Cornillé, either because he felt instinctively that the latter would have need of diversion in the absence of Lord Badger and his daughter, or because, for the moment, he had really enough of traveling. A yet more extraordinary fact was that Grimmitschoffer also declared that he wished to remain in Babylon. In vain Miss Nelly impressed it upon him that they were going to coast along the shores of ancient Chaldea and that he would probably make interesting discoveries. Grimm put on his most solemn and enigmatic air, affirmed that he had nothing further to learn from Chaldea and that the excavations which he had been able to undertake, "thanks to Lord Badger's bounty," added he, bowing courteously, were too important to make it possible for him to abandon them. On the day set for departure, Badger, his daughter, Fatma, Jack Adams and Monaghan were, therefore, the only ones to embark on the *Electricity*. Captain Laycock had insisted that they should hasten to take advantage of the last days during which the Euphrates would still be navigable to its junction with the first affluent which it meets with below Hillah.

When the little ship weighed its anchor, handkerchiefs were waved on both sides, as if a long separation were in question. A quarter of an hour after the departure, Miss Nelly could still perceive in the distance a flag which floated from the top of the tower on the Kasr.

From Babylon to Divaniyeh, the Euphrates offers nothing remarkable. The banks are very low; rice-fields, as far as the eye can reach, where now and then an Arab, bending forward, his bare legs half sunk in the muddy soil, is occupied in laboriously transplanting the stalks of rice.

The current, rapid at first, allowed the *Electricity* to descend the river quickly; but, little by little, the water diminished in breadth and depth. If this continued much longer, they might well ask themselves whether a sufficiently large channel for navigation would be left. Captain Laycock, standing in the middle of the bridge, attentively watched the course of the vessel through these narrow channels.

"It is singular," said Miss Nelly to him at dinner, "the Euphrates becomes narrower as it approaches the sea. It is thus the very opposite of the other rivers, which are almost inlets of the sea at their mouths. Just look at the Thames, the Seine, the Gironde, the Scheldt, the Danube."

"Patience, Miss Badger, the Euphrates will soon do as the other rivers, and will proudly bear the tribute of its abundant waters to the Indian Ocean. The cause of its present narrowness is accidental. Have you forgotten then that the canal of Hindiyah, which begins above Babylon, turns off a portion of its waters to feed the sea of Nedjef? But let this same Hindiyah return, and you will see the Euphrates regain its normal width."

Meanwhile, the river dried up more and more. In the neighborhood of Lamlum the marshes began. The banks, on both sides, were now but immense plains of reeds, from which the sound of the steam, escaping noisily from the boiler, caused myriads of aquatic birds to fly up. The captain was furious at not being able to send a few good shots after them. His sporting instincts were aroused at sight of these innumerable fowls. But delay was not to be thought of—not a minute was to be lost—if they did not want to run the risk of seeing the vessel run aground. It is in the midst of these marshes that the Euphrates has its narrowest point—a little over two hundred feet in width. Its depth also diminished visibly. Several times there had already been heard, under the hull, a singular noise, which gave the captain great uneasiness.

"The boat is grazing the muddy bottom," said he. "If the level of the Euphrates sinks a few inches yet, we shall be unable to advance any farther."

The Euphrates fell over seven inches on that very day.

At four o'clock in the afternoon a violent concussion shook the vessel, whose hull had sunk deeply into a sand-bank. Miss Nelly and Fatma, who were sitting in the saloon, were suddenly thrown to the floor. The very thick carpet softened their fall, so that they received only some light contusions. The other passengers were more or less hurt, but none seriously. A sailor only, hurled head foremost against a corner of the engine-ladder, was picked up unconscious.

In an instant everybody was on deck.

"What is the matter? What has happened?" asked the two young girls, while the men remained silent and impassive.

The captain did not stop to reply to his passengers. He had other cares at that moment than to play the agreeable towards the ladies. He must assure himself before all that the engine was not in danger and that no leak showed itself. The *Electricity* was solidly built and had not suffered. This result ascertained, and then only, the captain returned to his companions and explained to them what had just happened so unexpectedly.

"The ship has run aground on a sand-bank. Have no fear; there is no danger. Is anybody hurt?"

They showed him the sailor, who was still unconscious. He examined him and found that the swoon was caused simply by a rather severe concussion of the brain. By his orders, the wounded man was conveyed to the sailors' quarters and caused to inhale salts. A quarter of an hour later he appeared on deck again, still somewhat stunned, but in a fair way to recovery.

And now, what was to become of them? Would it be possible to extricate themselves? The captain had the engine work backwards. The vessel trembled, but did not back an inch. After an hour's efforts, nothing remained for them to do but to fold their arms. Night had set in. It was best to wait until next day before deciding on what course to take. They descended to the saloon, took supper as if nothing extraordinary had occurred, and went quietly to bed.

Yet the situation might become critical; they were sunk in the mud, amidst an inextricable forest of reeds, and distant from all assistance. But the characteristic of English courage is calmness. We others—we Frenchmen—are second to none as regards intrepidity. Only, we must act this intrepidity *en virtuose*. Our courage is expansive, talkative, exaggerated if need be. To die singing is an essentially French device. If an Englishman were obliged to find its pendant, to die silently is what he would probably inscribe on his escutcheon. According to one's disposition, or perhaps also according to circumstances, one is at liberty to give the preference to English courage or to French valor; one thing is beyond doubt, that the two nations have always found it to their advantage to unite and employ their similar yet different qualities towards a common end.

Next morning, on awaking, Miss Nelly was agreeably surprised to feel the ship moving. She looked out of the cabin window; it was not to be denied, the *Electricity* was running at full speed on the Euphrates; reeds and marshes had disappeared.

"Then I have dreamed last night," she said to herself.

She dressed hastily, without waking Fatma, who was still asleep, and ascended to the deck, where her father was alone with the captain. The latter was saying to his lordship:

"There has been a fresh rise in the water last night. Thanks to this fortunate circumstance, we have been enabled to set the vessel afloat again, and to get off from the sands. We have passed the dangerous point, and we now have nothing similar to fear."

"I felt no uneasiness at any time," replied Badger. "And you, my daughter?"

"Nor I either. You know well, father, that with you I should go without fear to the end of the world."

"You see that I was right, Miss Nelly," said the captain to the young girl, "the Euphrates has regained its original width."

"The Hindiyah has returned then?"

"Yes, we passed its mouth at six o'clock in the morning. You were still asleep. But wait a little, we are soon going to pass a branch of the Tigris."

"How, a branch of the Tigris?"

"Yes, that is strange, isn't it? Above Babylon it is the Euphrates which discharges a part of its waters into the Tigris. Below, it is the Tigris which flows in part into the Euphrates; these alternations show what a small difference in level there is between the basins of the two rivers."

A half hour had hardly elapsed when the *Electricity* passed opposite to the derivation announced by the captain. It was, however, but a broad canal, offering nothing remarkable. Its waters were nevertheless sufficiently abundant to visibly enlarge the bed of the river, and from then on navigation became much more easy.

The region through which they were passing had a less wild appearance. The cultivations became more important; cities were passed. Nazrieh, built at the junction of the Shat-el-Hai—the new derivation of the Tigris and of the Euphrates—held the attention of the travelers to a high degree.

"Why, look, we have come back to Europe," cried Miss Nelly; "see, there are houses like in England."

"We are nevertheless still in Mesopotamia," replied Jack Adams; "only Nazrieh was built by a Belgian engineer, who thought of nothing better—although the climatic conditions were diametrically opposed—than to construct, on the banks of the Tigris and of the Euphrates, a city which was the exact copy of those on the shores of the Meuse or of the Scheldt. At Liberty we have been better inspired."

Nevertheless it was decided to visit the city, as much from interest as from curiosity. Nazrieh might offer peculiarities useful to imitate at Liberty. It is always good to consult the experience of others.

The vessel was passing through ancient Chaldea, the one country in the world which has perhaps exercised the most decisive influence on the destinies of humanity since the times that can be called historic. It is here that the invention of phonetic writing is generally laid. It is true that it is also attributed sometimes to the Phœnicians and to the Egyptians. These employed it for common uses, while the hieroglyphic writing was reserved for sacred uses. It is perhaps correct to attribute the same discovery to several nations. At a certain point of intellectual development, it may happen that nations, having attained the same degree of civilization, make the same inventions simultaneously.

Be that as it may, whether the priority in the most marvelous of man's discoveries belongs to Chaldea or not, there is another kind of glory which cannot be denied it—that of having been the religious instructress of the white, Semitic and Japhetic races. The native land of the three great monotheistic religions—Judaism, Christianity and Islamism—our traditions, our legends come to us from her, and, thanks to the European spirit of initiation and of propagation, they will soon have made the tour of the world.

Alas! Chaldea has fallen greatly from its ancient splendor. Entire cities here are built of reeds. Our travelers saw an example of this when passing before Suk-e-Sheyukh. The successors of those who instructed the world have now only slight branches to shelter them from the inclemencies of the weather. This results from the difference of the races. If the soil is less fertile, if the pestilential marshes and barren sands have replaced well-tilled fields and fertile plains, the fault must be charged to the carelessness of the present inhabitants. The ancient Chaldeans were courageous and industrious men, the modern Arab returns to nomadic life.

After a journey of several days the *Electricity* arrived at the junction of the two rivers. A large village, Kurna, is situated at the very extremity of the point.

The appearance of the two rivers differs entirely.

"You might believe yourself to be at Lyons," said Miss Nelly, "at the junction of the Rhone and the Saone. While the Tigris is the Rhone with its impetuosity and its dizzy rapidity, the Euphrates represents the slow and majestic course of the Saone."

"Do you know the signification of the word Tigris?" Monaghan asked the young girl.

"Not at all."

"Tigris means arrow."

"Then it is very well named. You call to my mind that, according to my old professor of geography, Rhone comes from the Celtic and signifies rapid river, but *arrow* seems to me a more happy name."

The stream of water formed by the union of the Tigris and the Euphrates, and which bears the name of Shat-el-Arab, presents a magnificent appearance. Its broad sheet seems boundless. The banks are low; river, plain and sky are confounded in one undecided line. The blue of the firmament tinges the waves; the rays of the sun cause the sands of the desert to glisten far and wide; all is but one sheaf of light, one immense glow.

"How beautiful it is!" Miss Nelly murmured again and again, leaning on the balustrade of the ship. "I have never seen anything like it."

In the neighborhood of Bassorah the landscape was not the same. The plantations of date-trees formed veritable forests. The view, instead of extending boundlessly towards all points of the horizon, was bounded on the right and on the left by a curtain of verdure.

They were rapidly approaching the sea. The tides began to make themselves felt.

These tides are not very strong, for the Persian Gulf, which is, as it were, a pendant of the Red Sea, or Arabian Gulf, is, like the latter, deeply embanked in the land and communicates with the Indian Ocean only by the narrow inlet of the Strait of Ormuz. Nevertheless, on account of the small elevation of the banks of the river, its waters, mingled with the waves of the sea, inundate the forests of palms twice a day at high tide.

Under the influence of this constant moisture, and of the sea-salt which forms an excellent manure for them, the date-trees of Bassorah give the best dates in the whole world.

They stopped a whole day at Bassorah. Badger was desirous of visiting some of his compatriots who have established important banking and commercial houses in this city. This time they had returned entirely to civilization. The new city, built on the banks of the river, is wholly European in appearance, in manners and in language.

For all that, or perhaps even on account of that, it had little attraction for our travelers. A striking proof of the facility with which one becomes disaccustomed to the civilization of the cities if one has only tasted free and independent life.

Old Bassorah interested them more. Like Venice, it is built on canals, the walls of its buildings plunging directly into the water.

The interrupted voyage was resumed with pleasure. They were in haste to reach the shores of the sea. Down to Fao, a small city situated at the very mouth of the river, the panorama remained the same —forests of date-palms, fruit-trees in abundance, well-cultivated fields, which seemed of an extraordinary fertility; at times immense surfaces covered with wheat.

"One cannot imagine the fertility of the soil," said Monaghan. "There are years in which the abundance of the crops is such that the natives feed their cattle with wheat, and the cattle even being unable to consume it entirely, they are compelled to use it as fuel."

"And to think," remarked Jack Adams, "that at the same time whole villages are dying of hunger in India! Yet it would be easy to transport this excess of wheat over there."

"Yes; but the inertia and the fatalism of the populations stand in the way. They would sooner die of hunger than seek their food abroad."

"You must also take into account the indifference and the severity of the European governments. When they pose as the guardians and protectors of populations which are subjected, professedly in their own interest, they take charge of souls and should fulfil all the duties of a good father of a family to his helpless children."

At Fao the expedition left the *Electricity* to proceed by caravan to the southwest extremity of the Persian Gulf.

As they left the Shat-el-Arab all trace of vegetation gradually disappeared and they found themselves once more in the midst of the barren and desolate desert.

At last they perceived in the distance the great Indian Ocean, whose blue waves were dying away on the golden sands.

The camp, which was to stand for five or six days only, was fixed at a little distance from the shore.

Opposite, and separated from the main land by a narrow arm of the sea, lay a small, sandy island, the island of Waraba, and, farther off, out at sea, another island, larger than the first, that of Bubian. It was on these two islets that Jack Adams had thought he would be able to place the apparatus destined to convert the waves, the tides and the winds into electricity.

... The day has been warm and the journey fatiguing. The evening is splendid. The sky is studded with thousands of stars, among which several constellations, unknown to the skies of the north, shine with an intense brightness.

The fires of the bivouac have been lit. The waves reflect the flame in long, red columns, which seem to repeat themselves endlessly. The chardavars, stretched out on the sand in a state of complete immobility, are sleeping, entirely enveloped in their white burnous. Only Badger and his companions are still talking of the object which has brought them so far from their country.

These men, who appear so small and so mean in the presence of the boundless space which surrounds them on all sides, these men possess the lever which moves the world—they have faith. They believe in the almost illimitable power of science. They have confidence in the word which has promised to man the empire of the world: "Replenish the earth and you shall subdue it." That is to say, make use of the very forces of nature itself for subduing it and compelling it to execute the orders of intelligence and thought. A day would come when the wind, which now uselessly raised the sands of the desert, would serve to illuminate the reconstructed cities; when the waves which were dying away at the feet of Badger and of Jack Adams would serve to move the railways which would place the Mediterranean and the Indies in communication.

Next morning the necessary preparations were made for passing over to the two islands. They had brought with them a small steel boat that could be taken apart, sufficiently large for crossing small arms of the sea without danger.

In half an hour all the parts of the boat scattered on the sand were fitted together, and the little craft was ready to go to sea. Guided by Captain Laycock, who held the rudder, and propelled by two stout oarsmen, it had quickly crossed the strait which separates the island of Waraba from the coast.

After a minute examination on the part of Jack Adams and Monaghan, they went back to the boat, which had passed around the island and was lying at the shore opposite to that on which they had landed.

The arm of the sea which separates the two islands was also crossed without difficulty, and they set foot on the soil of Bubian.

Waraba is but an islet; Bubian is much larger and its height above the level of the sea much more considerable.

After having studied the geological formation and drawn the topographical plan of the two islands, Monaghan and Jack Adams desired to fathom the depth of the arm of the sea which separates Waraba from the mainland and Bubian from Waraba.

This operation finished, they entered the boat again to return to camp. On the same evening, after dinner, Monaghan and Jack Adams, having written out their notes and verified their calculations, were able to acquaint Lord Badger with the result of their investigation.

Here, in a few words, are the conclusions at which they had arrived: the island of Bubian was larger and more elevated above the level of the sea than they had supposed. It alone would be sufficient for setting up the apparatus.

Waraba, much smaller, would be sacrificed in part. Two dams were to be constructed at each of its extremities, intended to connect it on one side with the mainland and on the other with Bubian.

"In this way," continued Jack Adams, "I shall obtain a lake of which Waraba will be the centre. That island will disappear almost completely beneath the waters, for I shall make use of its sands for constructing the dikes."

"Then the sea does not suffice you any more?" observed Miss Nelly. "At present, behold, you need a lake!"

"Certainly. I shall fill this lake at the time of high tide by opening flood-gates, and, at low tide, I shall open other sluices in order to precipitate the waters of the lake into the sea."

"I understand now; you will cause the water to fall on turbines, which will set dynamo-electric machines in motion."

"That is it, exactly, Miss Badger. Not only will the turbines turn when the lake becomes empty, but it will also be possible to set them in rotation when the lake fills up. In this way there will always be but little time lost during the day."

"It seems to me," said Monaghan, "that I have heard another means for utilizing the tides spoken of favorably."

"Yes; but it appears to me much less practical than the first. It consists in making use of the rise of the waters for compressing the air in a receiver."

"What is the disadvantage of this system?"

"It requires apparatus that are too complicated and too costly."

"But," said Lord Badger in his turn, "do you not fear that the construction of your dikes will require considerable labor and will, consequently, be very expensive?"

"I do not think so. The result of our soundings has been to show that the depth of the water does not exceed fifteen feet in any place."

"That is little, indeed. And where do you intend to place your mills?"

"On a series of isolated knolls formed of resistant sand, which lie not far from the shore towards the eastern part of the island. On these heights nothing will obstruct the action of the wind. Besides, they will have the advantage of standing near to the site marked out for the construction of the hydraulic works."

Four days had sufficed for completing the studies and surveys which were the object of the journey. They retraced the road followed before and embarked again on the *Electricity* at Fao.

At Bassorah they heard news from London. The *Davy* and the *Faraday* had finished loading and were on the point of going to sea again.

All went well as far as Kurna, the point of junction of the two rivers. Above Kurna the navigation on the Euphrates became difficult. At Samava they had to abandon the idea of ascending farther. They said adieu to Captain Laycock, who returned to Bassorah to await the arrival of the two transports there, and procured the necessary horses and mules for returning to Liberty by the land route.

This last part of the journey was marked by an event which might have had tragical consequences. The road followed by the caravan ran along near to the banks of the river. During a halt Miss Nelly and Fatma had separated a little from the rest of their companions to pick some flowers which grew among the reeds. A profound silence reigned around them, and wholly engrossed in their pleasure, the unfortunate girls little suspected that a terrible enemy had been watching them for several minutes. While they were advancing joyously to the edge of the water to draw the stalks of the flowers towards them, laughing when one of these stalks slipped from their grasp, an enormous crocodile, which slept extended on the sand, had waked up and was attentively following all their movements. Suddenly it rushed forward in their direction, opening its wide jaws, ready to devour them.

At the noise which the broad feet of the monster made in passing over the sand, the young girls turned around and uttered cries of terror. They tried to flee. Their road was closed on all sides. On the right and left, an inextricable mass of reeds; in the middle of the road left open, the crocodile, which was slowly advancing.

As if assured that its prey could not escape it, it stood still for a few seconds. This short interval sufficed for Fatma to come to a supreme resolution. Feeling that she was lost, she and her mistress, the poor girl determined to save her companion at the risk of her own life.

Advancing in front of the crocodile, which was watching her with its green eyes:

"Good-bye, dear Nelly," said she; "save yourself."

Comprehending Fatma's admirable self-sacrifice, Miss Nelly sprang forward in her turn to hold back her friend. It was too late. The crocodile had already seized the border of the dress of the unfortunate girl, who, thrown down by the shock, had rolled over on the grass. Suddenly, at the moment when the monster rushed forward a second time to seize her in the middle of the body, a gunshot rang out and the crocodile sank heavily to the ground. Three seconds later Monaghan, his still smoking gun in his hand, raised up the unconscious Fatma, while Miss Nelly, who had come up beside her, tried to bring her to. As the crocodile still gave some signs of life, Monaghan discharged a second shot point blank at it, shattering its head.

When Badger and Jack Adams, attracted by the sound of the two shots which the geologist had fired off, and by Miss Nelly's cries of distress, came up, they found Fatma recovered from her swoon and sobbing, a prey to a nervous fit, a very natural result of the terrible shock which she had received.

"What has happened?" asked Lord Badger, anxiously.

Monaghan told him how that, while hunting wild ducks near by, he had heard the cries of the two young girls and had hurried to their assistance. It was high time, for he had found Fatma thrown down and the crocodile preparing to devour her.

As to Miss Nelly, she had fallen on her father's neck, trembling all over. As soon as her agitation permitted her to speak, she told him how Fatma had wished to sacrifice herself to save her.

"Dear, dear Fatma!" exclaimed Badger, with tears in his eyes, clasping the young girl in his arms; "brave and generous soul! From this day on I have another daughter. Were it not for your admirable sacrifice it would be all over with my Nelly. And you, my dear Monaghan," added he, after a moment, grasping the geologist's hand, "you have done your duty nobly. Count on me at all times."

"My lord," the latter replied, simply, "what I have done every one else would have done in my place. Besides, I am amply rewarded by the very service itself that I have been able to render our two companions."

They slowly retraced the way to the encampment. Fatma, supported on one side by Lord Badger's arm, on the other by Miss Nelly's, gradually recovered. She told them that from the moment when she advanced towards the monster she no longer knew what happened. Stunned by the shock, she had immediately lost consciousness and had not even heard the two shots fired by Monaghan.

"I thought," said Badger to the latter, "that there were no crocodiles in Mesopotamia, no more in the Euphrates than in the Tigris."

"The opinions are divided on this subject," replied the geologist. "Some naturalists assert that they are met with, others deny it absolutely. At any rate, it is certain that these animals are extremely rare. But we have to-day obtained the proof that there are still some in existence and that this malevolent species is not wholly destroyed."

On their return to camp Badger proposed that they should defer their departure until the day after, and rest during the remainder of the day and the following night, so as to give Fatma time to recover completely. But Monaghan was of the opinion that the diversion and the fatigue of the journey could only be favorable for the convalescent by effecting a happy diversion on her nerves.

The journey to Babylon was, therefore, resumed in the evening, and a few days later the caravan had the pleasure of being once more in

Liberty. No, traveling in summer was decidedly not agreeable. It was decided that they should quietly await the return of the cooler days of autumn before undertaking new expeditions. The life which they led at Liberty then resumed, outwardly, its accustomed course; nothing was changed, apparently. Yet, any one who might have possessed the gift of reading hearts could have prognosticated, without fear of being mistaken, that it was all over with the delightful and peaceful intimacy of former times. Already it became easy to foresee that many storms were on the point of breaking forth, the consequences of which would compromise not only the happiness of those concerned, but the very prospects of the work itself.

The success of this work had been due in a great measure to the perfect harmony which, until then, had not ceased to exist between all the members of the association. Under the inevitable pressure of human passions this harmony was on the point of disappearing.

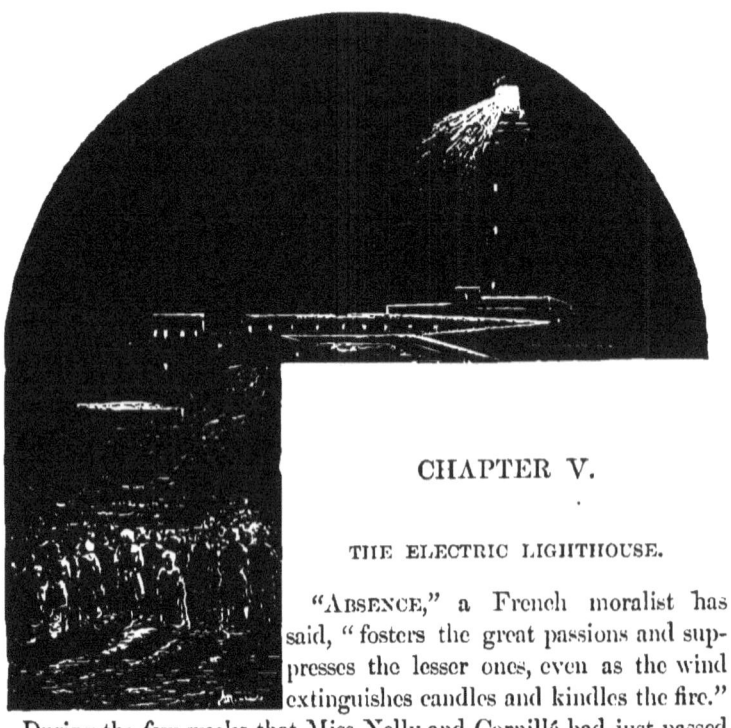

CHAPTER V.

THE ELECTRIC LIGHTHOUSE.

"ABSENCE," a French moralist has said, " fosters the great passions and suppresses the lesser ones, even as the wind extinguishes candles and kindles the fire."

During the few weeks that Miss Nelly and Cornillé had just passed at a distance from each other, they had had ample leisure to examine their hearts carefully, and to ascertain whether the sentiment which they felt for each other was simply a deception of the heart, a fancy of the imagination, born of the circumstances which had brought them together during many months, or whether it had the positive and earnest character of an affection capable of orienting a whole lifetime.

The result of this inward inquiry was the same for both of those concerned. Cornillé decided that he would never love another woman than Miss Nelly; she, for her part, after having well examined herself, felt entirely ready to sacrifice prejudices of rank and fortune for the man whose name, she rightly thought, she would one day be not only happy, but proud to bear.

Women possess a great advantage over men; they are rarely mistaken as to the sentiments which they inspire. Miss Nelly was thus in advance of Cornillé inasmuch as she was absolutely certain of the young Frenchman's love, while he was still asking himself whether he was really the preferred one.

Since the scene in the hall of the electric motors, no particular incident had occurred between the two young people. Miss Nelly seemed even to avoid being alone with Cornillé, and to seek Jack Adams' society in preference. It was he to whom she now applied when she had some information or an explanation to ask for. It was his company which she demanded when a visit to the Kasr or to Babel was in question.

Cornillé, a novice as yet in the study of the human heart, was hurt by this conduct. "Is she not free," said he to himself, "to choose whom she will; why this manœuvre of seeming to hold equal balance between two men who are friends to-day, as if she wished to make rivals of them to-morrow?" And he was almost disposed to accuse Miss Nelly of coquetry.

In this he was completely mistaken. The young Englishwoman was too proud; she had too just a consciousness of her worth to take such an attitude. In trying to react against the sentiment which drew her towards Cornillé, and which she felt to be governing her greatly, she was, on the contrary, obeying the most noble feelings.

By the very reason of her more refined nature and the perhaps higher conception of duty which she has formed, the consequences of a bad choice are still much more to be dreaded for woman than for man. Every young girl feels this truth instinctively, even before her reason is sufficiently developed to enable her to account for it. Hence, when a choice is to be made, there is a hesitation which hardly ever exists with the young man, and which has often the appearance of caprice and coquetry.

Our friend Cornillé had allowed himself to be deceived by this appearance like any ordinary mortal. It was not long before he was undeceived.

A few days before their departure for the Persian Gulf, Jack Adams, Miss Nelly and Fatma were walking one afternoon towards the Kasr, when, at a turn of the road, they met Cornillé, who, for his part, was going to the works at Babel. Cornillé greeted them politely; but his face immediately took on so sad an expression that Miss Nelly experienced a feeling almost of remorse. She asked the young man to accompany them to the top of the tower. Cornillé hesitated an instant. The eyes of the young girl were fixed upon him at this moment. They expressed so sincere an astonishment and so eloquent a reproach, that it would have shown bad grace indeed to be sulky notwithstanding. The four together, therefore, continued the way to the Kasr.

"Poor Cornillé," said Fatma to her mistress, at a moment when they had allowed themselves to be distanced by the engineers, "there were tears in his eyes when he saw you pass with Mr. Jack Adams."

"He is wrong," replied Miss Nelly, simply, "for he loves me, and I love him, too."

The visit to the Kasr passed off most smoothly; they talked machines, electricity; they spoke of new Babylon and of its destiny. The conversation kept in a serious channel, without deviating towards any of those subjects which come almost naturally in a conversation between young people:—their tastes, each one's predilections, the estimate of a book, of a piece of music—and where, each one's personality being necessarily implicated, it becomes easy to hint at what one does not wish to express plainly. Nevertheless, Cornillé appeared to have completely recovered his serenity. The truth is that a really sincere person possesses a moral ascendency which it is impossible to escape. Miss Nelly's look—that look marked by an undeniable honesty—had been sufficient to cause Cornillé, who was surprised in his injustice, to be pierced to the depths of his heart with regret at having even been able to suspect her.

Nevertheless, from this day on until the one fixed upon for the departure, Miss Nelly, under the pretext of having preparations to make, remained almost always locked up in her room, except at meal hours and in the evening, when, the whole party being gathered together, she was sure never to run the risk of finding herself alone with Cornillé or Jack Adams. She came but seldom into the parlor, and went out only when accompanied by her father. A new occurrence, which it is time to mention, imposed this rigorous caution upon her.

Absorbed by another sentiment, and not very vain by nature, Lord Badger's charming daughter had never said to herself that Cornillé was not the only one to live in a daily intimacy with her, and that, also young, good-looking in appearance, and likewise destined for a brilliant future, Jack Adams might believe he had the right—for the same reason as his French colleague—of loving her, and flatter himself with the hope of being also loved by her.

It was during the visit to the Kasr that she had, for the first time, a sudden intuition, as it were, of the situation. Then, recalling to mind many apparently trifling circumstances, to which she had attached no importance, and observing attentively Jack Adams' attitude, she no longer retained any doubt: Cornillé was not the only one who loved her; Jack Adams and he were rivals, and rivals without knowing it.

This discovery, which might perhaps have exalted an ordinary woman with pride, filled Miss Nelly, on the contrary, with sadness. She immediately comprehended the seriousness of the situation, reproached herself for her innocent Machiavelism, which had perhaps encouraged the hopes of Jack Adams, whom she esteemed, although she had little sympathy for him. In an instant her resolution was taken. For several weeks she was going to be separated from Cornillé and in constant relation with Jack Adams. The latter must understand from her attitude that he was forbidden to hope.

As to the former, she must examine herself seriously on his account, and, if she felt herself resolved to sacrifice all to be his wife, not hesitate to pledge him her faith. In the opposite case she must, even at the risk of being misjudged, confess to him honestly that she had been mistaken as to the nature of the sentiment which she felt for him, and bid him renounce all hope of ever obtaining her hand.

It was with this intention that she had left. Her handshake with Cornillé at parting expressed an affection at the same time so grave and so moving, that the young man understood that his fate was to be decided forever. There was such a harmony between these two beings, an esteem so complete and absolute, that Cornillé did not doubt that, whatever his beloved one's decision would be, it would be worthy of her and of him. He felt within him the power to await the decree which was to decide his fate, if not without anxiety, at least with a calm and manly resignation.

This digression, absolutely indispensable in order that the sequence of events may be understood, has caused us to turn back for several weeks. Let us now return to the point at which we discontinued our story, that is to say, at the return of the caravan to Liberty.

"How is your thermo-solar pile getting on?" asked Miss Nelly smilingly of Cornillé, when she found herself alone with him for a moment after lunch next day.

"Very well. My expectations are being realized; it will be completed in the month of November, and in the spring it will be possible to set it in operation."

"Good! Until then you must not think of anything else. Your first duty is towards your work; as long as it is not completed, no diversion is permitted."

"You depend greatly upon my courage, *mademoiselle?*"

"I count very much on my own. So, is it agreed?"
"Your wishes are orders."
"Thank you."

She held out her hand to him, and he kept it for an instant between his own.

"Miss Nelly! dear Miss Nelly?"
"Hush," said she, disengaging herself, while happy Cornillé, stand-

ing motionless in the same place, seemed like a man who was suddenly to see the sky open over his head.

In thus postponing the time at which she should authorize Cornillé to declare himself officially, Miss Nelly had had no intention of imposing a time of probation upon him, which she deemed useless, for she was quite sure of the engineer's love. She dreaded the consequences of an avowed rivalry between him and Jack Adams, and hoped, by gaining time, to see all traces of this rivalry disappear. Already Jack Adams seemed to have understood the significance of her more marked reserve towards himself; in a few months, thought she, he will be completely cured of a passion without a possible issue, and will resign himself philosophically to his friend's happiness.

Miss Nelly had decided that Jack Adams' ruling passion was pride, and she believed him to be but little accessible to sentiment. In this she was not mistaken; but what she was not aware of, was the extremes to which wounded pride can drive a violent nature and a vindictive mind.

At present, everything was quiet as yet. The labors were pushed on without intermission at the works of the Kasr and of Babel. Jack Adams and Cornillé united their efforts so that everything should be finished at the commencement of the rainy season. Work was not wanting.

The *Davy* and the *Faraday* had arrived at Bassorah in the first days of July. There was no possibility of transporting the new material to Babylon by way of the river. They had thus found themselves under the necessity of having all of it carried on camels' backs. A slow, expensive, and inconvenient way; but there was no other course to take.

The hydraulic works of the upper Tigris were kept in regular electric communication with Liberty. In the middle of the month of August all were finally completed. The underground wires connected them with the central works of the Kasr. They were only awaiting the first rains of autumn and the rising of the Tigris in order to send torrents of electricity to Babylon and charge the accumulators to repletion.

During the months of August and September the weather remained dry; but, from the first days in October, the telegraph reported abundant rains in the valley of the upper Tigris, and on the 17th the manager of the works at Jezireh telegraphed to Lord Badger that the waters of the Tigris were high and the machines ready to work.

At noon precisely the electric fluid arrived like an impetuous flood at the extremity of the wires. From the wires it was caused to pass into the accumulators, which were to be charged successively.

Badger and his companions, collected together in the hall of the accumulators, are anxiously following the movements of the apparatus. The engineers, the builders, and the foremen are there to watch the progress of the final experiment. Everything goes on as well as could be desired. The first accumulator only has been placed in communication with the wires. At the end of eight minutes the bubbling is heard which is produced by the tumultuous escaping of oxygen and hydrogen, announcing that the accumulator is completely charged.

Jack Adams takes his note-book and his pencil and puts down some figures. When his calculations are finished:

"Gentlemen," says he, "in twenty-four hours we shall have charged two hundred elements; that is to say, the wherewithal to begin the electric lighting of Liberty. To-morrow evening Babylon will be lit up by the force drawn from the sources of the Tigris."

The engineer then placed the wires in communication with the first series of the accumulators. All those present watched him work with curiosity. The hands of the works, less familiar than their superiors with the theories of science and with mathematical abstractions, loudly expressed their astonishment at sight of these long copper wires, covered with silk and gutta-percha, proceeding in all directions in an apparent disorder. That which seemed most extraordinary was to persuade oneself that these wires were really traversed by streams of electricity.

"It is certain," said Badger, "that all this strangely confuses the imagination. The mind refuses to believe in such wonders."

"I confess it is amazing," replied Jack Adams. "More than once I too have stopped, pensive, before the iron wires of a telegraph. Eh! what, I said to myself, is it possible that at this moment words, sentences are circulating in this wire? I am in London, and there, through this base metal, through this inert matter, there comes from Calcutta the announcement of a brilliant inheritance, of a birth, of a death. All is silent around me, and yet here is passing the message which traverses continents and seas with the rapidity of lightning."

"When a vessel," added Cornillé, "passes through the Mediterranean from Gibraltar to the shores of Asia Minor, as our *Electricity* has done, the passengers sail more than once over cables which bind the continents together, without thinking that human thought is passing at a few yards below their feet. Yes, my dear friend, you are right, there is something here to astonish even those who are the authors of these wonders."

"As for me," said Miss Nelly, "it seems to me that I am the plaything of a dream. I cannot imagine that this inert wire, offering absolutely nothing extraordinary either to the sight or to the touch, should be at this moment the seat of a current of force which started over six hundred miles from here a thousandth of a second ago. I cannot believe that this force

is accumulated in these equally inert bits of lead."

"And yet, miss, to-morrow evening you will certainly be obliged to believe it, when the place here will be lit up as in broad daylight."

In support of his words, Jack Adams showed, in all its details, the electric lamp destined to throw a bright light over all the region.

"Your lamp," observed Cornillé, "is truly of gigantic proportions. I have never seen the like of it."

"This is true. It was necessary to have in our possession a luminous source of considerable intensity. Electricity shall not fail us, and it is a question of illuminating a very large area."

"What is the power of this lamp?"

"I estimate it at thirty thousand Carcel lamps at the least. This intensity of light corresponds to one hundred and fifty horse power, expended at this moment in any one of the works of the upper Tigris. That is about one-fifth of the total force over which we can dispose up there. You see thus, my dear Cornillé, that this lighthouse, notwithstanding all its power, will consume for itself but the fifth part of the electricity which the hydraulic works send to Babylon."

During all the afternoon of the following day Liberty was invaded by a numerous crowd, arriving from all directions. The report of the evening's experiment had spread quickly since the day before to Hillah and to the neighboring villages. Notwithstanding their supercilious affectation of indifference towards all that comes from the west, the natives had not been able to resist the temptation of seeing a new sun lit by the power of man.

The streets of Liberty offered a most picturesque spectacle. Groups of Arabs, squatting on the ground in oriental fashion, took their frugal repast in the shadow of the houses, and patiently awaited the night. Sheiks arrived, magnificently draped in their white burnous, their fine weapons sparkling in the sun, and mounted on mettlesome and richly caparisoned horses. Curious people of lower degree had united to travel by caravan. The tents raised around the city, the camels and the asses tied to stakes fixed in the ground, gave Liberty the appearance of a sort of intrenched camp. Yet, in this varied multitude, there was nothing of the din and tumult, the deafening uproar of the European crowds. This gathering, composed only of men, and where neither the silvery voices of women nor the joyous cries of children were heard, remained impassive and calm, at least in appearance, notwithstanding its feverish expectation.

Badger received the visits of several sheiks and caids of the oases, some of whom, already known to him, introduced their friends and relatives, who were desirous in their turn to see the "great Christian chief." He talked long with them, and spoke to them of the experiments which he was going to try. On returning among the crowd, these sheiks in turn related all that the English lord had just told them. Curiosity was thus excited only the more, and the end of the day was awaited with great impatience.

At seven o'clock the last accumulator was charged. They had to telegraph to the upper Tigris to have the movement of the turbines stopped. The current being interrupted, it was unnecessary to let the apparatus act to no purpose. Next morning the turbines were to be set in motion again, and the accumulators charged anew for the illumination of the lighthouse.

At last the sun set. Badger and all his companions proceeded towards the plain which extended at the foot of the Kasr, so as to be well opposite to the projection of the luminous rays. He was followed by the hands of the works and by the crowd of natives. Not a cry was uttered. An almost religious silence reigned. All, civilized and native, collected amid these deserts, felt themselves under the influence of the strange, of the inexplicable. For the first time the electric light was to flash out in these solitudes and illumine the ruins of the most famous of ancient cities.

Twilight does not last long in these low latitudes; yet they desired to wait until it had been entirely night for some time, so that the sudden transition from darkness to light should be more striking.

Time passed slowly; the stars, becoming brighter and brighter, sparkled by myriads in the firmament, where the milky way extended like a broad phosphorescent belt.

"What a beautiful night!" murmured Miss Nelly into her father's ear.

"Yes, dear child, heaven favors our attempts. It loves the bold ones who strive to wrest its secrets from it for the good of humanity."

"Is it not strange that science is at times accused of impiety?"

"Very strange, indeed," said Badger, with a certain solemnity, "for science is God himself."

At this moment nine o'clock was heard to strike from the church of Liberty. Badger, rising immediately, set fire to a rocket planted in the ground before him. The rocket described a curve in the air, and, at the same instant, the lighthouse of Liberty was lit up by an immense jet of light.

Surprised and almost blinded, the Arabs remained for a moment speechless and startled. Then, all at once, the air resounded with their cries. Fond, above all, of the marvelous, this spectacle enraptured them to deliriousness, and their enthusiasm no longer knew any bounds. Allah! Allah! Allah! they repeated, prostrating themselves, and raising their arms toward heaven. Then there was a hubbub of confused voices, of varied exclamations. One thing that seemed to astonish them greatly was to see the excessively lengthened and intensely black shadows which their bodies projected behind them. Like great children, they amused themselves by making the most grotesque contortions in order to laugh at the images which they thus obtained on the sand.

Suddenly the light was extinguished. Darkness set in, black, thick, all the more intense as the transition had been more rapid. By an effect of contrast due to the strain on the retina under the too bright impression of the electric light, the sky, just before diaphanous, now appeared black as ink. The cries ceased instantly. At the end of three seconds the lighthouse was lit again definitely.

"Why this interruption?" Miss Nelly asked her father.

"That was in the programme, Jack Adams wanted to surprise the curious."

"Then he has well succeeded," said the young girl, laughing.

It was midnight when the lighthouse ceased to shine. Those present had been informed as to the hour at which the light would be extinguished, so that each one could reach his tent or his inn as easily as in broad daylight.

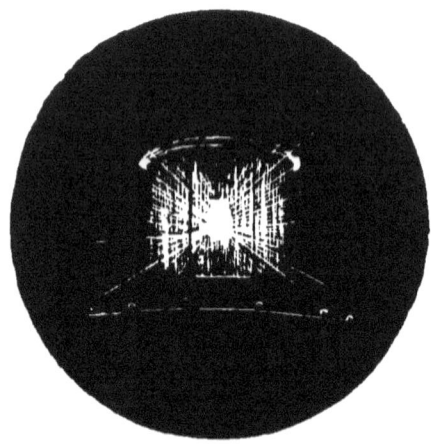

CHAPTER VI.

THE LIGHTING OF LIBERTY.

THE next day was still more fruitful in wonders than the preceding one. The lighthouse, notwithstanding all its power, was mere child's play for engineers such as Jack Adams and Cornillé. The question now was to light up the streets and the houses of Liberty. It was also necessary to light up the two works of the Kasr and of Babel, so that the work might be continued during the night.

Two different systems were to be employed for this purpose: the voltaic arc, obtained by Jablochkoff lamps, was to serve for lighting the streets and the halls of the Kasr and of Babel; as to the houses, it was expedient to make use of the incandescent light, softer and easier to handle than the voltaic arc.

During the whole day the workmen were in motion. The lamps had to be put in their places, the connection of the wires made sure of; in a word, it was necessary that nothing should be overlooked, so as to be certain of success.

Towards three o'clock the excitement began to be very great again in the streets of Liberty. The crowd of curious ones had grown still larger since the day before.

The rest of the afternoon passed in the greatest quiet. At the supper hour this crowd dispersed to take some nourishment, whether under the tents, or in the inns of the city, or simply in the open air, on the sand or the grass of the meadows. Liberty was abundantly provided with victuals of every kind. Badger had given orders that food should be distributed gratuitously to every one. The oriental people are remarkably moderate. A handful of farina, a little water, a few dates or dried figs, that is what, for an Arab, constitutes an excellent repast. The liberality of his lordship did not need, therefore, to involve him very deeply.

As on the day before, they waited until the darkness was complete before giving the signal for the illumination.

This time the effect was still more striking. As quick as lightning all the streets, all the houses, all the shops, were lit up wonderfully. Electric lamps were distributed everywhere in profusion.

The enthusiasm had been great on the night before; this evening it was indescribable. It was delirium—it was folly. The natives went through all the shops, into all the houses, and found new causes for amazement everywhere. The coffee-houses, sparkling in the light of innumerable lamps, especially excited their admiration.

Meanwhile the cry : " Fire ! fire !" rang out at one extremity of the city.

The crowd immediately rushed towards the fire. When it arrived, all danger was already over. It was only a board that had taken fire, and a large pail of water, thrown over it, had been sufficient to extinguish it.

Jack Adams, who was walking with Cahuzac in the neighborhood of the house where the fire had broken out, at the moment when the first flames were perceived, had immediately divined the cause of the fire, while Cahuzac extinguished the burning board. The two immediately came back to the place where their friends were, to reassure them as to the consequences of the accident.

"How did it happen?" Badger asked Jack Adams.

"That is very simple. We are lit up at this moment by more than six thousand lamps. The conductors, of a large diameter on leaving the works, grow gradually thinner, until they are turned into simple wires at the moment when they enter the houses. These conductors are of copper, and enclosed in tubes of iron from which they are separated by hemp and petroleum. Now, the heat developed in the copper wires being so much the greater as they are thinner, it happened that the current was intense enough to bring one of the wires to red heat and set fire to the board against which it was fastened. I had but to cut this wire in order to destroy the source of the evil. Our friend Cahuzac has done the rest by throwing water on the board."

"But is there no means of preventing this accident, which can become very serious in a large number of cases, and menace a whole city with conflagration?"

"Why yes, and this means is employed everywhere in Liberty. At the point where the wires enter a house, a wire of fusible metal is intercalated, which is intended to melt and to interrupt the current in the possible case that this current should become strong enough to damage the lamps or bring the inner wires to red heat."

"But now?" . . . remarked Cahuzac.

"In this case," continued Jack Adams, "it is probable that they forgot to put in this fusible wire. I shall go to assure myself of it to-morrow morning. With regard to this, observe the great superiority of electricity over gas as a means of public lighting. What precautions must be taken for gas when it is desired to interrupt the communication with the street-pipe! If this pipe is cut off, it must be hermetically closed in order to prevent the escape of gas. What dangers there are then to fear! With electricity there is nothing of this. The wire is cut, and that is all; the electricity cannot escape from the cut."

Recovered from the short panic caused by the threatened conflagration, the crowd had begun to move about again, less rough, however, more calmly and quietly, for one becomes surfeited of everything, even of the marvels and miracles of science. Besides, a new surprise was expected, and everybody proceeded towards the Kasr, which—at eleven o'clock precisely—was in its turn to be lit up. The crowds massed themselves on the immense meadows which separate the town from the works.

Eleven o'clock struck; instantaneously, as if by the stroke of a magic wand, the last vestige of that which once was great Babylon was one blaze from base to summit.

It was a gigantic pyramid of light, a formidable accumulation of electric lamps. All the details of the works appeared as if in broad daylight. At the top of the tower the lighthouse threw out its light far and wide over the plain. This time the spectacle truly approached the sublime.

"It has caused tears to come into my eyes," said good Monaghan naively to Badger.

The gates were opened and the public was permitted to move about in all parts of the Kasr. The crowd was seen to go up the spiral road and overrun the highest stories of the works. Ten minutes later there could be seen moving about on the platform above, and under the brilliant light of the lighthouse, thousands of heads surmounted by white haiks wound around with cords of camel's hair.

On that evening the steam and petroleum engines were also put into requisition. The accumulators, charged by means of the works on the Tigris, furnished the light of the lighthouse and of Liberty; the dynamo-engines, worked by coal and petroleum, served to light up the buildings of the Kasr.

Jack Adams turned the powerful rays of the lighthouse on to the ruins with which the plain of Babylon is studded. Some of these ruins presented a strange and truly fantastic appearance: under the intense brilliancy of the electric light, which effaces the penumbra, the tells resembled raging waves on a stormy sea.

At the foot of one of these hillocks, situated at about a mile from Liberty, a man was perceived, armed with a pick-axe, who was feverishly digging the ground. He was lit up in his work by a lantern suspended from the end of a stick. It was easy to recognize Grimm, who, since the electric experiments had begun, was more than ever bent on his excavations. He raised his head for a moment, looked in the direction of the lighthouse, and set to work at digging again.

After the ruins the turn came for the banks of the Euphrates. The city of Hillah and its oasis of palm-trees were caused to sparkle in the jets of light and to cast their reflections into the waters of the river.

A curious sight was then seen: the terraces of all the houses were occupied by the feminine population of the city, attracted by the

beauty of the spectacle. Believing themselves to be quite safe from indiscreet eyes, the young as well as the old showed themselves without veils and in the rich variety of their beautiful indoor costumes. The Europeans were thus enabled to see several pretty faces which, were it not for this fortunate circumstance, would have remained entirely unknown to them. Was the incident to the taste of all the husbands present at Liberty? That is a thing that it would be rash to assert; but we may at least be certain that, according to the custom in all countries of the world, there was not a single woman who, on the return of her lord and master, would not be able to persuade him that she had acted for the best.

Besides, the poor recluses seemed to take so great a delight in the enchanting picture which they had before their eyes, that one must have been more than pitiless to reproach them for it. The gestures, the attitudes, the signs and beckonings which were made from one terrace to the other were so expressive that one could guess at the exclamations and the words by which they must have been accompanied, and that one fancied one could almost hear the bursts of laughter issuing from all the half open mouths.

A certain number of women belonging to the working or poor class, and whose dignity did not confine them within the walls of their dwellings, had even ventured, but closely veiled, these, on the road from Hillah to Liberty. The children, who in the East seldom leave their mothers, accompanied them. This evening's gathering thus had an animation and a picturesqueness which the most brilliant festivals rarely have in the Mussulman countries, where the absence of the feminine and infantile element brings a tone of gravity even into joy and pleasure.

The feast did not end until very late at night. It was only towards two o'clock in the morning that the visitors, intoxicated with light and astonishment, retired to their tents and to the inns.

Next morning Liberty had resumed its usual appearance. At daybreak the Arabs had all reached their homes again.

The experiments had succeeded perfectly on the whole. Excepting a few unimportant accidents, like that of the fire that broke out, everything had gone on as well as could have been desired.

There had, indeed, been here and there some momentary extinctions, some defectiveness in the conductibility of the wires; an accumulator had been damaged. But these are things which are inevitable in all works, and above all at the beginning of so considerable an experiment.

"We shall remedy the few defective points," said Jack Adams to Badger. "Now that we are rid of the crowd, we shall be more at ease to continue our trials."

"If the crowd inconveniences you," replied Badger, "it will be easy to keep it at a distance."

"You think, then, that there will always be an affluence of visitors?"

"I am convinced that a still greater number of curious people will come here than during the last two days. These oriental populations are slow to come out; but when once you have succeeded in setting them in motion there is a veritable invasion."

On that very day they had proof that his lordship's conjectures were correct. Captain Laycock and Monaghan were walking about on the upper terraces of the Kasr, when they perceived in the distance, on the road to Bagdad, a large caravan which was advancing rapidly towards Liberty.

They hastened to inform Badger, who mounted with them to the summit of the tower, and all three turned their glasses in the direction indicated.

The party was still too far off to distinguish anything, unless it be that it consisted of at least five to six hundred persons and was composed for the greater part of Arabs, who formed a multitude of white points, against which a few black spots stood out.

These black dots indicated that there were several Europeans with the Arabs. Badger and his companions now awaited with impatience the arrival of the troop. Perhaps it brought information from London; perhaps, who could tell? even friends.

The caravan did not make its entry into Liberty until three hours later. Badger and Captain Laycock went to meet it. They had not been mistaken: at the head of the troop there rode some fifteen Europeans, five or six of whom were acquaintances; the English consul at Bagdad; the French consul; Sir Edward Barthing, one of Badger's warmest friends; Captain James Colson, an old acquaintance of Laycock; two journalists, one of them a correspondent of the *Times*.

Sir Edward Barthing and Badger, Captain Colson and Laycock fell into each other's arms in ecstasy. The English consul introduced to his lordship his colleague, the French consul, and some ten of the principal inhabitants and the native authorities of Bagdad. The latter, mounted on superb horses, had put on their finest costumes for the occasion. His lordship bid his new guests welcome and conducted them to his dwelling. As to the throng that followed the Europeans and the Arab chiefs, it was soon dispersed in the coffee-houses of the city and in the environs.

"And now explain to me how this caravan was formed?" asked Lord Badger, when they were all collected in the parlor before a lunch which, though an improvised one, was none the less sumptuous. "How have you been able to know so quickly that we had begun our experiments? Yet I had expressly forbidden them to telegraph the news to Bagdad in order to avoid obstruction."

"It was your experiments themselves that informed the inhabitants of Bagdad," replied Barthing. "The day before yesterday, at six o'clock in the evening, the news suddenly spread that a strange phenomenon was showing itself at the horizon towards the southwest. The population repaired in a body towards a knoll which rises at the highest point of the city and from where you command the view of the desert. I hastened there also, and saw a bright light sparkling above the horizon, throwing, as it were, jets of gold on the sand. I immediately saw that it was an electric lighthouse, and the consul, who was with me, declared that you had begun your experiments. Then, without losing time, we informed a few friends and acquaintances, and, mounting on horseback, we took the road to Babylon. We

were followed by a large crowd, eager to see, which has accompanied us to this place."

The conversation continued with animation. Badger and his daughter were happy to have late news from London, which Sir Edward Barthing had left a short time since. The papers and reviews arrived regularly at Liberty, and a voluminous correspondence was received there, but in regard to those thousand nothings which alone can render well the character of the absent native land, Barthing, who was well known in society, could furnish details, piquant through their newness.

The experiments of the day before were repeated during the night.

After having visited the city, the halls, the thousand wonders of the Kasr, Badger caused the Europeans and the native chiefs to mount to the top of the light-house tower to witness the experiments in lighting.

Liberty was lit up to its darkest corners. The Kasr sparkled in innumerable lights, and at one o'clock in the morning they descended again to Liberty, every one absolutely enraptured by the beauty of the spectacle which he had had before his eyes.

CHAPTER VII.

THE GREAT WORKS.

On the 17th of November all the experiments in electric lighting were terminated. The works of the upper Tigris operated with the greatest regularity. Our people were in possession of an immense quantity of electricity, renewed each day.

It was, therefore, time to begin the great works projected. This Badger was in the act of demonstrating to his collaborators, collected around him in the common dining-room, after the fatigues of a well-employed day.

"Until now everything has favored our enterprise," said he. "The death of poor Flatnose is the only misfortune that we have had to deplore. The results obtained have been satisfying; the Arab, Kurdish and Turkish populations do not show themselves hostile to our experiments. Their curiosity, strongly excited, holds their judgment, in a measure, in suspense. If they will show themselves hostile, it will not be until later on; let us take advantage of the moment when all is quiet and when nothing seems as yet to menace us, to push on vigorously with our works. We do not know what the future has in store for us. The farther our work will be advanced, the less easy will it become to destroy it.

"We possess a source of electricity such that no one before us has had a like quantity. The admirable invention of a Frenchman, Mr.

Marcel Desprez, enables us to transmit the electric fluid to great distances and to make it serve for setting machines in motion. What we have already done and what we shall yet do at Babylon will be but the starting-point of a succession of enterprises destined, thanks to the invention of your compatriot, and to your own, my dear Cornillé, to transform completely the surface of the planet. What steam had already begun towards bringing the nations together and for the fusion of the races, will soon be finished by electricity.

"Let us hasten, therefore, to leave the beaten tracks and to engage in new experiments. With the electricity come from the turbines of our works on the upper Tigris let us set in motion the dynamo-electric engines which will serve us for digging canals and for draining a large part of the sea of Nedjef."

"Thus," observed Miss Nelly, "it is the falls of the Tigris which come to work at digging the canals and at draining the sea of Nedjef."

"It's wonderful!" cried Cahuzac, enthusiastically.

"No," said Jack Adams; "it is only natural. For science there is nothing wonderful. Man is surrounded by overflowing force uselessly spent. The rule of progress consists in utilizing this force better and better. That which is wonderful for the common run of people is only very natural for the scientist."

"You are evidently right, my dear Adams," said Cahuzac. "Yet permit me to call your attention to the fact that there is one thing that is wonderful, for it is not natural."

"Which?"

"That is the scientist himself."

At this everybody began to laugh, and they went up to smoke cigars on the terrace. . . .

It was on the 10th of December that the labors were inaugurated. It was necessary to take advantage of winter, for during the hot season this work would be impossible. Badger did not wish to build his city in the midst of a desert. Nobody would come to live in it. Before all, it was necessary to render the soil productive, to cover it with rich crops. It was necessary that, on arriving, the new colonists should find immense fields of wheat, laughing orchards, forests of date-palms and cocoanut-trees. Babylon must be built in the midst of a verdant oasis, arisen almost suddenly from the aridity of the sands.

In reasoning thus, Badger saw correctly: the future of civilization lay in the zone of heat and light. But, to live there, it was necessary to modify nature and to transform the desert into a great garden before founding cities there.

This is how the work had been distributed: Jack Adams was charged with the drainage of the lake of Nedjef; Cornillé took the direction more particularly of the works in the plain of Babylon.

Concerning this choice, a little incident had occurred which had a certain importance and had thrown a new light on the situation of three of our principal characters. The two engineers desired to remain at Babylon. But as it was impossible to satisfy them both, recourse was had to lot. Badger wrote the names of Jack Adams and Cornillé on two slips, which were then carefully folded and placed in the bottom of a hat. Fatma drew out one of these slips; it was Jack Adams' name which emerged. The names of Babylon and Nedjef were put down on two new slips, and Jack Adams was asked to draw out one.

Unhappily for him, fortune, which had favored him at the first turn, wished without doubt to justify her name as a fickle goddess, for she abandoned him at the decisive moment, and he drew the name of Nedjef.

When Miss Nelly heard this result, she could not repress a movement of joy, which, almost imperceptible and fugitive as it was, had not escaped her father, whose eyes were at that moment fixed upon her.

Since some time before this Badger had acquired the certainty that his daughter loved one of the two engineers; but which one? He could not have stated it precisely. The drawing by lots had seemed to him an excellent means for ascertaining this; that is why, during the whole time that the operation lasted, he had but seldom taken his eyes off his daughter.

The gleam of pleasure which had crossed Miss Nelly's eyes when Jack Adams read the name of Nedjef had told him what he desired to know. Now it was settled—his daughter loved Cornillé.

This discovery did not displease him. Jack Adams and Cornillé were both perfect gentlemen, equally distinguished, equally intelligent, equally industrious, the one like the other. If Badger had been asked which of the two seemed to him most worthy of esteem it would have puzzled him to reply. Yet, if his daughter had loved Jack Adams, his affection, with quasi-maternal intuitions, would have experienced alarms which it did not feel at all concerning Cornillé. An optimist by nature and also somewhat from reason, he had yet too much penetration and experience in men not to have divined in Jack Adams the germ, if not of a coarse and vulgar egoism, at least of an unbounded self-love which time and successes would but develop. Cornillé, on the contrary, seemed to him endowed to a degree greater than ordinary with that happy qualification to which we are pleased to give the name, somewhat odd, perhaps, but after all expressive and well-invented, of altruism. In short, it seemed to his lordship that his daughter's happiness would be better assured with the Frenchman, and for his fatherly heart that was above all the important point.

Jack Adams accepted his relative exile with good grace.

"Fate has been just," he said to Cornillé, stretching out his hand to him. "When I have gone to the frontiers of Persia or to the shores of the Persian Gulf you have remained alone; it is now my turn to exile myself a little."

"Quite an easy exile, my dear Adams," replied Cornillé; "from the sea of Nedjef to Babylon is but a step; you will manage to cross it frequently."

"Be sure that I shall not fail to do it," replied Jack Adams.

Indeed, it might be said that, during the four months that his mission lasted, there was not a week in which Jack Adams did not come to pass a day at Liberty.

Towards the middle of the month of January, about a month after the commencement of the work, an exact account could already be rendered of the plan of the whole. It was, in fact, of an extreme simplicity. On the site of ancient Babylon an immense square of about two and a half miles on each side had been marked out. There the new city was to arise, dotted with verdant clumps of trees, intersected by canals of running water, and over which the canopies of date-palms would wave about like gigantic fans destined to cool the atmosphere.

The original square had been divided into sixteen hundred other squares by means of forty parallel lines drawn in the direction of the river and forty other lines perpendicular to the first. An immense chess-board had thus been obtained, each square of which covered over two acres, that is to say, measuring about one hundred yards on each side.

As Babylon was to be a gigantic city, the streets would have a breadth of one hundred yards by a length of two and a half miles. Cahuzac had made a remark with regard to this that was not devoid of a certain interest: that is, that the inhabitants of one side of the street would not be annoyed by the curiosity of the inhabitants of the opposite side. Besides, added he, the gossips would not be able to chatter and speak ill of the neighbors across the street.

Large covered galleries, stretching from right to left, along the whole length of the street, would, during the day, shelter the pedestrians from the heat of the sun, already tempered by the brooks of running water and a double row of trees. By an ingeniously contrived system, the part of the roadway left open to the sky could also be covered by canvas stretched from one roof to the other of the covered galleries.

Modern Babylon might have been reproached with being quite monotonous, and with resembling the cities of the United States, over which—according to the expression of an American author—the god of architecture seems to have cast a malediction.

In order to avoid a similar disgrace, and not to inflict on the old earth, which had seen so many wonderful cities arise, the pretentious and irritating vulgarity of our modern cities, Badger had resolved to borrow all his effects at once from the constant source of all beauty:

nature. And, certainly, he was in a centre where he could draw freely on its treasures. By causing water to circulate in abundance in his nascent city, he could make of it a fairy-like city of trees and flowers. Under the luxuriant foliage, under the variety of the leaves, the inevitable poverty would disappear.

In order to break the monotony, large places had been conceived, half of which were to be converted into parks, in which they would try to collect together the species belonging to different zones of culture, and the other half of which were to be reserved for the markets, the places of reunion, the great public monuments. It would have been unjust to ask more, the rest was the affair of the architects. It was hoped that they would come, like the rest, when the moment had arrived. Ah! if only the Arabian genius had been able to rise from its torpor!

"The time is not yet ripe," murmured Grimm, mysteriously, putting the forefinger of his right hand to his brow.

To see the birth of a city is assuredly one of the most curious and attractive spectacles that can be imagined. In order to bring such an enterprise to a successful end, there is perhaps not a single branch of human activity which it is not necessary to lay under contribution. It is a complex work in which every one is interested according to his qualifications: the poet like the artist, the artisan like the man of the world, the illiterate as well as the learned. What, then, is it when— as in the case of new Babylon—it is a question of causing it to issue all in a piece, and furnished with the complicated organism of modern life, from a desolate soil, abandoned for a long succession of centuries!

The digging of the canals greatly interested Miss Nelly and Fatma. Not a day passed on which they were not seen in one part or the other of the work-yards. Badger often accompanied them; but it also frequently happened that he left them alone under Cornillé's care. He knew them to be safe and well taken care of. He had an absolute confidence in the character of his daughter, and in the honesty of the engineer. When the two young people were betrothed, he knew that he would be the first one to be informed of it.

The canals had not only for their object the bringing of water to the city, they were to serve for irrigating the plantations and cultivated lands which extended all around over a vast perimeter. And so, for several miles around, interminable staked-out lines were seen to extend, representing the future irrigating canals.

That which greatly excited the curiosity of the young girls was, above all, the working of the machines which were taking up the mud and the sand. Let us say a word about the method employed by Cornillé.

The canals to be dug had little depth and little width, for they were to serve only for irrigation and not for the transport of ships or even

of simple boats. The machines for digging the ground were similar to those which served for piercing the isthmus of Suez and that of Panama. But, instead of working by the aid of steam or of compressed air, they received their movement from electricity.

For this, large wires, stretched along the ground, placed the electric works of the Kasr in communication with the extracting apparatus. It was a truly curious spectacle, these powerful engines which worked without the eye being able to surmise where the motive power was. No fire, no smoke, nothing but a silent fluid, circulating in a stream in the copper wires.

The happiest of all during these labors was certainly our archæologist, Grimmitschoffer. He abandoned his singular excavations in the form of trenches, for they became unnecessary; the digging of the canals replaced them with advantage.

"Now, what are you looking for in this manner?" Monaghan asked him one day when he saw the archæologist carefully inspecting the bottom of a ditch that had just been dug. "It seems to me that, until now, the archæologists contented themselves with making excavations in the ruins of the ancient monuments, and not with digging ditches across the plains."

"You are right," answered Grimm. "But, if my colleagues act thus, it is because they are content with searching the common remains

of the palaces or temples. As for myself, I have a grander object in view, of which no one has thought until now."

"And what is this object, Mr. Grimm?"

"Hush!" replied the *savant*. "I shall soon have gained it, and you will be astonished at the boldness of my researches."

"Be it so," said the geologist; "I have too much respect for the secrets of others to question you any further."

The labors brought to light a large number of curious objects, stones with inscriptions, foundations which threw a new light on the palaces of Babylon, statuettes, an immense quantity of articles which would make Badger's museum the richest in the whole world with regard to the ancient oriental civilization.

The objects found belonged by right to his lordship. If Badger gave up all rights to his finds to Grimmitschoffer, those of the association were legitimately his. The scientist contented himself with gleaning. His ambition no longer lay there; he was seeking the philosopher's stone of archæology.

What was it? No one knew it, if not Grimmitschoffer. Did he know it himself? The future will soon tell us.

CHAPTER VIII.

TILLAGE AND COOKING BY ELECTRICITY.

AT the same time that the work of digging the canals was begun, another operation, more common, but no less useful, was being performed. The ground comprised between two canals was being tilled and sown by means of electric machines. Ploughs and drills were moved by the aid of motors similar to those which served for the excavations.

It will be remembered how fertile the soil of Mesopotamia becomes as soon as it is supplied with a little water. Well, now it would not be wanting, and magnificent crops might be expected. For the first year, two hundred and fifty acres were thus sown, about a mile and a half from Liberty.

The electric tillage, moreover, presented no difficulties whatever.

Cornillé, who was the organizer of this work, had but to copy several famous experiments already made in France, principally at Sermaize.

The ground tilled and sown, it was still necessary to think of the future. The grains committed to the earth were to germinate and give birth to numerous ears. The essential point was to irrigate the plantations. Now, water was not far off, since the fields were surrounded by a belt of ditches in communication with the Euphrates. But from the ditches the liquid had to be led to the roots of the stalks of corn. To arrive at this result pumps had to be set up.

This irrigation required a new application of electricity. Each pump was furnished with a little electric motor, and each electric motor had to be connected by a special wire with the accumulators of the works on the Kasr. Thus this strange spectacle was afforded of solitary pumps working all alone, with no apparent motive power.

Cornillé had yet to occupy himself with the utilization of electricity for a domestic use of great interest. It was a question of nothing less than electric cooking and heating at Liberty.

Chef Green was overwhelmed with joy. Just think! Green was to be the first to heat his kettles, to roast his chickens by the aid of electricity. It must be admitted that this was enough to turn the brain even of a cook.

"Electric soup!"

"Roast venison, *mode electrique!*"

"Asparagus, *sauce electrique!*"

"Electric vanilla cream!"

Such was the *menu* which Green now saw every night in his dreams. Cornillé in a few days transformed this dream into reality. On the 5th of February, at four o'clock in the evening, Green's kitchen was heated and lit up exclusively by electricity. From that day on not a single particle of coal appeared in the scuttles.

What cleanliness now! This was no longer a kitchen, it was a parlor. No more of that dreadful coal which blackened the walls, no more smoke, no oven spreading heat and bad odor at random around it.

A strange kitchen, in truth, where the most fantastic apparatus replaced the common cooking-stove.

"You see, Miss," said Green to Miss Nelly, who had come to witness the first experiments in electric cooking; "I press this button, and behold the water boiling in the kettle. I press this other button, and there the chicken turns slowly before the hot roaster."

At the moment when Green was speaking thus he was standing up before a board provided with buttons, similar to those used for electric bells. Before each button a copper plate contained the indication of the corresponding apparatus and its use.

Hot water, meat to boil, gridiron, roaster, stove No. 1, stove No. 2, etc.

It was sufficient to push a button in order to set the corresponding apparatus in action. By pushing another button, situated a little below the first, the electric current was interrupted and the operation brought to an end. Several apparatus were even automatic. Thus the current ceased spontaneously as soon as the temperature of the water reached the boiling-point and was re-established of itself when the temperature became too low.

It is interesting to know how Cornillé had solved the problem of electric heating.

To the same extent that electric lighting has been a problem studied in all its phases, that of electric heating has been neglected. This fact is easily explained: the means of economical heating abound around us. Coal, wood, petroleum, are not high in price, and, thanks to them, we obtain a steady heating. The need of heat borrowed from electricity has, therefore, not yet made itself felt.

But at Liberty the problem deserved the trouble of being closely examined. The quantity of electricity which they had at their command was so considerable that it became possible to replace heating by coal by electric heating.

Cornillé had found himself under the obligation of inventing the necessary apparatus himself. He had only availed himself of the property which the electric current possesses of bringing a fine platinum wire to red heat.

Each time that the electricity circulates in a metallic wire it develops more or less heat. The temperature is the higher as the diameter of the wire is smaller.

Cornillé had chosen platinum, notwithstanding its high price, lying between that of gold and that of silver. But platinum had one immense advantage, that of being fusible only at an excessive temperature, and, above all, of not being attacked by the substances which would enter into the composition of the food.

This last point was of the greatest necessity. A copper wire, for example, would have gradually dissolved in the food and would have ended by poisoning the guests.

"Now," said Cahuzac, "Green poisons us sufficiently already, without electricity coming to the rescue."

Simply a joke, having but the force of a witticism, for *chef* Green was really a model cook, having never disturbed anybody's digestion.

The culinary instruments were divided into two categories—the roasters and the boilers. The first were to be brought to a high temperature, to a violent red heat, radiate and roast the meats turning near them. The object of the second was to boil the water and bring it to ebullition.

The roasters were composed of platinum wires brought to incandescence by the electric currents. As to the boilers, they were spirals of platinum immersed in the liquid that they were to boil. The spiral of platinum became red hot in the air. But in the mass of water it communicated its heat to the liquid, which was rapidly brought to ebullition.

The 5th of February was a holiday for Badger and his companions. A grand banquet united the principal collaborators of his lordship around the same table. Jack Adams was present and gave his colleagues an account of the state of the works in the lake of Nedjef. They were advancing rapidly and would soon be finished.

The feast was merry, and a considerable number of toasts hailed the new electric cooking. One only, Cahuzac, found fault. At each new dish he was seen to make a grimace.

"Why, what is it that you object to in this cooking?" Cornillé at last asked him, out of patience.

"I find," replied the photographer, smacking his tongue against his palate, "I find that it has a slight odor of electricity."

After the electric cookery Cornillé did not rest yet. He set up two electric lifts, one at the Kasr, the other at Babel. From the same time dates also the appearance of the first paper at Liberty. This journal, which bore the title of *Babylon Electrified* and from which we have borrowed the greater part of our narrative, appeared but once a week. The paper was printed on a rotary press, set in movement by electricity. Thus thought was set down in indelible characters at Babylon by means of the falls of the Tigris. A unique event in the annals of

BABYLON ELECTRIFIED.

journalism—*Babylon Electrified* was distributed gratuitously to all its subscribers.

Furthermore, the works of the Kasr and of Babel were connected by telephonic wires with the dwellings of the engineers at Babylon. The principal houses of the city were also connected with each other.

Cornillé delighted the inhabitants of Liberty by setting up electric clocks in the streets. Finally, an accident also gave Monaghan an occasion to show a new and original application of electricity. They

came to tell him one day that one of the workmen at the Kasr had had a finger torn off. The unfortunate man's hand had been caught in one of the gearings of the steam-engine. It was lucky for him that the accident had had no worse consequences. He had run the risk of losing his hand, his arm, and perhaps even of being entirely crushed between the wheels.

Monaghan went to the place of the accident. The amputation of the finger was found to be necessary. It was then that the idea came to him of utilizing the electric current for cutting off the crushed part.

Monaghan took a long platinum wire and brought it to a white heat by the passage of electricity. Then, using this wire like a knife, he cut the patient's finger in a few seconds. The operation succeeded perfectly, and the invalid, notwithstanding the loss of his finger, felt relieved at once.

This operation was naturally spoken of in the evening at the common table.

"How is it," asked Cornillé, who had witnessed the operation of the geologist-doctor, "that not a single drop of blood was lost, and that the patient did not show signs of a very intense pain? Yet it seems to me that the artery cut by the wire would let blood flow, and that the section of the nerves would bring on the sensation of acute pain. Add to this that a burn is always very painful."

"You forget one thing, my dear Cornillé," replied Monaghan; "that is that the platinum wire was brought to the temperature of red heat. Now, at this temperature, the cuts are cauterized, the arteries and veins closed, and the nerves so instantaneously destroyed that all pain is suppressed."

"That is true," replied Cornillé. "That also calls to my mind a certain accident of which I was the victim quite recently. I desired to show some persons with what facility the electric current brought the platinum wires to a red heat. Well, through forgetfulness, I had kept one of the extremities of the platinum wire between my fingers at the moment when it was traversed by the current. I felt no pain whatever, and it was only through the smell of the burned flesh that I was apprized of the fact that the wire had penetrated my skin."

The conversation then continued on the subject of other applications of electricity to medicine, and especially to surgery. Monaghan recalled that a great number of dynamo-electric machines were made for the use of invalids, with alternating weak currents. These currents are caused to pass through the sick parts, and real relief is at times obtained.

Cornillé told of another very curious surgical application of which he had been a witness. It was a question of extracting a small fragment of iron from the eye of a smith. A pair of iron pincers were arranged so as to serve as a magnetic nucleus for a powerful electromagnet. The piece of iron then attached itself fast to the pincers, and could be drawn out.

As they were in the humor for story-telling, Captain Laycock mentioned a curious occurrence that had happened in Brazil during a short sojourn that he had recently made in that country. An invalid was afflicted with elephantiasis. A physician subjected the excrescence of flesh to an electric current, which finished by reducing the swelling and liquefying it, so to speak.

"I have also heard it told," said Miss Nelly, "that the interior of the human body could be lit up, and the exact place seen where a projectile had lodged itself."

"That is perfectly correct, Miss Badger," replied Monaghan. "Unfortunately this procedure, so simple and so ingenious, can be applied only in cases where the projectile is situated in the neighborhood of the stomach or of the lungs. A small electric lamp is introduced into the stomach of the wounded person. Thus the interior of the body is strongly lit up, and it becomes possible to perceive the position of the opaque projectile."

"How ingenious this all is!" said Miss Nelly. "How convenient electricity is, and how it is applied to innumerable uses."

"Yes, Miss Badger," replied Cornillé. "Electricity is certainly the most convenient form in which force can be utilized, for we transform it at will into movement, heat, and light."

16

CHAPTER IX.

THE END OF AN ARCHÆOLOGIST.

For several months Grimmitschoffer had been showing certain signs of mental derangement. His madness had begun on the day when he returned to Babylon, after his excursion on the upper Tigris and the frontiers of Persia.

What characterized his morbid condition was that he seemed to have no aim whatever in his excavations. He neglected the really interesting finds, which were nevertheless not wanting, to search excitedly for "something" which he would not tell.

The conclusion is that he did not know himself what he was seeking—a characteristic sign of madness.

Yet, until then, they could still doubt. But doubt was no longer admissible when he was seen to abandon the hillocks and trace these interminable ditches in the midst of the plain.

This time it was no longer to be denied, the poor *savant* was completely mad. Every one had pity on him, let him alone, and only looked after him at long intervals. In short, his madness was mild; he was a great child, incapable of doing the least harm.

On the 18th of March, Grimmitschoffer came to Liberty in an agitation impossible to describe. Bareheaded, his clothes in disorder, his eyes starting from their sockets, he noisily entered Badger's dining-room. All were assembled at that moment, quietly talking of the

(242)

works which were being executed at the time and of those which were soon to be undertaken.

Jack Adams had left the lake of Nedjef on the evening of the day before, and was passing the day at Liberty.

A bomb bursting suddenly in their midst could not have produced a greater surprise. Miss Nelly and Fatma both uttered a cry of terror, and left their seats, ready to flee. Every one rose, thinking of an attack, a fit of raving madness.

But Grimm, on reaching the centre of the room, suddenly stopped; then, looking around him with a triumphant air, he slowly uttered these words:

"I have found it."

And, as every one remained silent:

"Yes, gentlemen, I have found that which I have been seeking for so long a time . . . Now, I can tell you to your face, you thought me mad. You pitied this poor Grimmitschoffer."

As several made a negative gesture:

"Do not deny it," continued Grimm, without giving them time to speak: "I saw it clearly by your looks. But to-day I come here with head erect, and I no longer fear your jests, for I have found it."

"Well, what is it that you have found?" asked Badger, when Grimm had calmed himself.

"What I have found, my lord?" cried the *savant*, raising his eyes towards heaven . . . "What I have found? . . . I prefer not to tell you, and to leave the pleasure of surprise to you. Come with me, and you shall see."

"Where must we go?" asked Jack Adams.

"Is it to the end of the world?" said Cahuzac.

"No, my fine Mr. joker," replied Grimm to the photographer. "I even advise you to take your apparatus along, for that which you are going to see is so wonderful that you should leave its image for the admiration of posterity."

"Where must we go?" asked Jack Adams a second time.

"To the seventh tell, on the road from Liberty to Bagdad," replied Grimm, "two miles from here."

"Let us go," said Badger, "I'll follow you. The weather is agreeable to-day; it will be good to take a walk. Gentlemen, are you of my opinion?"

Everybody replied affirmatively, and they set out, following Grimmitschoffer.

"Another fit of madness, more violent, this time, than the others," observed Cornillé.

"It is to be feared," replied Miss Nelly. "If this continues, he will have to be sent back to Europe in a strait-jacket."

It soon became impossible to follow Grimm. He walked on ahead, bounding at every tenth step, going now to the right, now to the left, like a drunken man. He was heard to speak between his teeth, sometimes to utter hoarse cries. They called him back when he was too far off; he then retraced his steps in the same wild manner.

He must no longer have seen anything before him, for he came near falling down every instant. He stumbled over the stones in the road; he became entangled in the bushes, he descended into the ditches and climbed over the heaps of sand.

"He walks like a somnambulist," said Monaghan.

Indeed, his look was fixed and glassy.

At four o'clock they had almost reached the tell indicated by Grimmitschoffer. Suddenly the latter stopped and said:

"Advance no farther! I shall tell you what you are going to see."

They stopped and surrounded the archæologist.

"Gentlemen," he began, "there is nothing new under the sun."

"*Nil novi sub sole*," said Cahuzac, who had studied his classics.

"Everything was invented in antiquity," continued Grimm, without allowing himself to be disconcerted.

"Not the railroads and the telegraph, at any rate," interrupted Cahuzac once more.

"That's just where you are mistaken, sir," cried the archæologist. "I expect to prove to you this very day that railroads were known and worked by the Babylonians."

At this they could no longer restrain themselves. Each one turned away to hide his uncontrollable laughter from the unfortunate man who was the cause of it.

Ten minutes later one could still hear the little smothered cries that the two young girls uttered. At last, after having composed themselves, they all drew near again to Grimmitschoffer, who had remained unmoved in the same place.

"I understand your emotion at this news," resumed the poor madman. "I can understand that tears rose to your eyes at this wonderful revelation."

"Let us go and see your discovery," said Badger, at length, to put an end to this situation, which was becoming painful.

"Not yet, my lord," exclaimed Grimmitschoffer, still impassive. "First let me tell you how I came to my discovery."

The uncontrollable laughter was succeeded by pity. Grimm's explanations were listened to in silence.

"Gentlemen," continued he, "there is a word that impressed me in the course of our journey on the Tigris. It was in the ruins of Khorsabad, after the discovery which I made of a warehouse of iron utensils."

"Ah! yes; I remember," said Jack Adams, "the day after your misadventure in an underground passage of the Kouyunjik."

"Alas!" replied Grimmitschoffer, turning pale at the recollection of his mishap. "Our lamented Flatnose, taking me aside, said to me: 'Lord Badger is envious of you. If you should discover a dynamo-electric machine in the ruins of Nineveh or of Babylon he would be nothing but a plagiarist.'"

"And then?" said Badger.

"Then, my lord, I searched. The more I reflected, the more I believed in the existence of these machines in the times of Babylon."

"And you have found an electric machine?" asked Badger, anxiously.

"No," replied Grimmitschoffer. "I have not found any electric machine, but I have found something just as important as that."

The *savant* interrupted himself an instant. Then, after having heaved a few sighs:

"I have worked well, gentlemen," continued he. "I have wasted my health, I have shortened my life, and I feel that I shall not long survive my discovery. My name shall become immortal—that will be my consolation. I shall have rendered a service to the universe, which will be honored by having given birth to a scholar like myself."

"What modesty!" Cahuzac could not refrain from saying.

But Grimmitschoffer no longer heard anything. He continued:

"Gentlemen, not finding any electric machine, I turned to steam-engines. I said to myself: there was a *depôt* at Babylon."

No one had the heart to interrupt the unfortunate man. Nothing is as painful as to witness the wreck of an intellect.

"Yes, I sought this station among the tells of Babylon. Not discovering it, I resolved to dig up the ground in all directions: I would thus hit upon the ancient railways. It was for that that you saw me dig ditches across the plain. Still I found nothing. Discouragement overtook me, and I was on the point of abandoning my idea. At last an accident set me on the road yesterday."

"On the railroad?" asked Cahuzac.

"I have discovered a locomotive!!!" cried Grimmitschoffer, with all the strength of his lungs. "Gentlemen, my locomotive is there, under that hillock. I have discovered the *depôt* of Babylon!!!"

The archæologist rushed towards the tell. They all followed him, running.

Strange! Yes, something could be perceived that resembled a steam-engine. Imbedded in the sand, amid a heap of bricks, three-quarters rusted a boiler appeared before the astonished gaze of Badger and his companions.

Grimmitschoffer was radiant. His arms crossed on his breast, he resembled a conquering god. He was enjoying his triumph; he was at the height of his glory.

Cahuzac approached the boiler and went all around it. He was seen to stoop down as if to read an inscription; then he came back towards Grimmitschoffer with a jesting air :

"My dear *savant* and friend Grimmitschoffer," said he to the archæologist, "permit me to congratulate you on your discovery. Draw near: you will be able to read on one of the sides of your locomotive the name of its maker."

"They all went forward towards the boiler, Grimm in front with Cahuzac.

"Stoop down," said the latter. " Look here; read :

CAIL & CO.—PARIS."

Grimmitschoffer uttered not a single word. The blood rose suddenly to his face; he turned two or three times on himself and fell heavily to the ground, against the boiler which he had just discovered.

He was raised up immediately and all necessary attentions were lavished upon him. It was useless; the apoplectic stroke had been fatal.

Grimm was dead! . . .

The loss of Grimmitschoffer without doubt was not likely to cause as much regret as that of good Flatnose; but, although the archæologist won but very little sympathy, and though, swelled with vanity, he had not succeeded in making himself liked by his companions, yet this unexpected death nevertheless spread consternation among the members of the expedition.

"Here are two victims in less than a year," said Badger, on the day after the accident;" if that continues, who of us will be left to witness the completion of the work?"

"That is true, my lord," replied Monaghan. "But it must be observed that the two victims have themselves been the instruments of their death. Flatnose would still be living were it not for his blind temerity and bravery. As for Grimmitschoffer, he died of pride. He would never have survived his disgrace as a *savant*."

"By the bye," asked Badger, " how do you explain the presence of this boiler, constructed at Cail's, among the rubbish of a tell?"

"I have made inquiries," replied Monaghan ; "here are the results : Some twenty years ago a steamboat tried to ascend the Euphrates above Babylon. The little vessel ran aground on a sandbank. The crew, after useless efforts to set it afloat again, had to abandon it to go to the mouth of the river in quest of more powerful means for saving the vessel. But, when they returned, the ship had completely disappeared. A band of Arab pillagers had carried off all that it was possible to take, then completed the destruction of the rest by setting fire to it. The steam-engine itself was taken off. But, not being able to bring away so heavy a weight, the plunderers buried it in the tell, where it was unfortunately found again by Grimmitschoffer."

"I do not understand," said Badger, "why Grimm had not read the inscription, yet plain enough, which was the cause of his death."

"Pardon me," replied Monaghan, "that is easily understood. Grimm, full of joy at the discovery, did not take the time to examine it. Entirely blinded by his fixed idea that locomotives existed at Babylon, he believed that his find was genuine. In the midst of a ruin, he would certainly expect to find only objects belonging to the same epoch as that ruin. It must be acknowledged that for a mind engrossed like his the mistake was easy to make."

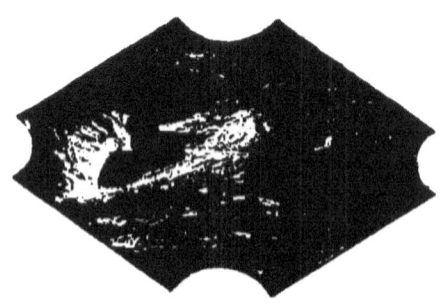

CHAPTER X.

A REVOLT.

WHILE setting up the numerous electric apparatus which we have described around Liberty and in the town itself, Cornillé had taken care not to neglect his thermo-solar pile. It was complete, and the time was approaching when it would become necessary to make use of it.

It was in the middle of May, and the turbines of the upper Tigris were beginning to slacken their movement. The waters, decreasing more and more within a fortnight, had suddenly fallen over three feet.

It was the end of the winter season for the hydraulic works; the summer season was to begin for Babel. After the electricity produced by the waterfalls, the electricity produced by the rays of the sun.

"After the rain, fine weather," as Caluzac said.

Indeed, the time was approaching when, as the turbines would cease to work altogether, it would become necessary to renew the supply of electricity by the thermo-solar pile. Cornillé was awaiting with an impatience easy to understand this day, which was to decide his future, when grave events occurred which well nigh compromised the future of the work and indefinitely deferred the welfare of our hero.

On the evening of the 21st of May the lighthouse and the whole town of Liberty were wrapped in the most profound darkness. This is what had happened.

For some time before this a secret restlessness reigned in the works. A week before, Badger had received a deputation from the European workmen, who demanded an increase in wages on account of the approaching heat which would make the work more fatiguing. Others, professing to be overworked, desired to return to England.

In appearance the demands of the workmen were just; in reality they were not. Living at Liberty was for them extremely cheap. They had dwelling, lighting, heating for nothing. The humblest laborer earned no less than from eight to ten shillings * a day. As to the victuals, they had to pay for them, which was but just; but there was a fixed price on all goods, and this price certainly represented the minimum of the cost price. Their lot was thus, in truth, preferable to that of the workmen in Europe, without even taking into consideration the facilities which would be afforded those who should desire to become colonists, and the future prospects that were open before them.

As to returning to their native land, no obstacle was laid in the way of any workman who asked to do so. Badger in that case furnished him with the sum necessary for reaching Bassorah, and to get from there to any part of Europe which he named.

But now it was no longer a question of one or two workmen asking to return to their country—there was a whole troop of them, and it was unreasonable to demand that Badger should pay the expenses of a desertion *en masse*, the consequences of which might be disastrous for his interests.

Badger, therefore, did not doubt for a moment that a ferment of

---

* About $2.00 to $2.50.—*Translator.*

discord existed at Liberty and that the workmen were incited by some ringleader. But where find this leader? How extirpate this ferment?

It was necessary to act with extreme prudence. Without promising anything whatever, Badger dismissed the embassy, saying that he would first have to consult his associates.

On that very evening, in fact, Badger gave his friends an account of what had passed during the day and explained the situation to them. They were all convinced, like himself, that there was among the workmen—as it nearly always happens in such cases—a firebrand who incited them to revolt.

The main point was to gain time.

On the following day, Badger received the delegates again. He showed them how worthless, how unjust even, their demands were; talked long to them of the exceptional situation which was given them by the association of which he was the principal, and concluded by declaring that he did not believe in the sincerity of their demands. He thought that they were concealing the truth from him.

The delegates tried at first to deny that there was any premeditation with them, or a secret motive for their proceeding. But, forced to their last intrenchments and driven against the wall by the inflexible logic of his lordship, they finally confessed the truth.

The truth was that the European workmen had yielded to fear. The native population of the town and of the works, so peaceful until then, was very much agitated for some time. The Arab workmen frequently assembled together, and the resolutions which they took in these private meetings, from which the foreign workmen were carefully excluded, were always kept secret.

One fine day, however, some European workmen were invited to attend one of these meetings. There it was made known to them that the native workmen, dissatisfied with their wages, were resolved to demand an increase. And as Lord Badger would no doubt have answered them that the European workmen showed themselves to be less exacting, the latter were called upon to demand an increase immediately for themselves.

The Europeans, who thought their wages were sufficient, declared that they would not obey this order. At this reply great was the wrath of the Arab workmen. They declared in plain terms that they were going to drive away the foreigners, put them all to death, and destroy the works from top to bottom.

It was then that the Europeans, alarmed, promised the Arabs to obey them and to demand a large increase in wages of Lord Badger. Some, more timorous than the others, even resolved to ask to depart immediately.

These revelations were grave. It was necessary to act with energy. Captain Laycock proposed nothing less than to fusillade all the Arab workmen.

"No," replied Badger. "We must be prudent. It is perhaps still

time to bring the rebels back to reason. Before having recourse to force, I want to exhaust persuasion. But if I fail I shall not hesitate to break down all obstacles."

"Another one who believes in the efficacy of kindness and clemency," said Cahuzac to himself. "If it were I, I should draw up all these blackamoors in a line, and, 'birr!' they would be struck down by electricity, which would do wonderfully well here."

After a short deliberation, it was left to Badger's skill to put an end to the conflict. The European workmen were called together. His lordship assured them that no harm should come to them as long as he were there, and urged them quietly to resume their work. On the other hand, he summoned the Arab workmen, promised them a slight increase of wages, and threatened them with the anger of the padishah if they persisted in their refractoriness.

For a few days everything seemed to be restored to order. But on the 21st all the workmen, natives and foreigners, refused to go up to the works on the Kasr.

That is why the town of Liberty was enwrapped for a whole night in complete darkness.

CHAPTER XI.

THE THERMO-SOLAR PILE.

This time there was no hesitating—the least appearance of weakness would have been the ruin of the expedition, the miscarriage of the dreams for the future, and perhaps the signal for a general massacre of the Europeans present at Liberty. But with men of the stamp of Badger and his associates, nothing like this was to be feared.

Without losing a minute, Badger telegraphed to the English consul at Bagdad, informing him of what had taken place, and requesting him to send Turkish troops with all possible speed. At the same time he asked him to inform the governor of his firm intention to arrest the principal culprits and have them taken under safe escort to Bagdad to be tried there.

Two hours later the consul answered that the governor gave Badger *carte blanche* to punish the guilty parties. He notified him, besides, of the near arrival of a hundred Turkish soldiers.

Badger went among the rebels immediately after, armed with his revolver. He was accompanied by Captain Laycock, by the two engineers and by Blacton, also armed; Monaghan and Cahuzac had remained with the two young girls, prepared for any emergency.

"Do not leave my father," had been Miss Nelly's whispered entreaty to Cornillé.

Badger informed the Arabs of his intention to arrest the culprits, and of the near arrival of the Turkish soldiers. As he finished speaking, one of the Arabs approached him, his eye aflame, brandishing a long knife. With a shot from his revolver, Badger stretched him at his feet.

At sight of this, there was a general stampede in the group of natives. Not that the Arabs lack courage, but every energetic use of force exercises a sort of fascination over them. Badger's action had invested him in their eyes with a prestige to which they submitted without even attempting to resist.

There remained the European workmen. They assured Badger that they had acted only under the threat of the Arabs, and that they were willing to take up their work again. Badger deemed it prudent to arm them, for fear of a more general uprising on the part of the Arabs. Those among the latter who had openly taken part in the revolt did not return, either on that day or on those following. A few came back to Liberty and humbly asked to enter the works again. Badger, thinking the revolt quelled, complied with their request.

One of them attracted notice by his supplications and his protestations of repentance. It was a laborer who had settled in Liberty not long before. Dressed like an Arab, his appearance and speech would cause him to be recognized rather as a Kurd. Badger gave him permission to enter the works again like the others. But if he had seen the glance full of hate which the Kurd darted at him when he had crossed the threshold, Badger would have comprehended that the man whom he had killed was neither the principal nor the most dangerous culprit.

When the Turkish soldiers arrived, three days later, all was quiet at Liberty. Nevertheless, as the return of similar occurrences might be feared, it was decided that they should remain in the town.

The departure of a part of the workmen had fortunately brought no serious disturbance into the labors at the works. On the 25th of May they were ready to set the thermo-solar pile in motion.

It had been decided that they should await the time when the sun already stood high over the horizon before beginning the working of the apparatus. At ten o'clock, the rays would fall in an almost perpendicular direction, and the maximum yield would be obtained.

From nine o'clock on, Cornillé was at his post on the platform of Babel. He had no doubt as to the result. He had made so many preliminary experiments that he believed himself able to foretell with certainty the quantity of electricity that could be collected in the accumulators. Nevertheless, since the morning, he was prey to a great agitation.

Suppose that the sun which was rising, instead of shining on his triumph, was going to light up his defeat? It would only be a drawn game, after all; he would begin again; he was sure of his calculations. But it was not only a question of success that was at issue; it was not his fortune, his ambition, which were at stake, it was his love, his happiness. Miss Nelly had said to him: "Until then, think of nothing else." From this day forth, he would therefore be permitted to aspire openly to her hand, to allow not a day to pass without proving his affection to her, without striving to win her own. They would then form projects together for the future. Was it really possible, such a dream? Was not some evil spirit watching in the darkness to prepare a terrible awaking for him?

But no, everything favored him: the sky was splendid; not a cloud, however light, to hide the rays of the sun. No moisture in the air to diminish the intensity of its rays. A burning heat, pouring down on the copper plates of the pile, and quite ready to be transformed into electricity.

Cornillé placed the two poles of the pile in communication with the wires which led to the accumulators in the works on the Kasr. He carefully examined the wires which connected the elements of the pile, so as to avoid any interruption of the current. He was desirous of having a hand himself in the final preparations and to leave nothing unthought of, so that he should be able, whatever happened, to bear witness to himself that he had kept the promise made to his beloved one, to think of nothing but the final success. Ah! if she were only there.

The hand on the dial of Babel was drawing near to ten o'clock, when two persons, who were no others than Miss Nelly and Fatma, appeared at the end of the terrace.

For those who believe in the effects of inspiration, there will be nothing surprising in this appearance. Since morning, Miss Nelly also was tormented by a distressing expectation. She also had wished to be alone. She had shut herself up in her room and had refused to accompany her father and his friends, who had gone to the accumulators in order to be enabled to ascertain immediately the result obtained.

She was feverishly watching the clock slowly marking the minutes, when, moved by a sudden resolution, she took her hat, her parasol, her gloves, and, leaning on the arm of her faithful companion, she proceeded towards the Kasr.

Somewhat out of breath from a rapid ascent, the two young girls stopped a moment before advancing towards the engineer who, absorbed in his work, had not heard them coming. Miss Nelly advanced alone, and found herself opposite Cornillé just at the moment when he raised his head, after having finished his examination.

"You here, Miss Nelly!" cried he, overwhelmed with joy and surprise.

"I wanted to come myself to inspire you with courage and confidence," replied his lordship's daughter. "Was I wrong in violating orders?"

"Can you speak so?" said the engineer. "I have never been wanting either in courage or in confidence; but now that you are here, my good genius, my patron fairy, I am certain of success. Thank you, Miss Nelly, thank you."

These words agitated the young girl. But, overcoming her emotion, she said to the engineer, in a still faltering voice:

"And now, attention to your calculations; you run the risk of being behind time, and my father is punctuality itself. There is no longer any one here: Fatma and I will wait quietly in some corner."

However quickly this scene had taken place, it had lasted several minutes. Violent strokes of the hammer rang on the bell of the telephone which placed Babel and the Kasr in communication.

Cornillé hastened towards it and put the instrument to his ear.

"What has happened?" asked Badger; "it is already five minutes past the hour, and there is still nothing."

Cornillé drew out his watch, an excellent chronometer; it showed indeed five minutes past ten.

"An involuntary delay," he replied immediately, "I'll set it in motion."

And, running towards the ends of the wire, he put them in communication with the poles of the pile.

This done, he went back to the telephone, waited five minutes, and asked:

"What result?"

"Perfect," replied Badger, a minute later, Cornillé anxiously repeating all his words. "The figure announced is even exceeded by five units."

"My best congratulations, Mr. Engineer," Miss Nelly then said, advancing and roguishly outlining a ceremonious courtesy. Then, pressing Cornillé's hand, first with the grave tenderness of a sister, and then with the tender and fond affection of a *fiancé*, "Charles," she said to him—it was the first time that she called him thus by his Christian name—"Charles, I authorize you to ask my father for my hand this very day."

Before he had even found the strength, in the ecstasy of his happiness, to stammer a word of thanks or at least to fall on his knees, as a well-bred lover would not have failed to do, Miss Nelly had taken Fatma's arm again and was hastily descending the stairs.

Cornillé saw her go down the slope, light as a bird, and soon disappear in the direction of the Kasr.

"I do not know what I should have done," he muttered, "if she had married another than myself."

In a moment his imagination transported him to London; he beheld himself occupying a high rank in English society, the husband of the handsomest and richest heiress of the three kingdoms. His face became gloomy.

And if Lord Badger refused to give him the hand of his daughter? Might he not have high pretensions for her, want a son-in-law that was noble, wealthy, bearer of an illustrious name?

Was not his name illustrious now? To-morrow it would be in every one's mouth; soon it would have gone around the world. Is the fame of to-day not equal to that of the past? Is the glory which one owes to oneself not superior to that which one has received from one's ancestors? No, he was proud to have been chosen by Miss Nelly; but Miss Nelly might be proud to be his wife.

Cornillé owed it to himself, as well as to Miss Nelly, to make his request on that very day.

After lunch, when the others had retired one after the other, Cornillé approached Lord Badger and requested a moment's conversation with him. His lordship immediately asked him to step into his private room. As soon as they were alone:

"I expected you, my dear Cornillé," said Badger, simply. "My daughter has told me all. You love her, she loves you. You have come to ask her hand of me?"

"Yes, my lord," replied the engineer, surprised, for all that, by this abrupt entering upon the subject—for the French have always some difficulty in becoming accustomed to the simple way in which the question of marriage, so complicated in France, is treated in England—"yes, my lord, I come to ask Miss Nelly's hand of you."

"My daughter has chosen you. I approve of her choice. From to-day on consider yourself as betrothed to my dear child."

Cornillé had never seen his lordship so moved. Tears flowed from his eyes in spite of him. These men of iron, who shrink from nothing, have the tenderest hearts. Badger passionately loved his daughter, the living image of his well-beloved wife, and he said to himself that he was no longer the first in her affection.

In the presence of this overflowing of paternal grief, Cornillé wanted to apologize for his happiness. Badger gave him no time to speak; he hurriedly entered his daughter's room, and soon came back, holding her by the hand; then, placing this hand between those of Cornillé:

"My daughter," said he to her, "behold your future husband. From this day on you are his. Love him as your mother loved me."

The two *fiancés* then knelt before his lordship, who blessed them, and, having raised them up again, drew their heads to his breast.

Fatma was asked to come and share the joy of this family scene. Had she not become Badger's second daughter?

"My children," Badger then said, "I now require a promise of you. Your marriage will be solemnized a year from now in London. In a year our experiments at Babylon will be ended and we shall return to England. Until then I desire absolutely that no one shall be able even to suspect what has occurred here. For everybody my daughter and the engineer Cornillé are to each other what they were in former days, and nothing more. I have serious motives for acting thus, which you shall know when the time comes."

"You wish it, my father," replied Cornillé; "without trying to discover what the reasons are for your conduct, I promise on my honor to follow your intentions."

"As to my daughter, I will answer for her," resumed Badger. "She has shown what she can do in the way of dissimulation," he added, laughing, "and I know that I can also count on Fatma."

"You know that I should be killed sooner than speak," said Fatma, resolutely.

They could, indeed, count on her; to spare those whom she called her deliverers the shadow of a care, the poor girl would have consented to pass through fire.

The dinner party which ended this memorable day was full of spirits and cheerfulness. The joy over the results which had been attained was so exuberant that it hid the black spots which still showed themselves at the horizon. Dreams of the future were formed at a time when the present was hardly assured.

Jack Adams, as fervent in his enthusiasm for the present time and his worship of science as the late Grimmitschoffer had been with regard to the past, extolled beyond measure the triumphs of mind over matter.

"See whether man has the right to govern nature," cried he with vigor. "What would she be without him? A mass of incoherent or injurious forces. The force which we have borrowed from the waters of the Tigris and which we have utilized here, of what use would it be were it not for us? Simply to round off the pebbles in the bed of the river and to wear off the edges of the cliffs on its banks. And the sun, instead of scorching the sands of the desert and burning the earth with its fires, will now have to work more usefully."

"You are right, my dear Adams," said Badger; "but do not forget that if man governs nature, it is by using nature herself. Man is but a wonderful organizer, an admirable worker, and that is enough for his glory. Happy when he remains faithful to the *rôle* which the creative will assigns to him and when he does not himself become a destructive power."

It was late when they separated. Cornillé was the last to retire, still rocked in his dream of happiness. He had just attained that height of destiny which it is given to so few men to reach even once in their lives. One and the same day had made him happy and famous. It now remained for him to drain the series of deceptions and trials with which fortune requires her favors to her chosen ones to be paid. This is right, after all; otherwise man might be tempted to think himself a god.

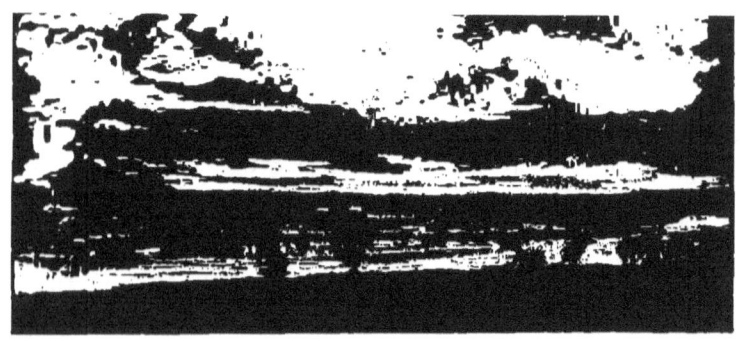

CHAPTER XII.

THE CALM BEFORE THE STORM.

ON the following day, May 26th, the thermo-electric pile was put in operation at six o'clock in the morning.

At three o'clock in the afternoon they came to inform Cornillé that it was becoming necessary to interrupt the current. All the accumulators were already charged to their utmost capacity.

They had too much electricity!

At this news Badger called his collaborators together. He asked them what it was possible to do in order not to lose this precious force. It was regretable to see themselves under the obligation of allowing the pile to work only during part of the day, at a time when they could collect a good third more of electricity.

"An abundance of good things does no harm," observed Monaghan. "You will escape with losing only the excess of fluid."

"Might not new accumulators be constructed?" said Blacton, in his turn.

"No," replied Badger, "this means is impossible. We cannot make accumulators here. It would be necessary to have them sent over from England and erect new buildings on the Kasr, which is already rather narrow."

"I know a very simple way," said Jack Adams. "It has been planned by one of my friends, Mr. Ayrton, an engineer. It was a question of decomposing water under very high pressure by means of electric currents. It would be possible to condense in this way in one and a half cubic feet of a mixture of oxygen and hydrogen the force capable of producing the work of one horse-power during sixty hours."

"Why, but that is magnificent!" cried Badger. "Is it possible to set up this apparatus here now? Have we the means of constructing a receiver to hold this gaseous mixture?"

"Perfectly, my lord," replied Jack Adams. "I'll undertake to set up this receiver myself and to have it working in a week."

"Be it so," said Badger. "Mr. Jack Adams, I count on your skill and on your devotion."

In spite of himself, Badger somewhat emphasized this last word, devotion.

It is now time to tell why his lordship had required of Cornillé and of his daughter the oath to keep their promise of marriage secret.

Badger had observed a little coldness on the part of Jack Adams for three months past. The cause had escaped him at the beginning; but the scene which had taken place with regard to the drawing lots for the distribution of the works at Babylon and at the lake of Nedjef had completely opened his eyes.

Yes, there could be no doubt about it, there was rivalry between Jack Adams and Cornillé, rivalry in science and rivalry in love.

Jack Adams was jealous of the invention of the thermo-electric piles made by Cornillé. He was jealous of Cornillé's love for Miss Nelly.

Badger, who was a sharp observer, had acquired very many proofs of it. Quite recently, at the time of the revolt of the Arabs, he had observed with sadness the voluntary effacement of Jack Adams. He had said nothing, done nothing; but one could feel that this unpleasant mishap did not displease him too much. This revolt of the Arabs, which had retarded the working of Cornillé's pile, served his jealousy.

Then, even on the day before, when Cornillé's success had been so complete and so brilliant, Jack Adams had joined but feebly in the general congratulations.

On the other hand, Badger had observed Jack Adams' assiduous attentions to Miss Nelly. For several weeks he had even believed that his daughter had a secret inclination towards the engineer. She had sought his society by preference, avoiding that of Cornillé. But he had quickly discovered his error. "Tell me whom you avoid," he said to himself in thinking of his daughter, "and I shall tell you whom you love."

Badger had thus acquired the certainty that Jack Adams loved his daughter, but that his daughter did not love him.

Now, above all, it was necessary to avoid a rupture. The success of his attempt was at stake. It was impossible for him to deprive himself of the services of Jack Adams, a scientist of the first class, and an engineer of consummate ability.

Not that he believed Jack Adams to be capable of a base action. Certainly not; in his opinion, the engineer had too noble a soul and a heart too much above the common. That a base creature should yield to his animosity, was to be feared; but, as for Badger, this heroic and proud man, who judged his fellow-men by his own standard, he could not suppose that another would be capable of doing what he himself would not have done.

In short, it was best to avoid any surprise. He therefore believed himself to be acting wisely in carefully keeping secret the betrothal of his daughter to Cornillé.

Jack Adams worked with ardor at the construction of the receiver which was to contain the mixture of oxygen and hydrogen. Materials were not wanting, nor the means for employing them.

In order to resist a pressure of several half-scores of atmospheres, it was necessary to use thick sheet-iron. Now, there had just been brought from England a whole collection of steel plates cut and arranged for constructing a gas-vat. It is true that this receiver, similar to the gasometer in the gas-works, had originally been intended for another use.

It will be remembered, in fact, that it was designed to set up works on the shores of the Persian Gulf for utilizing the waves of the sea. The system consisted in making use of the waves for setting in action a powerful pump which would compress air in a reservoir.

Now, it was this reservoir which Jack Adams wanted to use for the decomposition of water by the thermo-solar pile. So long as Cornillé's pile furnished such quantities of electricity, it became useless to go far away to collect the natural forces of the wind, of the tide and of the waves of the sea.

Badger, consulted with regard to the abandonment of this part of the programme, was the first to advise it. In his opinion, the trial experiments had given such results that it was advisable to finish them as quickly as possible, to publish them, to found a great joint stock company for the construction of new Babylon, and to make an appeal for capital.

Besides, to tell the truth, the utilization of the wind, of the tides and the waves of the sea seemed to him still too much in its infancy. In the waterfalls, and above all in the rays of the sun, there were the means for furnishing sufficient electricity to the future colony. It would always be time to finish the experiments with the rest.

When the receiver was constructed, it was necessary to find a suitable site for it. It was decided to place it on the top of Babel, in the vicinity of the pile. There, it would be near to the electric source, and under the immediate supervision of Cornillé.

Ten days after the events which we have just related, the new establishment was completely finished. It had a vague resemblance to gas-works. By means of thick platinum wires, the water was decomposed into its two elements by the electric current. Oxygen and hydrogen, subjected to a pressure of thirty atmospheres, were accumulated in the receiver.

Thanks to this arrangement, they possessed a considerable source of heat: for it is known that an excessively high temperature is obtained by the combination of oxygen with hydrogen.

A month has passed away since the revolt of the Arabs. The works of the Kasr have now taken on their usual appearance again; the town of Liberty is quiet. Were it not for the presence of the Turkish soldiers, nothing would have recalled the painful scenes of the threatened riot of the 21st of May.

Babel, which appeared to slumber for so many months, has in its turn become a centre of activity. Now it is the soul of Badger's enterprise, for at its summit electricity is produced, the source of every movement.

It will be remembered that one of Badger's great projects was the construction of electric railways. Since Cornillé's thermo-solar pile furnished streams of electricity, it was now possible to think of the construction of the most useful railroad.

This latter was quite naturally indicated among the three principal lines which were to start from Babylon. These three lines were: that of Bagdad, that of the Persian Gulf, and lastly that of the Mediterranean. The line of Bagdad presented serious disadvantages if it was built first, for it would permit the hostile populations of the East to come easily to the new city. Badger desired, on the contrary, to isolate Babylon as long as possible from the rest of Mesopotamia, which is watered by the Tigris. The line of the Persian Gulf would not be of use until later on. There thus remained only the railroads which, ascending the Euphrates, would proceed across Syria to join the Mediterranean.

For this year, they desired simply to construct a short branch of about twelve miles, quite sufficient for the preparatory trials. The work advanced rapidly, especially as to the embankments which were to protect the railway from the inundations of the river.

Thus, everything seemed to proceed as well as could be desired. And yet disquietude reigned in all hearts.

What an anxiety seizes you suddenly in the middle of a fine summer's day at the approach of a violent storm? Nothing, in appearance, disturbs the purity of the sky, and yet every one has the presentiment of an unknown danger. The bird becomes silent in the branches, the insects go back below the ground, the grass itself trembles and withers. Man, uneasy, examines the horizon, and looks in the distance for the cloud which is to bring the lightning.

Thus Cornillé, a more sensitive nature than the others, perhaps, more particularly felt the storm approaching. Two things gave him especially much uneasiness: the revolt of the Arabs and the care which Badger had taken to keep secret his betrothal to Miss Nelly.

It is true that the Arabs were now quiet. But it seemed to Cornillé that this calm very much resembled that which precedes a storm. He no longer found the same sympathy as formerly among these workmen.

Always sparing of words, they worked silently, retired within themselves, as if impatiently awaiting a much longed-for coming event.

Cornillé had tried to make them speak. They had answered him that no one bore Badger or him any malice, that they all liked their masters, whom they found good and generous.

What displeased them was the work accomplished by his lordship. They foresaw that they would be driven out of Mesopotamia in the near future. They had been told that Badger wanted to found a large city on the site of Babylon, and people it with Europeans, that is to say, Christians. They, the Arabs and Mahometans, would therefore be obliged to flee and to return to Arabia, where existence was so hard and the soil of such little fertility.

Then, he had further learned that the dervishes looked unfavorably on the works executed in their country. All that was being done at Babylon was the work of the evil spirit. The wonders which had been witnessed could be explained only by his intervention. On their return home, after having seen the electric lighting of Liberty and the lighthouse of the Kasr, the Arabs had shown less religious fervor than before. It was therefore necessary to root out this ferment of indiscipline and of relaxing in faith. If care was not taken, Christianity would soon replace the religion of Mahomet.

"Death to these dogs of Christians!" had said the marabouts in the mosques. Sooner or later, an outburst of rage and hate was to be expected on the part of the populace against Badger's enterprise. The only thing which could yet save Badger and his companions was the support of the Sultan and of the armed force. But it is known how feeble is the influence of the Sultan in Mesopotamia. Every year witnesses the outbreak of considerable revolts, of which the Turk gets the upper hand only with much difficulty. If religious fanaticism was mingled with it, there was everything to fear.

The commander of the faithful himself seemed to lend a favorable ear to the complaints which were addressed to him against Badger.

The fact was, therefore, that he too feared the influence of the powerful English lord on the populations of Asia Minor.

We have also said that one of the things which troubled Cornillé, was the silence which Badger desired to preserve in regard to the betrothal of his daughter, and the reason for which he found it impossible to discover.

Uneasy for a time at the favor with which Jack Adams seemed to be regarded by Miss Nelly, he had long ago recovered from his jealous fancies and had ceased to see a rival in his colleague. Still less would he have suspected him of base envy. He had always considered Jack Adams as his devoted friend, and continued to esteem him as such.

Man is ingenious in tormenting himself. Cornillé came to think that his betrothed had already been engaged to some one in England, and that, for this reason, Badger did not wish to divulge her engagement with another. He spoke of it to Miss Nelly, who assured him that her heart had always been free, and that she had never been engaged to any one.

"My father simply wished to know whether you were capable of keeping a secret," she sometimes said, laughingly.

At bottom, she was only too well assured of the wisdom of his lordship's injunctions.

She feared the terrible consequences of an open rivalry between the two young men as much as he—more than he, perhaps. Yet happiness makes blind, and Miss Nelly was yet in the age when hope in the future is strong enough to counterbalance and silence dismal presentiments.

In spite of the uneasiness which this cause for anxiety gave her, the sentiment which predominated with her was the joy of knowing her life to be joined forever to that of Cornillé.

What delightful projects for the future were exchanged with Fatma.

"You will stay with us," said she to her companion, "you will see how happy I shall be with him."

"Pshaw!" replied Fatma, "when you are once married you will no longer care for my society."

"You naughty girl. That is to say that it is you who will leave me to be married in your turn."

"Oh! as for that, I don't say no," replied the young girl, blushing.

"There! now I think of it, you will marry Jack Adams."

BABYLON ELECTRIFIED.

"Never," cried Fatma, with an energy which surprised Miss Nelly.

"Why? Is he not young, handsome, amiable?"

"I don't like him," resumed Fatma. "It may be that he is good, but he has a hard look. He has the eyes of a harsh man! I should be afraid of him if he were my husband. Oh! I beg of you, my dear Nelly, do not think of making me marry him. I would die rather than become his wife."

"Fear nothing, my dear Fatma," said Miss Nelly, embracing her, "I shall never be the one to advise you to marry any one whom you do not love. We shall try to find a husband for you who will please you better than Jack Adams."

Thus the two young girls chatted. While the storm was rising above the horizon and threatening to engulf everything, the two weak creatures, full of faith in the future, slept in peace, peacefully and smiling.

CHAPTER XIII.

NEW CAUSES FOR ANXIETY.

CORNILLÉ's fears seemed chimerical, for everything remained quiet during the months of June, July and August. The intense heat which reigned at this period considerably retarded the progress of the works. No European would have been able to bear an excessive fatigue with a temperature which often exceeded forty-five degrees centigrade. They worked only a few hours each day—in the morning at the rising of the sun, and in the evening at its setting.

Jack Adams had taken the management of the construction of the railroad; Cornillé continued to dig canals all around the future Babylon.

Badger often inspected the works, taking Miss Nelly and Fatma with him. He allowed the young girls to go out alone only as little as possible. In order to avert Jack Adams' suspicions, and at the same time not to displease Cornillé, he was careful to visit the workyards of the canals one day and those of the railway the next.

He hoped thus to gain time and to escape any ennui until the time of his return to London, which was to take place the following summer.

The construction of the railway was a sight worthy of attracting attention. The embankments were executed by means of electricity. It was a question of digging up the ground in order to get earth out of it, which was then heaped up so as to form an embankment, on which the rails were laid. The railway was thus protected from the inundations of the Euphrates, the windings of which it followed.

The machines serving for the extraction of the earth had already been in operation on the borders of the lake of Nedjef for digging a harbor. The powerful dynamo-electric motors received their movement by means of wires laid from the works of the Kasr to the point where the work was going on.

But the most interesting was the laying of the rails. It was necessary to make use of the forge every moment, in order to rivet them and join rail to rail, so as to establish the electric communication from one end of the line to the other. Jack Adams had invented portable forges, with which he utilized the mixture of oxygen and hydrogen produced by the excess of electricity of the thermo-solar pile.

It had been an easy matter. It is known that the mixture of oxygen and hydrogen, in the proportion of two liters of hydrogen for one liter of oxygen, gives, in burning, a heat capable of melting the most refractory metals, even platinum.

Jack Adams therefore collected, in very strong cases, a certain portion of this mixture, compressed at a pressure of thirty atmospheres. These cases were then brought to the spot where the work was going on, and served to set the forges going. For that, it was simply necessary to cause the gaseous mixture to pass through a caoutchouc tube to blowpipes constructed in a peculiar manner. There, the mixture was ignited; a long flame was thus obtained, which, in an instant, brought the thickest bars of iron to a temperature of white heat.

We have just said that the mixture of oxygen and hydrogen was ignited at the end of the blowpipe. This was possible only on the condition of having a blowpipe specially constructed for this use. It will be seen why.

When a mixture of oxygen and hydrogen is ignited, a fearful detonation takes place. If this mixture had, therefore, simply been lit at the end of the blowpipe, without taking any special precaution, the case which contained the gases would have been caused to burst.

Fortunately, there is a means, already employed by Davy in his safety-lamp for miners, permitting the ignition of a detonating mixture at the end of a blowpipe, without at the same time causing the explosion of the whole mass. It is sufficient to insert, along the tube which brings in the gases, a great quantity of fine wire-gauze of platinum. Under these conditions, explosions are no longer to be feared: the fire cannot spread from the flame of the blowpipe to the explosive mixture contained in the reservoir.

The works of the electric railroad advanced but very slowly. At the end of the month of August, no more than five miles of rails had as yet been laid.

It was useless to hurry. They would have all winter to hasten the completion of the line. Besides, they were in want of rails, a new supply of which would not arrive until the beginning of autumn.

Meanwhile, in the last days of the month of August, the events became grave again. The Arabs, very quiet until then, again showed hostile intentions. Every day emissaries arrived at Liberty, sent by the enemies of Badger's projects, who gained over the Arab laborers, inciting them to revolt or to desertion. The mutterings which arose increased each day.

Badger lost patience at last. Nothing irritates intrepid men so much as these daily broils, which one feels must become dangerous in time, and against which one is disarmed. The brave man delights in finding himself fairly in the presence of danger. Having it before him, he fears it no longer and feels himself strong enough to brave it.

Badger therefore resolved to hasten matters. He decided to discharge the Arab laborers at the works, and to expel them also from Liberty and even from the precinct granted by the sultan on the site of Babylon. He would retain only the Europeans.

The enemy would no longer be with him, it is true; but it was to be expected that this hostile act would draw upon him the animosity of the Arab populations of the neighborhood. The peril would perhaps become greater; but he would have the advantage of knowing exactly where the enemy was to be found and how he would have to fight him. Fortifications would be raised around Babylon, they would be armed with cannons, Turkish troops would be placed here, determined to defend Badger's work.

For this, they would have to come to an understanding with the authorities of Bagdad and of Constantinople. It was necessary to enter into negotiations which would require time and shrewdness. Badger called his companions together. He made known to them that he would leave for Bagdad that very evening. He would come to an understanding with the governor and return immediately after. He asked Laycock whether he would consent, in case it should become necessary, to proceed to Constantinople to see the sultan, so as to obtain all the indispensable authorizations. It is unnecessary to say that Laycock consented and held himself entirely at his lordship's command.

It was then the 2d of September. Badger left for Bagdad on the same evening, accompanied only by four trusty servants, courageous and capable of resisting an attack of plunderers. Mounted on excellent horses, they could easily, in two days, cover the distance which separates Babylon from the capital of Mesopotamia. Miss Nelly would gladly have accompanied her father, but that was impossible. Badger was obliged to double his stages; at that period of the year the young girl would not have been able to stand so great a fatigue.

The leave-taking between the father and the daughter did not take place without a certain emotion on both sides. Fortunately, Miss Nelly was still ignorant of the dangers which threatened them all; otherwise her sorrow at seeing herself separated from her father would have been much greater. It was, therefore, Badger who was most deeply moved, but he took good care not to allow it to be seen. What was going to happen at Liberty during his absence? He recommended calmness and coolness. If anything serious happened, they should immediately telegraph to him at Bagdad.

Three days after his departure, that is to say on the 5th, a despatch was received from Bagdad at eight o'clock in the evening; his lordship announced that everything went well and that Captain Laycock was to hold himself in readiness to leave for Constantinople immediately after his return. Badger announced at the same time that he would leave Bagdad on the second day after and that he would arrive at Liberty on the 8th, during the night.

Badger, in fact, needed the following day to see the governor again and to consult with the English consul. The English government would have to act at the court of the sultan in Constantinople and to exert its influence to procure the necessary authorizations for his lordship.

Everything being finished and in a fair way at Bagdad, Badger retraced the road to Babylon on the day fixed by his telegram. He returned full of hope in the future and believed that he was certain to overcome to advantage the ill-will of the natives and of the marabouts.

The little band was but a few miles from Liberty, on the night of the 8th, when another party of several horsemen was perceived before it. Ignorant of the intentions of the newcomers, they cocked their carbines and drew their revolvers.

The two parties were now only twenty yards or so apart, when Badger heard a voice crying out: "A friend! I am Captain Laycock."

It was, in truth, the captain who had come forward to meet his lordship.

"What is the matter?" asked Badger, eagerly, when he was face to face with Laycock.

"Bad news, my lord," replied the captain. "We have been informed from the works at Jezireh that the Kurds of the mountain have revolted, that they are descending in a body towards the Tigris and threatening to destroy our establishments."

"Curse it!" cried Badger. "The villains, not being able to hurt us at Liberty, now deal their blows at our hydraulic works on the upper Tigris!"

They made for Liberty at full gallop, reaching it an hour later.

Immediately, and without taking a minute's rest, Badger placed himself in telegraphic communication with the manager of the works at Jezireh. The latter answered that there was nothing new, but that they were momentarily expecting the most serious events. He asked for help at the same time.

Badger called his collaborators together. It was decided forthwith that Captain Laycock and Monaghan should leave immediately for the upper Tigris. Their arrival might, perhaps, save the works from a complete destruction. As to Captain Laycock, who was to go to Constantinople, he would proceed to that city after having pacified the revolted Kurds.

Next morning the captain and the geologist took the road to Bagdad. They were armed with his lordship's full authority and abundantly supplied with the sinews of war, that is to say, with gold.

"I rely on you," said Badger to them, effusively pressing the hands of Laycock and Monaghan. "Your mission is not without peril. Try to recall to reason the spirits misguided by superstition and ignorance. Do not oppose their beliefs, but prove to them that we are not enemies of God, but, on the contrary, advocates of progress."

Alas! Badger himself had not entire faith in the efficacy of these means. He felt clearly that humanity was not yet ripe for pacific progress, and that, for a long time to come, perhaps, it would still be necessary to impose it by force.

CHAPTER XIV.

JACK ADAMS.

DURING the whole week there was—between Liberty and the upper Tigris—an incessant interchange of telegrams. The excitement continued among the populations of Kurdistan. The works were visited every moment by numerous bands of rebels. So far they had not attempted an attack by force of arms, and contented themselves with uttering threats.

Badger had informed the managers of the works of the coming of Laycock and Monaghan. The chief point was to gain time; to inform the Kurdish chiefs who had promised their alliance, and, with their aid, to try to calm the most hot-headed fellows. The gold of Laycock and Monaghan would do the rest.

It might, therefore, have been hoped that everything would soon be restored to order, if a new complication had not been added to all those of an already perilous situation. To the dangers from without internal discord was to be added. From this day on the hours of the existence of Badger's work were numbered.

The poor human being, in a great measure through his own fault, no doubt, is so little accustomed on this earth to feel himself in possession of an unalloyed happiness, that, if such good fortune comes to him, he is always in great danger of allowing himself to be found out, whatever interest he may have in concealing his precious secret. In spite of the efforts which he makes to be lost in the crowd, a happy man does not resemble other men—a naive satisfaction with himself and with others, a general benevolence and optimism form a sort of halo for him which betrays him without his suspecting it. If the heedless eyes of an indifferent person are rarely mistaken in these symptoms, how is it with the envious look, constantly on the alert, of a jealous and proud rival?

At his rival's air of satisfaction, even in the midst of the anxieties to which he was a prey; at the radiance of happiness which transfigured Miss Nelly, Jack Adams could not long deceive himself, and he soon arrived at the conviction that the two young people had mutually pledged their faith.

In the paroxysm of excitement and rage into which this discovery threw him, he resolved not to content himself with suspicion, and to have, as we say, his mind clear about it. Quite full of this idea, he proceeded one afternoon to Badger's dwelling, fully decided to demand an explanation of him.

As he advanced, however, the uselessness and even the ridiculousness of his proceeding gradually appeared to him. Exact an explanation of his lordship? to what purpose? Express his resentment to him? by what right? Had not Badger and Miss Nelly acted in the fulness of their liberty? Had there ever been any promise exchanged between the young girl and him?

What was to be done, therefore? He wanted to challenge his rival; fight with him and kill him. He wanted to stab Miss Nelly. He wanted . . . all that a man wants who is blinded by rage, that is to say, that he did not know exactly what himself. He no longer thought, he was out of his senses.

Exposed to the tumult of a thousand conflicting passions, he was prowling like a wild beast around Badger's house, with haggard look and discomposed countenance, when he saw Fatma come out alone and proceed to the right, as if to go towards the Kasr.

In his present state of mind nothing was more apt to exasperate Jack Adams, for he did not doubt for a single instant that Fatma was commissioned to take a message to Cornillé from her mistress. He restrained himself, however, and, trying to set on a calm face, he accosted the young girl.

"Young lady," he said to her, "I have serious matters to talk about with you. We are alone here; nobody can hear us. It concerns Miss Nelly."

"I am listening to you, sir," replied Fatma.

"Is your mistress betrothed to Cornillé?" asked the engineer.

On hearing these words Fatma could not help trembling. But, recovering herself, as if the most simple matter in the world had been in question:

"You think so?" said she. "Well! in what way does that concern you? Has not Miss Nelly the right to be betrothed to whom she likes?"

"Wretch!" cried Jack Adams, violently seizing the young girl's wrists, "then you don't know that I love your mistress, and that if she marries Cornillé I shall kill them both!"

"Let me go," said Fatma, whom this sudden rage frightened. "Let me go; you hurt me."

"Answer me," continued Jack Adams, beside himself, "is your mistress the *fiancée* of Cornille; yes or no?"

"I know nothing about it."

"You lie, your mistress conceals nothing from you."

"Mr. Jack Adams," replied the young girl, who had succeeded in freeing herself from the engineer's grasp, "if she whom it pleases you to call my mistress, and who treats me like a sister, hides nothing from me, not even her most inward secrets, it is, no doubt, because she has absolute confidence in me, and it is not you, a gentleman, who would want to force me to betray this confidence."

When he heard himself thus recalled to self-respect and to a sense of honor by this maiden who stood before him, Jack Adams could not help himself from a profound feeling of shame; it wanted but little, and, hiding his face in his hands, he would have fled far, very far away from every evil temptation. But ever since he yielded to the perverse instincts of his nature, his conscience lost more each day.

"I am not here to listen to moral dissertations," sneered he; "it is immaterial to me to be a gentleman or not to be one. I am descended from a violent and vindictive race. I have sworn revenge, I shall revenge myself. I shall be up there quicker than you, and if I find Cornillé, woe to him ! . . . I shall kill him !"

"You will not do that," said Fatma, who, believing the engineer to be, on the contrary, capable of anything in the state of exasperation in which he found himself, was determined to pacify him at any price.

"No, you will not do that," she continued in an entreating tone, drawing nearer. "Cornillé is your friend, and he would be prepared to face the most cruel death, for his part, in order to save you from no matter what danger. Miss Nelly loves him, you say? Let us admit that this is true, since you think so. But, Miss Nelly is not alone here, I am also pretty, and . . . I love you !"

"You love me, you, Fatma?" exclaimed Jack Adams, overwhelmed with surprise.

"Yes," replied the poor girl, in an almost faltering voice. "But . . . you made me afraid and I did not dare to tell it to you. You gave me much pain, I assure you, when you occupied yourself incessantly with Miss Nelly without pretending to notice me. And . . . just now, again . . . when you told me that you loved her. . . . Ah ! now I understand jealousy myself, too."

"Do you speak the truth, Fatma," continued Jack Adams in a low voice, "is this not a generous falsehood in behalf of her whom you call your sister?"

"To prove to you that I speak the truth, ask my hand of Lord Badger to-morrow, this very evening, when you wish. . . ."

Choked by her emotion, the young girl staggered and seemed about to faint.

"Fatma !" cried Jack Adams, supporting her. "Yes, you are handsome and you also deserve to be loved."

"Now, leave me," the young girl suddenly said, disengaging herself. "I hear some one . . ."

"*Au revoir*, Fatma !"

Uncertain, agitated in spite of himself by what had just taken place, Jack Adams descended to Liberty again, while Fatma went towards Babel.

As soon as she knew herself to be alone, the poor thing sat down on a bank of grass, and, pressing both hands upon her heart, as if to prevent it from bursting, she said to herself that it was ended, ended. Ended her happiness and the pleasant dreams of the future. She would be the wife of Jack Adams, whom she did not love, and who loved another. And yet, she would be a faithful wife to him. She would strive to make him better.

Fatma's devotion was all the more heroic, as Jack Adams inspired her with a veritable terror. But, with somewhat savage natures, gratitude—so rare with the civilized—is an absolute, almost religious sentiment, from which any sacrifices may be expected. Without any hesitation, without a look backward, Fatma had invented this generous subterfuge: to protect the happiness of her benefactress, she had immolated her heart by offering her hand to the man whom she abhorred, just as, to save her life, she had, but a few months previously, thrown herself before the monster ready to devour her.

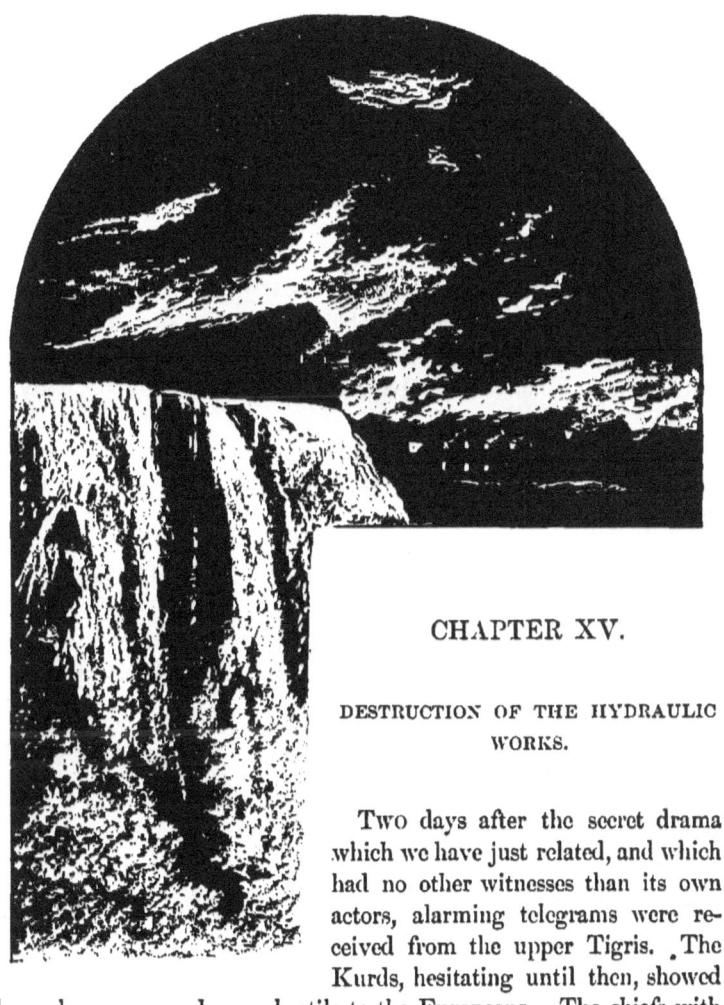

CHAPTER XV.

DESTRUCTION OF THE HYDRAULIC WORKS.

Two days after the secret drama which we have just related, and which had no other witnesses than its own actors, alarming telegrams were received from the upper Tigris. The Kurds, hesitating until then, showed themselves more and more hostile to the Europeans. The chiefs with whom Badger had made alliance at Julamerk, on the Greater Zab, were unable to restrain the fanatical populations. Numerous emissaries, come from the south of Mesopotamia, preached the destruction of the sacrilegious works of the infidels.

The patriarch of the Chaldeans, at Elkosh, had tried in vain to intervene. His efforts had proved powerless before a hostility which nothing could any longer suppress.

Badger despaired. Laycock and Monaghan, gone only a week ago, could not reach Jezireh before a month. Would they arrive before the commencement of hostilities? Would not everything be already destroyed?

What exasperated his lordship and his companions most was the consciousness of their powerlessness. As if by an irony of fate, they almost came to curse this science which permitted them to be informed, hour by hour, of the events which hurried along and brought on their ruin, while they found themselves confronted by the impossibility of remedying it.

"Science is still very incomplete," exclaimed Cornillé in despair. "Why are there not means of transport which abolish distance as the telegraph abolishes time!"

The 20th of September was an unlucky date. It was learned that day that the telegraphic communication was interrupted between the works of Bodia and those of Jezireh.

The emotion felt at Liberty on receipt of this telegram will be understood. Badger immediately asked for the cause of this rupture.

"*We do not know. No news received from Bodia and Egil before the breaking of the wire.*"

Such was the laconic reply of the manager of the works at Jezireh.

Alas! this reply was sufficiently clear. The works at Bodia had been attacked unawares by the Kurds, and the telegraphic wire cut.

Two long days passed in the most painful expectation. At Jezireh they were still in ignorance as to the fate of the inhabitants of Bodia and Egil.

At last, on the morning of the 22d, the following telegram was received:

"*Managers and workmen of Bodia arrive safe and sound at Schebleh. Works completely destroyed. Kurds have designs only upon the buildings, not upon the persons.*"

Thus the fears were confirmed; the Kurds were beginning to put their threats into execution. Fortunately, until now no loss of any human lives was to be deplored.

Badger breathed more freely. "The works can be rebuilt," said he to his companions; "they can be made finer than they were, but life cannot be restored to a dead man."

It was probable that the works at Egil had met the same fate as those of Bodia; but, on account of the distance which required a three days' journey, they were not certain of it until a few days later.

Badger had still a gleam of hope. "It is possible," said he to his daughter and to Cornillé, who seldom left him, no more the one than the other, during these terrible days, "it is possible that the Kurds, satisfied with their revenge, stop at Bodia and return to their mountains. The works of Schebleh and Jezireh will then be spared."

"I do not think so," replied Cornillé, with sadness. "The one that directs the Kurds must be hostile to us to the death. Be convinced, therefore, that he will not stop half-way."

"Let us hope that the captain and Monaghan will arrive in time," said Badger.

He had no more than finished his sentence when the bell of the telegraph rang. They rushed towards the apparatus.

"*Works of Schebleh on fire.*"

A sentence which, in its brevity, expressed a great deal.

Cornillé was right. The enemy continued his work of destruction without intermission. Descending the course of the Tigris, he burned everything on his way.

A profoundly sorrowful sight was then beheld. Badger, this man of so manly an energy, of an inflexible will, Badger wept. Before the destruction of his work, before the ruin of his hopes, this strong spirit had a moment of weakness.

Cornillé, no less moved, respected this deep sorrow. At this solemn hour, every word of consolation would have been out of place. Cornillé was also touched in his most lawful ambitions; like Badger, he was on the point of despairing of the future.

Soon, overcoming his emotion, Badger went to the telegraphic apparatus and sent off this telegram:

"*Set fire yourself to the works and to the dwellings of Jezireh. Wait for your comrades from Egil, from Bodia, from Schebleh; return all together to Bagdad, where I shall await you.*"

"Why at Bagdad, and not at Liberty?" asked Cornillé with astonishment.

"My dear Cornillé," said Badger, laying his hand firmly on the engineer's shoulder, "in a week Liberty will no longer exist."

CHAPTER XVI.

THE REVENGE.

FATMA's admirable devotion had, for a few days, brought a happy diversion to the schemes for revenge which absorbed all the faculties of Jack Adams.

The young Greek was, in truth, very handsome. Her beauty, more absolute, obtruded itself even more, at first sight, than that of Miss Nelly. Happily favored on the score of intellectual endowments, she was kind-hearted—every one knew it—even to entire forgetfulness of self. It was impossible that the voluntary confession of her love should not have made a vivid impression on a young man, inclined to extreme passions.

But pride is the chief fault of the Englishman, as it is the chief weakness of England. If Cornillé had not been in love with Lord Badger's daughter, or if only he had been an Englishman himself also, it is more than probable that Jack Adams—placed between two equally

(285)

charming young girls—would have felt himself drawn by preference towards the young Greek. And it is a fact that Fatma—a few years younger than her companion, of a more pliant and malleable character, consequently, let us say the word, of a more contestable intellectual superiority—would have better answered the ideal which Jack Adams had formed of woman, than the proud Miss Nelly, who had the extravagant pretension of becoming the companion and the equal of her husband.

It is also probable that if Jack Adams had acted differently he would have succeeded in gaining the love of the young Greek. The despotic and stern air which she found in him would not have been capable of frightening her long, accustomed as she was from her infancy to see woman accepting without a murmur her complete subjection to her husband, and to recognize with a good grace the immense distance which separates them. The love of this man, apparently of such little tenderness, would have moved her and . . . all would have been for the best, for everybody would have been satisfied.

Unfortunately it was not thus that matters were to end. Since Cornillé presumed to aspire to win the love of the mistress, how could Jack Adams demean himself so much as to think of the servant! No, his honor and that of England were at stake, the victory must be disputed with the *Frenchman* and, finally, gained by himself.

These sentiments of pride and of ambition, which, unknown, perhaps, to Jack Adams, had from the beginning had a greater part than real affection in his passion for Miss Nelly, now returned more violently to the charge to whisper their detestable advice to him and cause him disdainfully to repulse the charming girl who had pledged her faith to him.

Marry Fatma, a former slave, a girl picked up in the midst of a field, never! It is true, Fatma was the adopted daughter of Badger, who, without doubt, would endow her richly. A further reason for not accepting her as a wife, for he would owe his fortune to Miss Nelly's father, who, no doubt, would consider him very happy, while he did not think he was doing too much for Cornillé—the odious rival —in giving him the hand of his own daughter. He even reproached himself, as for an unworthy weakness, with having hesitated an instant when Fatma had come to offer him her hand.

Everything seemed to conspire, moreover, to stir up the evil passions which devoured Jack Adams' heart and to bring his hate against

Cornillé to its height. So far it was always that part of the general work of which he had taken charge which was sacrificed—the works of the Persian Gulf, abandoned; the works of the upper Tigris, destroyed by the Kurds, then burned by the orders of Badger himself.

He had been the first to recognize the necessity of these sacrifices and to advise them. It was none the less true that it was Cornillé who triumphed, that it was to him that the final victory belonged; his, consequently, the honor and glory of the success, for the contemporaries, as well as posterity, remember hardly anything but success.

It was on the 22d of September that the destruction of the works on the upper Tigris was entirely consummated. After having sent his telegram, Badger had called together those of his companions who remained at Liberty; he informed them that he had himself given the order to burn the works of Jezireh.

"And now," asked he, "what remains for us to do?"

"That will depend on our situation at Babylon," said Cornillé, who was the first to speak. "If we can still count on a year of quiet here, nothing will prevent us from finishing our experiments. The destruction of the hydraulic works is certainly a great disaster for us; but at the present time all our experiments as to the possible utilization of the waterfalls are finished and the results fully obtained. The important point to-day is to construct an electric railroad along the Euphrates, which places Babylon in communication with the Mediterranean and the Persian Gulf. Now, the thermo-electric piles will be fully sufficient. They will furnish us with enough electricity for working our railroad during the first period of the trials."

"Always his pile!" murmured Jack Adams, with an evil smile.

"You are right, my dear Cornillé," replied his lordship. "The whole question is, in fact, to know what our situation will be at Liberty. What will take place when the Arab workmen are informed of the revolt of the Kurds and the destruction of the works? I hope that the presence of the Turkish soldiers will suffice to keep them in awe. I am, besides, resolved to blow out the brains of the first one who will dare to threaten us."

"How unfortunate that Captain Laycock and Monaghan are not here," said Jack Adams.

"Yes," replied Badger. "I have sent a telegram to Bagdad to let them know of the events as soon as they arrive at Mosul and to tell them to return at once to Liberty, where their presence has become necessary."

"They cannot be here until three weeks from now, at the earliest," remarked Cornillé.

"And between this and then, what events may happen! After all, gentlemen, the best is to trust in God and in our firmness. It is, perhaps, still possible to bring our enterprise to a good end. In the space of a year we can finish everything here and then return to England to prepare the final work. One never obtains one's object but at the price of long efforts and hard sacrifices. We have not had too much to complain of so far."

"Assuredly not," replied Cornillé. "Our experiments have been satisfying in every respect. Whatever happens, we may be proud of the results obtained. We wanted to prove that the natural forces can be transformed into electricity, this electricity then conducted to a given point and adapted to all the daily uses. Very well; I think that this principle is henceforth an established fact."

"And all this has been done by you, gentlemen," said Badger, addressing himself to Jack Adams and Cornillé—"the one by bringing to Babylon the motive power of the falls of the Tigris, the other by seizing the power of the solar rays in the midst of the desert. You have deserved well of science and of humanity. When, later on, New Babylon will have reappeared on the ruins of the ancient, your names will be graven in letters of gold on a triumphal column, for you will have been its new founders."

"You show too much modesty, my lord," replied Cornillé. "We have worked under your orders. It is you who have united in a single group so many separate minds. In union only there is strength. He who groups the different talents so as to cause a grand and durable work to spring from the common effort, he has more merit than the others, and his name will be famous and honored."

"The conclusion of all this, my dear collaborators," said Badger, smiling, "is that each one of us, like the laborers of whom the Gospel tells, has done all that is in his power to do, and, consequently, deserves his reward. But, before loading ourselves mutually with eulogies, let us think of the difficulties of the present. When we shall have finally triumphed, we shall wait with patience to be crowned with laurels."

"In that case," said Cornillé, "we risk waiting a long time. Gratitude is a virtue that is very long in coming to men."

"It never comes for contemporaries," said his lordship; "too many prejudices stand in the way. To do good to men is to make an investment at a long date. Fortunately, the true reward of having been useful to one's fellow-men does not depend upon the others. One inherits oneself of the good which one has done, by the very satisfaction which one feels at it. To have formed part of the creative and beneficent spirit, is that not enough for a mortal?"

There was a moment of silence.

"Enough of philosophy like that, gentlemen," said Badger, rising. "I perceive that nothing makes a philosopher of one so well as misfortune. Let each one return to his work. Let us have a reciprocal confidence in ourselves. Count on me as I count on each one and on all."

All of those present came forward in turn to press the hand which Badger held out, and went out, taking away a little more confidence in the future.

Cornillé passed last. Badger gave him to understand that he wished to speak to him in private.

"My poor friend," he said to him as soon as they were alone, "I want to speak frankly with you. I am afraid," continued he, in a grave tone; "yes, afraid. It seems to me that we are on the very brink of our ruin."

"Why, what is the matter, my lord? Just now you seemed to hope."

"We are surrounded by implacable enemies who wish our ruin. Do not ask me where or who they are, I know nothing about it. If I knew it I should not be afraid. We have been struggling for some time in a net the meshes of which are drawn closer each moment."

"Does the danger not appear greater to you than it really is? It is far from here to the land of the Kurds. Here, the soldiers of the sultan protect us."

"Alas! I wish I were mistaken; but I perceive certain signs which make me fear everything ... Cornillé, I have a service to ask of you."

"Whatever it may be, count on me."

"If I die," continued Badger, a prey to a strong emotion, "promise me to watch over my daughter and to protect her."

Then, going to his writing-desk and taking out of it a sealed envelope which he gave to Cornillé:

"This is my will," said he to him. "On your return to England, you will marry my Nelly, my dear child, the only being that ... "

"My father, I implore you, leave these gloomy thoughts. Why speak already of your death? Am I not here to defend you? If you perish, be sure that I shall be dead first."

"I forbid that," resumed Badger, warmly, drawing Cornillé to his breast in a strong embrace. "You have not the right to die, is not my daughter your betrothed? As for myself, I must be the first in the conflict which is near at hand. I am your leader, it is my duty to defend you."

At this moment the bell rang violently.

"Come in," said Badger, with great calmness.

Blacton entered with a dismayed countenance:

"All the Arabs are already acquainted with the destruction of the works on the Tigris," said he.

"You see it, Cornillé!" cried Badger, "I was right in saying that there is a traitor amongst us. The watch-word was given in advance.

The Kurds of Liberty know all about the revolt of the Kurds of the mountain. And what are the Arabs doing?" added he, addressing Blacton.

"They are unmoved and work as usual."

"A bad sign. That is not natural. If they are quiet, it is because they are getting ready to act. But where seize their leader? . . . "

Badger immediately called all his companions together again. He acquainted them with the news which Blacton had just brought him. Their astonishment was at its height.

"This is inexplicable," exclaimed Jack Adams, "we are the only ones here to know what has happened on the upper Tigris; how do the Arabs know it already?"

"There are but two explanations possible," replied Badger, coldly, "either there is a traitor among us . . . "

"No!" cried all of those present with one voice.

"I believe you, gentlemen," said Badger, relieved of a great weight, nevertheless, by the spontaneity of this protestation. "There is no traitor among us, but then there is, among the Arabs, a leader who conducts all. It is he who has stirred up the Kurds. I add that this traitor is here, for he alone can have informed the native workmen of the destruction of our works."

"This is but too evident," said Cornillé.

"Gentlemen," continued Badger, "let us observe the greatest vigilance. Let the approaches to Babel and to the Kasr be guarded night and day by the soldiers. As to us, let each one be at his post, armed and ready to blow out the brains of the first one who revolts."

The evening of this day of the 22d passed without incident. Everything remained perfectly quiet at Liberty and at the works. Nothing of the frequent going to and fro of the preceding days was observed.

"It is the calm which precedes the tempest," repeated Lord Badger several times.

For greater security, all the lamps were lit. As on the day of the inauguration of the electric lighting, one could see as well as in broad daylight at more than three miles from Liberty; but how the sentiments and the circumstances were changed! No more brilliant cavalcades and motley crowds, no longer any women on the terraces and on the roads. Everywhere the dismal solitude. Instead of the joy of triumph, sadness and anxiety depicted on all faces. In the place of unreserved admiration and enthusiasm, defiance and threat lurking silently. Yet the lighthouse explored in vain all night the most remote corners of the town, of the Kasr, and of Babel, nothing unusual was discovered. The Arabs slept more calmly than usual

Next morning not a man was wanting.

Ten o'clock had just struck. Badger and Jack Adams were walking on the terrace of Babel. Babel had been chosen as a point of reunion and of defence, on account of the more elevated and more isolated position of the hillock. From the terrace, one overlooked Liberty and its environs.

"By the bye," said Badger, suddenly, to his companion, "where can Cornillé and the two young girls have gone to? They were here not a minute ago."

"Oh! you know," said Jack Adams, "that Cornillé rather likes to isolate himself with Miss Nelly. They are, without doubt, cooing on one of the lower terraces."

On hearing these unseemly words, Badger stopped suddenly. He was about to reply sharply, when an incident as sudden as it was unforeseen prevented him from doing so.

A half-naked man had just crawled out from under the copper plates of the thermo-solar pile. With a single bound, he stood before Badger and Jack Adams.

"The ravisher of Miss Ross!" cried Badger.

"I have sworn to revenge myself!" said the Kurd. "You Christian dogs, you shall all die!"

It was indeed he, the ravisher of Miss Ross, this Kurd who had been wounded at the very moment when Flatnose fell, a victim to his courage. It was he whose face had expressed so much hate when— at the time of the revolt of the native laborers—he came out of the office where Badger, not having recognized him then, had just granted him the permission to re-enter the works.

At this unexpected apparition, a terrible light broke in on the mind of Jack Adams.

"I alone am the true culprit," cried he, taking his pistol in his hand and rushing at the Kurd; "this wretch has overheard my senseless threats, he must die only by my hand."

In order to understand the meaning of these words, it is necessary to go back a little.

It will be remembered that, on the day before, Badger had called his collaborators together twice in the same day. On leaving the first of these sittings, in which the abandonment of the hydraulic works had been unanimously decided upon as an absolutely necessary sacrifice, Jack Adams, a prey to an agitation impossible to describe, had gone into the hall of the accumulators on the Kasr.

The blood boiled in his veins; he strode through the spacious hall with long steps, seeing and hearing nothing around him. He murmured incoherent words, such as one may utter in the delirium of fever. The hate which he felt for Cornillé now extended to all his companions and to Badger himself.

"My works are destroyed! . . . Curse it! . . . Cornillé is a villain. He has taken Miss Nelly's heart away from me. No, he shall not marry her, I shall kill him first! . . . The wretches! They have destroyed my work . . . And this Cornillé who is victorious. His pile acts continually, for him . . . to think that it would suffice to hold a match to the cock which stops this reservoir in order to destroy everything . . . yes, a match would cause the mixture of oxygen and hydrogen to detonate, and a few seconds after, everything here would only be ruins and rubbish! . . . Cause all of those who have despised me and made game of me to die at one stroke! . . . Oh! what a horrible temptation! . . . But then, why has Cornillé been in my way? . . ."

Jack Adams was so absorbed in his thoughts, that he did not notice that some one had been watching him for several moments. An Arab had hid himself among the accumulators. He listened to the incoherent words which the engineer uttered in his irregular walk.

At the moment when Jack Adams conjured the frightful catastrophe which would cause the detonation of the reservoir, a hideous smile of ferocious joy contracted the face of the Arab. He glided like a snake through the accumulators and disappeared.

It was he who, springing up suddenly, had just uttered threats of death. At sight of him, at his unambiguous words, Jack Adams had understood all.

The wretch was hidden there, during his insane monologue, and it was he who undertook to commit the crime. Meanwhile Badger, petrified by the words which Jack Adams had uttered in springing at the Kurd, remained immovable as a statue.

This scene, however, had not lasted ten seconds.

The Kurd, as quick as lightning, proceeded at a run towards the reservoir of oxygen and hydrogen.

Jack Adams pursued him, trying to plunge his poniard into his body ; then, seeing that he would escape him, he discharged the chambers of his revolver in quick succession in the direction of the fugitive.

At the last shot, the Kurd fell to the ground, covered with blood, and rolled to the foot of the receiver. Then, making a supreme effort and uttering a terrible cry, he bounded to the cock, which he opened.

Jack Adams, understanding the intention of the wretch, threw himself on the Kurd ; but, at the moment when he stooped down to seize him, the latter, with a kick in the chest, sent him rolling ten steps before him, then, having opened the cock, he lit a match, and held it to the gas which was escaping with violence . . .

CHAPTER XVII.

RUIN AND DESOLATION.

A FEARFUL detonation rent the air. It seemed as if a hundred thunder-bolts had fallen on Babel at the same instant.

Lightning itself, moreover, could not have caused greater havoc than this explosion of over thirty-five thousand cubic feet of a mixture of oxygen and hydrogen at a pressure of thirty atmospheres.

Cornillé and the two young girls, who were chatting on a lower terrace, were far from suspecting what a terrible drama was unfolding itself above them. For a long while, Miss Nelly had no longer deceived herself as to the gravity of the situation. Knowing her to be strong and courageous, neither her father nor her betrothed had tried to lull her into a delusive security. Since misfortune was to come, it was better that she should be prepared for it. They themselves, however, could not suspect to what frightful extremes this misfortune was to go. Fatma, preyed upon by a keen anguish which she could not, which she would not confide to any one, had fallen into a gloomy melancholy, which she strove in vain to conceal from her brother and her sister, as she called the two young people. The latter, uneasy at this so sudden a change, tried to make the smile appear again on her lips, to open this young soul anew to the pleasant prospects of the future.

"You think I am uneasy as to my fate?" replied she, sadly shaking her head. "You are mistaken: provided that you are happy and that no misfortune happens to you, what does it matter to me what befalls me! I know well enough I am not born to be happy."

Astonished at these strange words and at the tone in which they were spoken, the two lovers were about to protest, when the sound of the two shots fired by Jack Adams showed that something unusual was taking place near by.

"My God!" cried Nelly, trembling all over, "what is happening up there? Let us run to my father's assistance!"

All three of them rushed towards the stair-case which led to the upper terrace, but, at the very moment when they were about to reach the first step, the explosion took place.

A light more intense than that of day illumined them. At the same instant a frightful noise resounded, and a violent concussion threw them down. The entire wall of bricks, which supported Babel, had oscillated on its foundations as in a violent earthquake.

They rose up again immediately.

A death-like silence succeeded the explosion. They rushed up the stair-case and arrived on the platform.

It would be impossible to describe the appearance of this plateau. Of the thermo-electric pile, nothing remained but shapeless fragments, scattered in all directions. The plates of copper, twisted by the action of the explosion, lay on the ground in the most frightful confusion.

At any other time the destruction of his pile would have wrung cries of anguish from Cornillé. Under the present circumstances he did not even take heed of it. What had become of his lordship and Jack Adams?

The engineer, Miss Nelly and Fatma proceeded to the spot where they had left their companions a quarter of an hour before.

"My God! my God!" cried Miss Nelly, no longer perceiving any one, "my father is dead; he has been killed by the explosion!"

"Nelly, my dear Nelly, have courage," said Cornillé, supporting the young girl, who was at the point of fainting away. "Stay here, I implore you; I shall continue the search."

Then, leaving his betrothed in Fatma's care, he explored the terrace in all directions. Not seeing any one, he ran towards the receiver, supposing that his companions were standing there at the time of the explosion.

In fact, he perceived a horribly mutilated body, in which, however, one could still recognize Jack Adams; the face had been better preserved than the rest of the body. It is probable that, in his fall, the engineer had rolled under a copper plate and his head had escaped contact with the flame.

As Jack Adams was already a corpse, it was useless to try to render him assistance. Cornillé laid his pitiful remains along the wall.

Had Badger shared Jack Adams' fate? Cornillé examined the surroundings of the receiver with his glances; he saw nothing. He was about to continue his search under a large heap of rubbish, when a great clamor arose below him. He rushed toward the parapet. He then had before his eyes a spectacle worthy of hell. The Arabs—completely revolted—had set fire to Liberty. The whole town was in flames, and the madmen, dancing and howling with joy, continued to spread the conflagration with torches. Unmoved, supporting arms, the soldiers of the sultan let them have their way.

Cornillé turned away his head. That which he saw exceeded the preceding horrors. The Kasr, in its turn, began to burn. From the top to the bottom of the works there was only a cloud of black smoke which rose towards the sky like a long column.

At this moment Miss Nelly entirely regained consciousness. At any price, the young girl had to be taken away from this scene of terror.

She rose with a bound and darted toward Cornillé. The flames, succeeding the smoke, formed an immense wreath of fire around the Kasr. Miss Nelly, her hands contracted, her eyes fixed, silently gazed on this gigantic brazier. Her mouth could not articulate any sound. Then, suddenly, she rushed towards Cornillé, crying:

"My father! Where is my father?"

Cornillé, his heart rent by so many emotions, no longer hoped to find Badger alive; paralyzed at the sight of so much ruin, he remained immovable and as if petrified.

"My father! Where is my father?" repeated Miss Nelly, sobbing."

"I have not found him yet," replied Cornillé. "Come with me, Nelly."

They proceeded together towards the spot where Cornillé had intended to search when the clamor had begun. It was evident that the force of the explosion had been specially directed toward this quarter.

There everything was broken and twisted.

Cornillé raised up several plates. He could then perceive a new corpse, crushed beneath the weight of the fragments of the pile. In a few minutes, aided in this sinister work by the two young girls, he succeeded in extricating the body. Alas! this could be no other than the corpse of Badger. This other victim of the explosion was completely unrecognizable. Entirely charred, nothing was left of the features of the face.

Miss Nelly, a prey to a terrible nervous convulsion, threw herself on the corpse and clasped it in her arms.

"My father! my poor father!" the unfortunate girl repeated again and again.

Suddenly a plaintive moan was heard at a few yards to the right.

Miss Nelly and Cornillé rose with a bound. At this moment a second moan was distinctly heard, more prolonged than the first.

Cornillé hurried to the spot from whence the groan had arisen. At the moment when he arrived there a plate of copper was seen to rise up; an arm, finally a head, appeared.

"Nelly! Cornillé!" cried a well-known voice, "where are you?"

There was no mistake about it; it was, indeed, the voice of Badger, but of an unrecognizable Badger.

His hair and beard were burned; his clothes had been half torn off by the violence of the explosion.

"My father! it is my father!" cried Miss Nelly, passing from the profoundest despair to the most intense joy.

Then, succumbing to this new emotion, the young girl lost consciousness a second time.

"Here I am, my lord," cried Cornillé, at the same time unable to believe his eyes and thinking himself the plaything of a dream.

It must not be forgotten that Cornillé and the young girls were ignorant of the presence of a third person at the time of the catastrophe. They, therefore, believed that they had found the corpses of Jack Adams and Badger. In reality, the second was none other than that of the Kurd, who, nearest to the flame, had been most completely charred.

As to his lordship, it was only by a miracle that he had escaped death. The flame, reaching the spot where he stood, had produced its effect, but with a relatively slight intensity. It is certain that the

fragments of the pile, of an enormous weight and hurled in all directions with a terrific force, might have struck him, and crushed him a thousand times.

"Where are you hurt, my lord?" asked Cornillé.

"I do not feel any pain," replied Badger, feeling himself, "but I am blinded. I fear that the flame has burned my eyes."

Five minutes after, his lordship, his daughter, Cornillé and Fatma were collected on the side of the terrace, in a spot free from *debris*. Miss Nelly, hanging on her father's neck, would not leave him any more.

Suddenly another explosion was heard. An immense sheaf of

300   BABYLON ELECTRIFIED.

flames sprang up on the summit of the Kasr, and charred fragments fell even on the platform of Babel.

"What has happened?" cried Badger.

"My lord," replied Cornillé, "it is the petroleum reservoirs of the Kasr which have just taken fire. Now, it is ended; there is no longer any Liberty, nor a Kasr, nor a Babel. Our ruin is consummated!"

CHAPTER XVIII.

A YEAR AFTER.

A YEAR has elapsed since the events which we have just described in rough outlines. We are once more in London, at Lord Badger's.

"Good-morning, father; how are you to-day?"

"Well; thank you, Cornillé," replies Badger to him who has become his son six months ago.

At the same instant, a young woman enters the room, in whom we easily recognize the Miss Nelly of old. Still as lovely as ever, her beauty has perfected itself by the certain something of calmness and seriousness which is given by the possession of happiness really worthy of this name.

"What has the doctor said to you to-day, father?" said she, kissing Badger on both cheeks.

"That I shall be completely cured in a few months, my dear Nelly. I see better day by day. He has still forbidden me to read to-day, but he has given me the assurance that I shall be able to resume my usual occupations in a month or two ... By the bye, my children," continued Badger, "I have received a long letter this morning from Captain Laycock."

"And what does he say, this honest Laycock?"

"Read it yourself," said his lordship, presenting a letter to Cornillé. "The captain is at this moment at Bassorah, on the Persian Gulf." Cornillé took the letter and read the following:

"My dear lord,
"I have returned this moment from Babylon with the *Electricity*. You had ordered me to collect the last fragments of the machines of the Kasr and of Babel.
"Alas! there are no destroyers comparable to these people of Mesopotamia. When I arrived at the site of that which had been Liberty, I found only the desert, silent as on the day of our arrival.
"The Kasr and Babel no longer show any trace of our presence. After the conflagration, the multitude of plunderers carried off everything, even to the smallest particle of wood and of iron. It would be impossible to-day, even for a new Grimmitschoffer, to find the framework of one of your machines among the bricks.
"I have therefore come back with empty hands. Of our expedition to Babylon, nothing is left but the remembrance, every material trace having totally disappeared.
"The elements themselves have desired to interfere. A typhoon, of a violence rare in these countries, has raised up mountains of sand and filled up the canals which Cornillé had dug so laboriously. . . . . "

"This letter is distressing," said the engineer. "It shows that nature, with the aid of man, has very quickly destroyed that which we had so much trouble in establishing."

"That is true," replied Badger, calmly. "But it proves also that we have been imprudent."

"How so?" asked Cornillé.

"We have relied too much on our strength, my dear Cornillé," replied his lordship. "We have been wrong in not taking sufficiently into consideration the hostility of the oriental nations towards everything that concerns the occident."

"Our efforts have nevertheless not been fruitless," said Cornillé, at the end of a few moments of silence.

"Most assuredly not," replied his lordship. "They have shown us which was the true road to follow. Then, we have been able to elucidate several questions not yet solved in practice. We have had, above all, the merit of working on a large scale, of making, on great spaces, experiments hitherto confined to separate laboratories or works."

"Have you still the intention of continuing the reconstitution of Babylon by means of electricity?"

"Always," replied Badger. "As soon as I shall have completely recovered my sight, I shall begin measures to form a powerful association."

"Do you think that you will gain your end rapidly?"

"I know nothing about it, my dear Cornillé; it will perhaps still require several years. But I count very much on the events to hasten the solution of my project. Public opinion in England is over-excited against the invasion of the Russians in Asia. A powerful colony, established on the banks of the Euphrates and the Tigris, would alone be able to uphold our influence in India."

"Your hands are, besides, all ready," said Cornillé; "our managers and workmen of the works of the upper Tigris and of Babylon will form an excellent nucleus for the future enterprise. It is truly fortunate that in the midst of our disaster we have not lost a single European. These fanatics decidedly had designs only on our work and not at all on our lives; but what a strange animosity against all progress come from the west!"

"All the more strange," said Lord Badger, "as these fanatics of to-day were our first instructors. Our ancestors of prehistoric times were but miserable savages, so long as the sacred spark had not been brought to them from the east. Later on, when the ancient nations had succumbed under the weight of the invasions from the north, a last offensive return of barbarity, did not these Arabs, to-day so rebellious against all progress, succeed in founding a wonderful empire where all the arts and sciences were held in honor? Amid the darkness of the Middle Ages, at that time when the last vestiges of the Greek and Latin civilizations were preserved with great difficulty in the monasteries, at times with more zeal than discrimination, did they not contribute greatly towards transmitting to us this precious legacy of antiquity? Were they not the first commentators of Archimedes, of Euclid, of Apollonius and of Ptolemy? Is it not to them, to their schools, that we are in a great measure indebted for having seen the spirit of discoveries and of inventions perpetuated in humanity?

"To-day, Europe has a duty of filial piety, of gratitude, to fulfil towards her old mother, Asia: she must tear her from her morbid torpor, bring back to her the torch which she has received from her. She must share with her the gifts which belong to her genius, the spirit of deduction and analysis, the application to work, the manly courage, the perseverance which triumphs over all obstacles.

"In this arduous task, where our most dangerous adversaries are precisely those who should rejoice most at our successes, let us take for our watch-word the motto of the youngest of the nations of European origin, of the one which, situated at the very extremity of the west, has moved forward so rapidly in the road of progress that in hardly a century it has outstripped its elders: *'Go ahead.'* Forward, always and everywhere. Our first efforts must not remain unprofitable, if for us, at least not for our successors. We must not abandon a work in which the first trials justify the greatest expectations. We must, on the contrary, persist in and renew our efforts, in order that one day the countries which have been the cradle of mankind may witness, on the ruins of Assyrian Babylon, the final and complete resurrection of *Babylon electrified!*"

JULY, 1889

Descriptive Catalogue

OF THE NEW

Publications and Importations

of

Gebbie & Company.

PHILADELPHIA:

GEBBIE & COMPANY,

900 Chestnut Street.

In presenting our Catalogue for the Fall of 1889, we respectfully announce that in addition to our NEW PUBLICATIONS there will be found quite a number of BOOKS specially IMPORTED by us for the American Market.

In regard to both the selection and manufacture of the NEW BOOKS, we believe they will be found worthy companions of those we commenced with last year, which, we are pleased to say, met with such gratifying approval from the trade.

It will be our endeavor to develop a line for ourselves both original and novel, and at the same time make a class of books that will be superior both in selection and manufacture.

CATALOGUE

OF THE

New Publications and Importations

OF

GEBBIE & COMPANY,

900 CHESTNUT ST., PHILADELPHIA.

Addison's Complete Works, including Poems, Dramas,
AND ESSAYS from the Spectator, Tatler and Guardian. With portrait and 8 illustrations, 6 vols., 12mo, Vellum cloth, leather labels and gilt top, (in box,) $10.50.
———Half calf, gilt, gilt top, (in box,) $16.50.

⁎ This is the most complete edition of Addison's Works ever issued. It contains much new matter, and upwards of 100 Letters not before published. A very full Index (108 pages) is appended to the 6th vol.

A'Kempis.—The Imitation of Christ:
By THOMAS A'KEMPIS. A new translation. Elegant edition with artistic borders and 20 photogravure steel-plate illustrations, by the Gebbie & Husson Co., Limited, selected chiefly from the old masters in the Gallery of the Louvre. 8vo, cloth, gilt extra, $4.00.
———Or, in mor. extra. gilt edges, $5.00.

⁎ The illustrations by the old masters are in the true spirit of holiness, and this beautiful volume has been finished in such an artistic manner throughout that makes it in thorough unison with the character of this Christian Classic, which has had, next to the Bible itself, the largest number of readers of which Sacred literature, ancient or modern, can furnish an example.

Apocryphal Books of the New Testament (The).
Being the Gospels and Epistles used by the followers of Christ in the first three centuries after his death, and rejected by the Council of Nice, A. D. 325. Illustrated with 32 engravings from ancient missals. 8vo, cloth, $1.25.

Babylon Electrified.—The history of an Expedition undertaken to restore Ancient Babylon by the power of Electricity and how it resulted. By A. BLEUNARD, Doctor of Science. Translated by FRANK LINSTOW

WHITE. Profusely illustrated with original engravings, by MONTADER, in one handsome volume, 8vo, cloth, gilt extra. $2.50.

*₊*This translation of a new author whose "Babylon Electrified" has had a large sale in Europe, may be best described as a Scientific Romance. There is a very interesting love story running through the narrative, but the most important feature of the work is, the marvel of applied electricity. At times the style reminds us of Jules Verne, but M. BLEUNARD is not one who deals with impossibilities, but measures all his statements and results with scientific care; his situations, nevertheless, are frequently marvellous, and will, without doubt, open the eyes of many readers, in a pleasant way, to the results that mankind may soon expect from Electricity harnessed by Science.

The plot is simple; an English Baronet of fabulous wealth, an enthusiast in matters of Science, undertakes, with the aid of two English Engineers, a French Electrician, and other scientists, to restore ancient Babylon, using electricity as the motive power. The most complete equipment, and an army of workmen, are shipped from London by way of the Suez Canal, to ascend the Euphrates to Babylon from the Persian Gulf, but Lord Badger and others of the travellers, landing at the mouth of the river Orontes, on the eastern shore of the Mediterranean, take the route of the proposed Railroad from the Mediterranean to the Persian Gulf, graphically describing the places of interest as they proceed, Antioch, Aleppo, and after they embark on the river Euphrates, the commerce of the river and the rich character of the soil in the valley of the Euphrates, (passing the site of the Garden of Eden,) with the manners and customs of the people—in the country and in its cities—Rakka, Deir, Anah, Jibbah, Hit, Butin and Hillah, (the modern name of Babylon,) besides the cities on the Tigris, Khorsabad, Bagdad, etc. In fine, this book although written to illustrate the accomplishments and possibilities of Electricity applied to Mechanics, is the best description of Modern Mesopotamia, (the original cradle of the human race,) ever given to the public.

Bible Stories and Pictures.

Three Hundred Bible Stories and Three Hundred Bible Pictures, being a pictorial Sunday Book for the Young, beautifully illustrated with 300 colored and other engravings. 12mo, cloth, gilt extra and colors, $1.25.

₊ This is a delightful volume that will always be an acceptable and profitable present to a Sunday School Scholar.

Bunyan's Pilgrims Progress, from this world to that

which is to come, with marginal references. LARGE TYPE EDITION. Illustrated with Portrait and Forty illustrations by SIR JOHN GILBERT, engraved by W. H. WHYMPER. Small 4to, cloth, gilt extra, red edges, $1.50.

Burke.—The Complete Works of Edmund Burke,

including the famous Speeches on the impeachment of Warren Hastings, with a General Index. 8 Vols., 12mo, Vellum cloth, leather labels and gilt top, (in box,) $14.00.

——Half calf, gilt, gilt top, (in box.) $22.00.

Burns.—The Works of Robert Burns.

A new and complete edition, *self-interpreting*, with copious notes and 60 new illustrations on steel. 6 vols., 8vo, cloth extra, gilt, $18.00.
——Half calf, gilt, extra, $30.00.
——**Edition de Luxe**, plates on India paper, 6 vols., large 8vo, cloth, gilt top, $30.00.

*∗*One of the principal features of this edition is, that it is prepared specially for English readers, the Scotch words being glossed at the end of each line in the English translation, so that American readers can easily understand the whole.

Extracts from Letter from Robert Clarke, Glendale, Cincinnati, O., one of the best-known Burns Students and Collectors in the World.

CINCINNATI, January 15, 1888.
GEORGE GEBBIE, ESQ.

My Dear Sir:—I have had it in my mind ever since I received the sixth and completing volume of your grand edition of Burns, to congratulate you on the very great success you have made of it. It is undoubtedly the best edition in every way ever produced. *I make it now my reading copy*, though I have many editions, all of the best ones. * * * * * Indeed, take the work as a whole, the editorial management of the work has been extremely judicious, and leaves nothing to be desired. You have profited fairly and intelligently by the labors of previous editors, rejecting errors, and improving previous comments by a great deal of original investigation, which adds very much to the value of the work and makes it FAR THE BEST READING EDITION.

From General Wilson, New York.

DEAR MR. GEBBIE:
I think I may safely say that your edition of Burns must be the final edition, and that nothing will be left for those who attempt to follow you.

Extract from a Letter from Mr. Carnegie, January 23, 1888.

Please retain half-dozen copies of *Edition de Luxe Burns* for me. I shall use them for presents to some Scotchmen dear to me on the other side. So glad to have America send them such a marvel. You have at last given mankind the edition of Burns' works upon which it (his fame) will rest. No other is ever likely to be required. That the land of Triumphant Democracy—of which Burns was the prophet poet—should give this to our and his native land, warms *my heart with rejoicing.* Yours always,
ANDREW CARNEGIE.
MR. GEBBIE, Philadelphia.

Columbus.—Christopher Columbus and the Discovery of

the New World, by the MARQUIS DE BELLOY. Finely illustrated with 8 Etchings and Photogravures and fifty-one Engravings on wood, designed and engraved by LEOPOLD FLAMING and others. In one handsome volume. 8vo, cloth, gilt extra, $3.25.

*∗*This work, published in Paris a few years ago, was written for the instruction and pleasure of his nephew, by the MARQUIS DE BELLOY. The book is in an easy and simple style, and when published, became so popular, that it immediately

took rank as one of the modern French Classics, and has since been translated into nearly every modern European language. Both historically and artistically it has been pronounced the best history of the voyages of Columbus that has ever been produced. Published in its present popular form it is expected to have a largely increased demand.

Comedians.—Celebrated Comedians. Containing 12 character portraits of eminent Comedians. Etchings, India proofs, $5.00.

1 Liston as "Paul Pry."
2 Hackett as "Falstaff."
3 Burton as "Toodles."
4 John Drew as "Handy Andy."
5 John T. Raymond as "Colonel Sellers."
6 Sothern as "Lord Dundreary."
7 Jefferson as "Rip Van Winkle."
8 Seymour as "The Admiral."
9 W. J. Florence as "Slote."
10 John S. Clarke as "De Boots."
11 Robson & Crane as "Two Dromios."
12 Ellen Terry as "Letitia Hardy."

Crowquill.—(Alfred Henry Forrester) The Laughing Philosopher. In the Middle of the Nineteenth Century. Edited by ALFRED CROWQUILL. With 140 illustrations, by CROWQUILL, CRUIKSHANK and JOHN LEECH. 12mo, cloth extra, $1.25.

☞ Rare fun and pleasant philosophy, treating of Medicine, Law, Smoking, Drinking, Sleeping, Marriage, Idleness, Racing, Oratory, Fighting, The Feelings, Punning, etc.

Dickens.—Character Sketches from Dickens.

By F. BARNARD. Containing 12 photogravures. India proofs, $5.00.

1 Caleb Plummer
2 The Two Wellers.
3 Rogue Riderhood.
4 Little Nell and her Grandfather.
5 Mr. Pecksniff.
6 Mr. Peggotty.
7 Mr. Micawber.
8 Captain Cuttle.
9 Miss Betsy Trotwood.
10 Dick Swiveller and the Marchioness.
11 Uriah Heep.
12 Bob Cratchet and Tiny Tim.

Dog (The). Its Management and Diseases.

By PROF. J. WOODROFFE HILL. Illustrated with 10 photogravures and numerous wood engravings. *New Edition Revised to date.* 8vo, cloth extra, $3.00.

⁎ This Volume treats very fully and clearly of all the diseases of Dogs, and is now the acknowledged text book used in the Veterinary College of London, England, and other places.

"A good work on the Dog was much required, and Mr. Hill has met the requirement. The directions for Management are based on sound principles. . . . . The diseases of Dogs are well described, some maladies finding a place for the first time, while the treatment recommended is judicious and appropriate."—*Lancet.*

"We have turned over the leaves of 'The Management and Diseases of the Dog,' with great care, and have come to the deliberate conclusion that the book is one of those invaluable guides which no owner of a dog who is concerned about the welfare of his pet should be without."—*Illustrated Sporting and Dramatic News.*

Drama.—The Old Dramatists' Library, consisting of the Dramatic Works of BEN JOHNSON, 3 vols. MARLOWE, 1 vol. MASSINGER, 1 vol. CHAPMAN, 1 vol., with memoir and notes, critical and explanatory, by GIFFORD, CUNNINGHAM and SWINBURNE. 6 vols., 12mo., half bound, gilt top, roxburghe, (in box,) $12.00.

Dumas (Alexander.)—The Lady with the Camellias. A new Translation. With a new preface by the Author, embellished with thirty-nine photogravure illustrations by ALBERT LYNCH. In one handsome volume. 8vo, cloth, gilt extra, $3.75.

*** Alexander Dumas' novel of "La Dame Aux Camélias," is well known as the subject of the Opera "La Traviata." Whilst the drama bearing the same name as the novel, was a great success on its first appearance in Paris, brought a fortune to its author, has been translated or remodelled in nearly every European language, and is represented on nearly every stage of the civilized world. The novel, "The Lady with the Camellias," which has gone through many editions in French, is now for the first time presented in English with all the original illustrations, in a portable form and at a popular price. The numerous beautiful illustrations are faithfully reproduced by the Gebbie & Husson Photogravure Co., Limited, of Philadelphia.

Francillon (R. E.) Romances of the Law:

With a frontispiece by H. D. FRISTON. 12mo, cloth, extra, $1.50.

*** The Twelve Tales comprised in the book bring out in broad relief the many peculiarities of the English Law, and are written in a highly entertaining manner, keeping the interest up from beginning to end. Such Tales as "Touch-and-go with a Great Estate," "A most Remarkable Will," "A Circumstantial Puzzle," "Only Ten Minutes," "Half a Minute Late," "A Cool Hand," "How I became a Murderer," are written with great power, and will be read with pleasure more than once.

"For variety of incident, ingenuity of construction, and general literary excellence, these twelve 'romances' will fairly stand their ground against any recent collection."—*Glasgow Herald.*

Fielding's Works.—Consisting of Joseph Andrews, Tom Jones and Amelia. With Notes and Memoir by THOMAS ROSCOE. Illustrated with the famous engravings by GEORGE CRUIKSHANK. 4 vols., 12mo, Vellum cloth, leather labels and gilt top, (in box,) $7.00.

———Half calf, gilt, gilt top, (in box,) $11.00.

Five Senses (The.)—Five etchings on Holland paper after Teniers, 5 Lichtdrucks after Hans Makart, and 5 photogravures by Goupil & Co., after Herman-Leo, Frappa and Chevilliard. Folio, cloth, gilt, $7.50.

GEBBIE'S SELECT PORTFOLIOS OF LITERATURE AND ART.

The Choice Works of Gerome.—Containing 10 photogravures from his most celebrated paintings. India proofs, $12.50.

1 Phyrne Before the Tribunal.
2 The Public Prayer.
3 The Christian Martyrs.
4 The Plain of Thebes.
5 Rachel.
6 The Grey Cardinal.
7 The Gladiators.
8 The Wall of Solomon.
9 The Flute Player.
10 Alcibiades and Aspasia.

The Choice Works of Hans Makart and G. WERTHEIMER. Containing 10 photogravures by Gebbie and Co., and Goupil & Co., from their most celebrated paintings. India proofs, $12.50.

1 Entry of Charles V. into Antwerp.
2 Diana Hunting.
3 An Egyptian King's Daughter.
4 Titian and his Model.
5 Rubens and his Model.
6 Cleopatra on the Cydnus.
7 Cleopatra Meeting Antony.
8 Revenge of the Flowers.
9 Kiss of the Siren.
10 Agrippina.

Burns.—Illustrations of the Cotter's Saturday Night and other Poems. Section I.
12 illustrations (photogravures and etchings) from designs by John Faed and George Harvey, etc. (photogravures by the Gebbie & Husson Co., Limited). India proofs, $5.00.

1 "The miry beasts retreating frae the pleugh."
2 "And weary o'er the moor his course."
3 "The lisping infant prattling on his knee."
4 "Comes hame perhaps to show a braw new gown."
5 "A strappin youth he takes the mother's eye."
6 "Beneath the milk white thorn."
7 "And let us worship God."

8 "The twa dogs."
9 "Farewell to Ayr."
10 "The Vision."
11 "Thou lingering star."
12 "John Anderson, my joe John."

Burns.—Illustrations of Tam O'Shanter and Auld Lang Syne. Section II.
12 photogravures and etchings. India proofs, $5.00.

TAM O'SHANTER.
1 "Auld Ayr whom ne'er a town surpasses."
2 "Where sits our sullen sulky dame."
3 "The souter tauld his queerest stories."
4 "The dreary hour he mounts his beast in."
5 "Kirk Alloway seemed in a bleeze."
6 "Warlocks and witches in a dance."
7 "But left behind her ain grey tail."

AULD LANG SYNE.
8 "We twa hae run about the braes."
9 "But we've wandered mony a weary fitt."
10 "We twa hae paidl'd in the burn."
11 "But seas between us braid hae roar'd."
12 "And there's my hand, my trusty fiere."

Goethe's Reynard the Fox.—Translated by Arnold,
(unabridged), with all of Kaulbach's 35 illustrations, etchings and photo-engravings. 8vo, cloth gilt, $1.50.

Grammont.—Memoirs of the Count de Grammont.
A new edition, copiously illustrated with 20 portraits by Scriven, and 17 photogravures from Leley's "Windsor Beauties," besides 25 new illustrations by Delort, (photogravures,) forming an elegant gallery of what Horace Walpole terms "The Court of Paphos." With notes by Horace Walpole, Sir Walter Scott and Mrs. Anne Jameson. The most complete and elegant edition of this graphic picture of the court and times of Charles II. ever published. 8vo, cloth gilt, extra, $5.00.

———Half calf, gilt, extra, $7.50.

———Without the 17 Plates of "Windsor Beauties." 8vo, cloth, gilt, $3.75.

———An **Edition de Luxe**, (limited to 500 copies,) with all the plates, on India paper, each copy numbered, 4to, full parchment or grained morocco, $12.50.

☞ Photogravure reproductions by the Gebbie & Husson Co., Limited.

"Grammont's Memoirs" is a famous book. It holds an unique place in the world of literature. It is the graceful day-book of the Court of Charles II. . . . . This inimitable edition of a remarkable book follows the translation by Horace Walpole with his Notes and those of Sir Walter Scott. . . . . Merely as a piece of beautiful book-making, we find it difficult to discover for it suitable words of commendation.—*Boston Daily Advertiser.*

It is an excellent edition at a reasonable price for those who admire the frank cynicism of this terrible indictment of the society of the reign of Charles II.—*Baltimore Sun, Dec. 5, '88.*

The present edition is so complete that it demands a word in regard to the general character of the worthy (Hamilton) . . . . a successful and beautiful edition of a famous work. —*Boston Post, Dec. 15, '88.*

Homer.—A Burlesque Translation of Homer in Verse.
By Thomas Bridges. An Entirely New and Modified Edition. Illustrated with all the original humorous engravings. 8vo, cloth extra. $3.00.

₀ This is a reprint of one of the most humorous productions of the last century ; being somewhat modified in language so as to adapt it to readers of the present time. Bridges in his book has kept close to the text of Homer, but burlesqued it in such a way that humor abounds in every line. The illustrations are an exact fac-simile of the original Rowlandson edition, and give an antique appearance to the book, the original of which is now very scarce and commands a high price.

Hueffer (F.)—Half a Century of Music in England.
By Francis Hueffer, author of "The Troubadours," "Biographies of Great Musicians," "Italian and Other Studies," &c. 8vo, cloth, extra, $2.50.

₀ *The Times*, (London,) of April 27th, 1889, in an exhaustive review of nearly two columns and a half, remarks incidentally : "As far as the work now under consideration is concerned, one consoling reflection will mingle with the regret universally felt at this sudden and unexpected close of a brilliant career; that had the proposed history been completed, the chapters musical readers would have been almost sure to turn to with the liveliest interest, are precisely those contained in the volume now before us—Wagner, Liszt, and Berlioz."

HAPPY-GO-LUCKY PICTURE BOOKS.

A Novelty in Picture Books. Alike Amusing to Young and Old.

Always Jolly!—An amusing Movable Picture Book by LOTHAR MEGGENDORFER. Containing several movable pictures in rich colors. With rhymes to each. Enclosed in a very striking cover printed in colors. Large 4to, boards, $3.25.

Curious Creatures.—A comical and movable Picture Book of the freaks and frolics of some funny creatures, by LOTHAR MEGGENDORFER. Containing several movable pictures in bright colors. With rhymes by LADY HOBHOUSE. Enclosed in a cover printed in many colors. Large 4to, boards, $3.25.

** The above are the successors to the volume "LOOK AT ME," that had such a large sale in England last year, and ran entirely out of print early in the season. As those books are nearly all made by *hand*, only a limited number can be secured, early application is therefore necessary.

"Remarkable for humorous ingenuity."—*Globe.*

"Most novel of the novelties perhaps that we have yet seen are the movable toy books by Lothar Meggendorfer."—*Daily Telegraph.*

"The new movable toy books will send little people into raptures of delight. Easy jingling rhymes in English accompany the quaint and amusing pictures."—*Daily Chronicle.*

"The best toy books for the nursery we have yet seen."—*Liverpool Mercury.*

"The most amusing as well as the most ingenious of gift-books which have come under our notice. They are sure to provide unlimited mirth for the nursery, and even grown-up-people cannot help being amused with the grotesqe effects which can be produced by making the figures 'act.'"—*Vanity Fair.*

Houssaye (Arsene.)—Seven years at the Comedie Francais. In one handsome volume. 8vo, cloth, gilt. $6.00.

——Illustrated with twelve fine photogravures (by the GEBBIE & HUSSON CO., Limited,) $7.50.

Indian Life.—(Hindu Muhammadan) Religious and Social. By JOHN CAMPBELL OMAN, Professor in the Government College of Lahore. 8vo, cloth, gilt extra, $1.75.

The *Saturday Review*, of April 8, 1889, in a highly interesting review of two columns and a half, concludes as follows: "Altogether, Mr. Oman has produced a neat volume in which intelligent observation is illustrated and not overweighted by apt quotation and scholarly research."

The *Nation*, of May 16th, 1889, in a long review, remarks: . . . . "They consist of sketches drawn direct from the life, of the manner in which the Hindu Religion as it exists to-day, affects, in his daily life, in his acts, and in his thoughts, the Hindu as he exists to-day . . . . but just as a sketch is, oftentimes a great deal more suggestive than the finished picture, so it is here."

"An extremely interesting little volume. . . . . We have seldom come across a work more readable, and the view of India presented by it is a truthful one conveyed in a pleasant form."—*The Athenæum.*

"Replete with valuable and suggestive information about less-known by-paths of Indian sociology. Mr. Oman is a shrewd and conscientious observer."—*The Academy.*

"Full of interest and instruction. . . . . The literary and scholarly qualities of the book are of a high order. It is a valuable contribution to the class of popular, and yet solid, works, calculated to increase our knowledge of our Indian fellow-subjects."—*Scotsman.*

Laughing Philosopher (The) in the middle of the Nineteenth Century. Edited by ALFRED CROWQUILL, with 140 illustrations by CROWQUILL, CRUIKSHANK and LEECH. 12mo, cloth, extra, $1.25.

Linton (Mrs. E. Lynn).
HISTORY OF JOSHUA DAVIDSON, COMMUNIST; Or the Modern Imitation of Christ—how it works on practical life in the nineteenth century. 12mo, cloth, extra, $0.75.

☞ This book was suppressed by the first American publishers.

"Joshua Davidson" was one of the first, if not the very first, of a now considerable list of fictions, dealing with the religious ferments of the day of which "Robert Elsmere" is the latest. "Joshua Davidson" is a strong work of its kind, and is recommended to those who are exercising themselves over Mrs. Ward's book.—*Philadelphia Telegraph, Dec.* 15, 1888.

Longfellow's Poem of Nuremberg.—Illustrated with
28 photogravures from views of the ancient city, and the 27 verses of the poem embellished with *illuminated initial letters from works of the middle ages.* Copied and arranged by MARY E. and AMY COMEGYS (*permission of Houghton, Mifflin & Co.*) 4to, cloth gilt, $7.50.

———Edition de Luxe (limited to 500 copies), with plates, on India paper, each copy numbered. 4to, full parchment or grained morocco, $12.50.

☞ The photogravures in this work are made by the Gebbie & Husson Photogravure Co., Limited.

. . . . "One of the most thoroughly satisfactory publications of the season. A miracle of good taste and delicate workmanship."—*Literary World.*

"This handsome volume containing Longfellow's fine Poem, is profusely illustrated with all the notable places, the churches and shrines of the city. . . . . In an art sense and for careful mechanical execution, 'Nuremberg' is a perfect book."—*N. Y. Times, Dec.* 16, 1888.

"It was a wonderfully good thought to make this superb book, just these views in old Nuremberg, in all the luxury of the art of printing, without a word of description, only the pithy poetry of Longfellow. Who that remembers his verses and has known the old city . . . . will not be gratified and charmed by this graceful tribute." . . . . —*New York Journal of Commerce.*

Macaulay (Dr.) Wonderful Stories of Daring, Peril
and Adventure, by DR. JAMES MACAULAY, editor of the *Leisure Hour,* etc., etc. Beautifully illustrated with full-page engravings by best artists. 8vo, cloth, gilt extra, gilt edges, $1.75.

⁎ Besides being very entertaining, this volume is full of instruction for both young and old.

"We are always ready to welcome instructive works by Mr. Macaulay."—*Times.*

"Boys of all ages will find plenty of reading at once wholesome and exciting in Dr. Macaulay's handsome volume."—*Guardian.*

"A book of stirring interest."—*Pall Mall Gazette.*

"It is a capital book for boys, and is sure to be popular."—*Record.*

"Dr. Macaulay deserves thanks for a book full of 'Wonderful Stories,' that are all true. They are well told, and have the further merit of admirable variety."—*Scotsman.*

"Taken altogether, this is a capital book for a boy."—*Church Times.*

"We can most cordially recommend this handsome volume, with its excellent illustrations, not only to the juveniles, but to the elders, of every household."—*Glasgow Herald.*

Manon Lescaut.—By the Abbé Prevost. Illustrated with

over 200 designs by MAURICE LELOIR, and *12 original exquisite etchings*, printed on Holland paper, proof before letter. 4to, cloth, gilt top, uncut, $12.50.

*** The most elegant edition of this celebrated French classic ever published.

"The Romance of 'Manon Lescaut' holds its place in the world's literature by virtue of its absolute sincerity in the portrayal of a certain type of womanhood. . . . . In the depiction of Manon and the mad infatuation of her lover, the Abbé Prevost, had distinctly a moral aim in view. . . . . The book will be a luxury to those who seek for choice specimens of the bookmaking art."—*Literary World, Nov.* 24, 1888.

"This is a new and incomparable edition of a book that will always be censured by large numbers, especially of those who speak the English language, but which will never cease to be read and admired by more than condemn it."—*Boston Daily Post, Nov.* 30, 1888.

"We know of no book which is so profusely and charmingly illustrated, none which shows such variety and ingenuity in design." . . . . —*Evening Bulletin, Nov.* 26, 1888.

"This edition of a French classic is an *edition de Luxe* and the most elegant of this book ever published." . . . . —*Hartford Courant, Dec.* 20, 1888.

NEW VOLUME BY MISS MARSHALL.

Marshall (Emma) Our Own Picture-Book of Many

Places and Many People. Illustrated with upwards of 150 engravings by several popular artists. 4to, cloth, gilt and in colors, $1.75.

*** This new book by the popular author of "Houses on Wheels," &c., &c., is what most of the friends of the little folks will be pleased to find; the descriptions of the pictures being written in that chatty and personal style that when read will appear as if spoken, and save many a hunt for a "Story." Whatever Miss Marshall writes is always entertaining.

Nursery Hours, containing Seventy-four Nursery Tales,

Rhymes and Songs, including all the old favorites. Beautifully illustrated with 217 colored illustrations by the best artists. Enclosed in a handsome cover, printed in colors. 4to, boards, $1.25.

*** This is, we believe, the most complete collection of nursery literature ever published in colors and in one volume. It comprises not only the most popular rhymes and songs, but all the old nursery tales that were such favorites with former generations. The coloring is bright and pretty, and altogether it makes one of the most delightful companions for the nursery.

Œuvres Choisies Des Grands Maitres Modernes.

Contenant 50 photogravures. Goupil et Cie. From representative paintings in the Paris Salons by French, Spanish, Belgian and American artists. With descriptive text by EUGENE A. REED, A. M., author of "French, German and Italian Art." Folio, full grained morocco, $20.00.

Phillips.--The Dictionary of Biograhical Reference.

By LAWRENCE B. PHILLIPS, F. R. A. S. New revised edition. Containing over 100,000 brief biographies of all eminent men who have ever lived in all times and countries till the present day. Revised and augmented to 1889, by FRANK WEITENKAMPF, of the Astor Library, New York. Upwards of 1,000 pages. Philadelphia, 1889. 8vo, half morocco, $5.00.

*** This work contains reference to all biographies included in over 50 Encyclopedias and Biographical Dictionaries, none of which includes more than 15,000 biographies—this contains more than 100,000.

From the Librarian of Congress.

WASHINGTON, D. C., Oct. 13, 1888.

Dear Sirs:—Phillips' "Dictionary of Biographical Reference" I have long used as the only trustworthy guide to the exact full names of all persons, *giving every Christian name in the vernacular language* of the country to which he belonged. I have had to buy no less than four copies of it for the use of my catalogue force. With high regard,

To MESSRS. GEBBIE & Co., Publishers. A. R. SPOFFORD.

MESSRS. GEBBIE & Co.

Dear Sirs:—You have conferred a service upon American students by republishing, with improvements, "Phillips's Great Index to Biographical Reference." A laborsaving, error-saving machine which should stand next to Worcester's and Webster's Dictionaries on the library shelf. Faithfully Yours,

S. AUSTIN ALIBONE.

NEW EDITION OF PLUTARCH.

Plutarch's Lives.—Newly Translated, with Notes, and a

Life. By A. STEWART, M. A., late Fellow of Trinity College, Cambridge, and the late GEORGE LONG, M. A. With copious Index. 4 vols., 12mo, Vellum cloth, leather labels and gilt top, (in box,) $7.00.
——Half calf, gilt, gilt top, (in box,) $11.00.

Quotations—Everyday Quotations:

A handbook of familiar Quotations and how to find them. by J. HAIN FRISWELL. 12mo, half bound, gilt top, $1.75.

Reed (J. E.)—The Lives of the Roman Emperors and

their Associates. From Julius Cæsar (B. C. 100) to Augustulus (A. D. 476.) Translated from the original text of Suetonius, Tacitus, Monges, Visconti, Crevier, and others. Edited by J. EUGENE REED, A. M. 5 vols., 8vo, cloth, gilt, extra, $15.00.

PROSPECTUS.

The preparation of the "History of the Lives of the Roman Emperors" dates from the days of the Cæsars. In their lifetimes their portraits were made in marble and bronze by famous artists, and their lives were written by contemporary historians, and although both the statues and the histories were engulphed in the dark ages that succeeded the fall of the empire, yet, as Europe in the Renaissance emerged from ignorance and barbaric desolation, the histories first were restored to the libraries, and, more slowly, the statues to the museums of Europe.

In the hall of the emperors in the museum of the Capitol at Rome, when we stop to gaze on the antique busts of the Cæsars, we naturally endeavor to trace in their sculptured physiognomies the characters of those princes who, for good or evil, were in their times masters of the destinies of a large portion of the human race.

In the present work we have these portraits faithfully copied, and their story graphically told. In every instance the source is acknowledged, so that the reader may authenticate our authorities as he proceeds.

DR. JOHNSON EDITION.

Shakespeare's Complete Works: With Biographical introduction, and an additional volume containing a complete compendium of each play, historical summary and account of the plot and characters of each play. With portrait. 7 vols., 12mo, cloth, gilt, $7.00.

———Half Calf, gilt, extra, $14.00.

₊ It is difficult to find a feature not already represented in all the possible forms of publication of Shakespeare's Dramas, but we have noted one very excellent form of Shakespeare's works entirely unrepresented in library shape, viz : the edition such as Dr. Johnson recommended as the best, in the following words : "Those who wish to become acquainted with Shakespeare for the first time, and who desire the fullest pleasure that the drama can give, should read every play from the first to the last, with utter negligence of all his commentators. When fancy is on the wing, it should not stoop at correction or explanation. Particular passages may be cleared by notes; but the general effect is weakened by the interruption. Obscurities and niceties may be investigated when time permits and inclination prompts; but from beginning to end it is best and safest to allow Shakespeare to speak for himself." Acting on this sage advice, we have adopted the text of Johnson and Steevens as revised by Clark and Wright, and give the complete works of Shakespeare in their unabridged and perfect purity in seven handy volumes, and in case of any reader needing explanation, we have added a thorough glossary of obscure words and phrases. In addition to this we have given a complete compendium and commentary of the plays and a concordance to all the most notable passages, as well as the characters in the dramas, besides other features not found with the current editions of Shakespeare.—*Publishers Preface.*

———**Compendium to Shakespeare,** containing historical summary, compendium of each play, and account of the plot and characters of each play, with 37 outline illustrations by HOWARD, being a supplement to the "Dr. Johnson" edition. 1 vol., 12mo, cloth, gilt, $1.50.

Shakespeare's Songs and Sonnets.—Illustrated by Sir JOHN GILBERT. Chromolithographed in many colors, by Vincent Brooks, (Day & Son,) London. With handsome cover beautifully printed in colors. Small 4to, boards, $1.00.

Shapley (Rufus E.)—Solid for Mulhooly.—A political satire. With 10 full-page new drawings, designed expressly for the work by THOMAS NAST. 12mo, cloth, $0.75.
———Paper, $0.50.

It is the keenest and most polished satire of the age. . . . . It will be the most successful gospel of municipal reform that has yet confronted our ring-ridden municipalities.—*Philadelphia Times.*

Those who hold aloof from city politics, indifferent or ignorant about them or their workings, would do well to read this book.—*New York Times.*
One of the brightest satires ever written.—*Louisville Courier Journal.*
The satire is so entirely true to the life, and written with such pungent wit, as to make its way at once to popular appreciation.—*Baltimore Gazette.*

Scotland and the Scots:

Essays illustrative of Scottish Life, History and Character. By PETER ROSS, author of "A Life of St. Andrew," &c. 12mo, cloth, extra, $1.00. The characteristics of Scotsmen are very carefully and accurately portrayed. The chapter on the "Scot in America" affords much interesting information regarding his influence upon the civilization of the New World.—*New York Sun.*

A NEW CHILD'S FAVORITE.

Story Telling (The) Album for our Boys and Girls.

Beautifully illustrated on every page with 205 large, fine engravings by some of the best modern illustrators for the young. 4to, cloth, gilt extra and in colors, gilt edges, $2.50.

** This new juvenile will be found of increasing interest by the little folks. The pictures are large and beautiful and the stories are written in that easy and natural manner that always delight the young. The binding is a rich harmony of gold and color.

Suetonius.—The Lives of the Twelve Cæsars. By

C. SUETONIUS TRANQUILLUS. The translation of ALEXANDER THOMSON, M. D., revised and corrected. Illustrated with 24 portraits on steel, from authentic antique statutes and busts of the emperors and their contemporaries, in the museums of Europe. 2 vols., royal 8vo, cloth extra, $5.00.
——The above 2 vols. in one, royal, 8vo, cloth, extra, $3.75.

****Suetonius' "Lives of the Cæsars" was held in such estimation that so soon after the invention of printing as the year A. D. 1500, no fewer than eighteen editions had been published, and nearly one hundred have since been added to the number.
This is the first American edition, with copious notes, and is printed from new pica type.

ENGLAND'S STANDARD CLASSIC.

Taine's History of English Literature, translated by

HENRY VAN LAUN. BEST ENGLISH LIBRARY EDITION. 4 vols., 8vo, cloth, $7.50.
——Half calf or half morocco, extra, $15.00.

** We are pleased to say that we have been appointed Agents for the American market of this handsome edition of the best book on English Literature.

Turner (F. C.)--A Short History of Art. By FRANCIS C.

TURNER, B. A. Illustrated by copies of some of the most famous Paintings and Sculptures. New Edition. Fully Illustrated, with numerous full-page Plates and Woodcuts, large 8vo, half bound, gilt top, (roxburgh,) $3.25.

"A clear and succinct account of the art of various nations. . . . Sure of a wide welcome. . . . He carries us successfully through the Indian, Egyptian, Persian, Assyrian, Greek, Roman, Italian, Spanish, Flemish, Dutch, French and English schools. He is especially full upon the art of the middle ages and the Rennaissance, and the illustrations which accompany the rest will be helpful to students."—*Times.*

"His sketches of the English school are very masterly and discriminating."—*British Quarterly*

"It is a most conscientious book."—*Daily News.*

Tennyson's Complete Works.—13 volumes bound in 3
16mo., cloth, $4.50.

⁎ This edition is printed from the large-type 13-volume edition published by Kegan, Paul & Co., and sold at 2s. 6d. per volume, cloth; it includes "Queen Mary" and "Harold," and all the minor poems till 1883.

White (Rev. Gilbert.)
THE NATURAL HISTORY AND ANTIQUITIES OF SELBORNE. Thoroughly revised, with notes by J. E. HARTING, F. L. S., F. Z. S. New Edition, with ten letters not included in any other edition. Profusely illustrated with the famous engravings by BEWICK, HARVEY and others. In one handsome vol., 8vo, cloth, gilt extra, gilt edges, $3.50.

"If any apology be deemed necessary for the appearance of a new edition of one of the most delightful books in the English language, the reader need only be reminded of the physical changes which have taken place since Gilbert White's day in the district of which he wrote, and of the vast additions which are daily being made to our knowledge in almost every branch of Natural History."—*Extract from Editor's Preface.*

Winton and Millar.—Steam and Electric Practice and Engineering.
A practical guide to improved methods of construction and the principles relating thereto, with examples, practical rules and formulae. By JOHN G. WINTON, Engineer, author of "Modern Workshop Practice." Assisted by W. J MILLAR, C. E., Secretary of the Institution of Engineers and Shipbuilders in Scotland, author of "Principles of Mechanics," etc. With additional American Examples, and an Introduction by JOSEPH M. WILSON, C. E., of Philadelphia. Illustrated with 900 engravings. 4 vols., 8vo, cloth, $12.00.

⁎ The object of the publication is to supply the practical engineer, ship-builder and mechanic with a trustworthy guide to the varied operations of the workshop and the building yard in a convenient form and at a moderate price. It is written by practical men, well acquainted with the operations which they describe, and seeks to convey to the workman detailed directions regarding his work in language such as he is daily familiar with, and, at the same time, to state clearly the higher principles upon which these operations are based and on which they depend for success.

www.ingramcontent.com/pod-product-compliance
Lightning Source LLC
Chambersburg PA
CBHW030734230426

43667CB00007B/714